FOOD PHILOSOPHY

Food Philosophy

AN INTRODUCTION

David M. Kaplan

Columbia University Press
New York

Columbia University Press
Publishers Since 1893
New York Chichester, West Sussex
cup.columbia.edu

Library of Congress Cataloging-in-Publication Data

Names: Kaplan, David M., author.
Title: Food philosophy : an introduction / David M. Kaplan.
Description: New York : Columbia University Press, [2019] | Includes index.
Identifiers: LCCN 2019019504 | ISBN 9780231167901 (hardcover) |
ISBN 9780231167918 (paperback) | ISBN 9780231551106 (ebook)
Subjects: LCSH: Food—Philosophy. | Food—Moral and ethical aspects. |
Food—Social aspects.
Classification: LCC B105.F66 K37 2019 | DDC 641.3001—dc23
LC record available at https://lccn.loc.gov/2019019504

Cover design: Milenda Nan Ok Lee
Cover art: *Herrings in a Bowl*, 1948. William Scott RA (1913–1989).

Andrea

CONTENTS

FOOD PHILOSOPHY

Introduction

WHAT IS PHILOSOPHY OF FOOD?

This book examines some of the philosophical dimensions of food production, distribution, and consumption. It analyzes what food is (metaphysics), how we experience food (epistemology), what taste in food is (aesthetics), how we should make and eat food (ethics), how governments should regulate food (political philosophy), and why food matters to us (existentialism).

This philosophical analysis of food is by no means the first. Philosophers have been examining it for thousands of years ever since Plato detailed an appropriate diet in Book II of *The Republic*. The Roman Stoics also discussed the importance of food and eating, as did Enlightenment philosophers Locke, Rousseau, Marx, and Mill. Since the 1970s, philosophers have broadened the discussion to include animal welfare, hunger, agricultural ethics, and food justice to name just some of the topics addressed. This book stands firmly in these traditions and draws on their literatures, but it also aims to show how philosophy can shed light on a host of other food-related matters, particularly how we make sense of it, how we taste it, and how it affects our identities.

The food philosophy addressed here is less of a unified perspective than a series of investigations that share three philosophical convictions: (1) food is always open to interpretation; (2) persons and animals deserve respect; and (3) food is about eating—and sometimes it's disgusting.

First, food is open to interpretation. There is very little consensus about how and what we should produce and consume. It is not even clear what food is or whether people have similar experiences of it. On one hand, it is recognized as a basic need, if not a basic right, common to everyone on Earth. On the other hand, it is hard to generalize about it given the wide range of practices and cuisines, and the even wider range of tastes. One would be hard-pressed to give definitive answers to practical and philosophical questions concerning food given the diversity of views about it. Instead, we make interpretations—claiming truth and normativity—that are open to debate. The better claims have better reasons and more moral force behind them; the worse ones are less plausible and less generalizable. For better or worse, there is no such thing as food-in-itself that can act as a standard to resolve disagreements about it.

Second, humans and animals have basic interests in life and freedom that should always be respected. All sentient beings have a fundamental dignity that should never be sacrificed for the welfare of others. But only humans have obligations to others—animals owe nothing to us (or to each other). Furthermore, only humans are entitled to all of the benefits and burdens of civic life. All animals care about their lives, and should be free to pursue their ends, but food animals are entitled to *some* civic benefits (protection, yes; voting, no), while wild animals are on their own. As for plants and ecosystems, they only matter to humans and to animals, not to themselves. That doesn't mean we can do whatever we want to nature—pollute it or trash uninhabited places for no reason (maybe graffiti the dark side of the moon)—it means that only sentient beings care about their own lives and that we owe a different kind of moral consideration to nature.

Third, food is unique in that it is the only thing we eat (and sometimes drink). Its edible nature means that we experience it differently than we do other ordinary objects. Specifically, only food satisfies hunger, and we can't help but taste what we put into our mouths. These acts of eating and tasting have tremendous bearing on how we approach food from a philosophical perspective. We think about what goes in our mouths differently than we think about things that do not. It feels more personal and subjective than what we see and hear, it exposes our vulnerabilities to poisonous and disgusting things, and it is bound up with a unique set of social practices that regulate how, what, why, when, where, and with whom we should eat.

The interpretive character of food, respect for human and animal dignity, and the act of eating are the threads that run through this book. (I'm tempted to say it has a hermeneutic and Kantian flavor, but I can't stand food puns.) Here is an overview of the main areas of the philosophy of food and a brief outline the topics investigated here.

Food metaphysics. Food is essentially whatever we eat and drink. Beyond that, it is hard to say what it is. We know it is edible, we know it provides nutrients that sustain living things, and we know it is typically made up of plants and animals, sometimes fungi and minerals (like salt) and chemicals if you include food additives. Drugs are often consumed but not considered to be food, or even food additives, for some reason. And not every edible thing is food, such as chalk, paper, and kibble. Food metaphysics attempts to define what food is. It analyzes food's very nature to arrive at an essence, much like a dictionary definition would do.

Take any food item and ask which properties make it what it is: is it the molecules, appearance, or social meanings? For example, is lettuce something with a chemical profile, a leafy green plant, or the key ingredient in a salad? Are hot dogs essentially ground pig parts, a variety of sausage served on a long roll, or something commonly eaten at a sporting event? Are the properties that make something food inherent in things, only in our minds, or products of the societies we live in?

These are metaphysical questions about the very nature of food. On an interpretive model, the answers take the form of different conceptions of food's essence. An interpretive model assumes we can never know what food is in itself but rather we understand it *as something* in relation to us. Something only becomes food for another, who interprets it as food. Yet, unlike a word or a law that is an entirely constructed reality, there is always something real about food for an interpretation to cleave to and articulate. The fact that people have different interpretations simply means that things can be carved up differently, not that all perspectives are equally valid.

In addition to questions about the ultimate nature of food, there are also puzzling metaphysical problems of classification where it is not clear how, or even if, something is food. Some things just miss the mark by a bit, for example, foods that are rotten or deformed beyond recognition—or things that people don't normally eat but could in a pinch, like service dogs or road kill. Then there are the things that resemble recognizable foods but don't quite pass for the real thing, like French toast bagels or puffy pizza with dipping sauce. What kinds of foods are these?

There is a broad class of foods that are clearly what they are intended to be but are not quite up to standard. They are bad versions of something. When Plato speaks about degrees of reality, he wants to distinguish between what is primary and derivative, genuine and fake. Perhaps we can speak of food in the same way. Maybe we can think of poorly prepared and inauthentic foods as poor examples of whatever it is they are trying to be. They resemble the originals but fall short. Or perhaps they are creative interpretations of traditional dishes. Food metaphysics can help clarify thorny cases of culinary identity and authenticity.

Food epistemology. Food metaphysics is bound up with epistemology: what one thinks food is depends upon how one perceives it. For example, we might experience food as something to be eaten, something to be avoided, something beautiful, or something that was once living. The same thing can be seen in a number of different ways depending on one's presuppositions and expectations. The food itself does not magically change as a result of an interpretation (that would be weird); instead, different aspects of it are highlighted or hidden depending on how we perceive it. Food is open to interpretation like any other ordinary object (except, probably, math and logic).

Yet food is about more than objects and essences; it is also about activities, traditions, and identities. We do things with food: we plant and harvest it, buy and sell it, prepare and eat it, and more. Chapter 2 examines the role of narrative knowledge in food experience. Narrative knowledge takes a historic approach by setting things in broad contexts that unfold over time in order to make sense of human affairs. And just as there are common conceptions of food, there are also common narratives about it, some better than others.

Yet food is different from other things we experience. For one, we don't simply experience it as an object outside of us (although we can, of course, look at, sniff, and consider it); we also experience it as something we taste, chew, swallow, and feel in the gut, sometimes hours later. We touch it, consume it, and then expel it in a radically transformed state. Furthermore, food experience is pulled by uncontrollable forces, unconscious motives, and desires, all of which are susceptible to social cues. Our own experiences of enjoying food and of starting and stopping to eat are not entirely ours to control. In addition, the knowledge from tasting food is notoriously hard to pin down. We all have different tastes, which seems to suggest taste is subjective; yet we can often agree about taste properties in food (whether something is sweet, salty, or spicy), which seems to suggest taste is objective, or at least found in objects, not only in our minds.

Although food epistemology is unusual, it nevertheless raises ordinary epistemological questions about justification and truth. We can have more and less reliable knowledge about flavors even though we have to rely on different senses than we normally do. The perceptions we have from the mouth and nose may not be the same as those from the eyes and ears, but we can still taste and smell accurately, can't we? Sniffing and tasting are different than seeing and hearing, but it is not clear to what extent those differences affect our knowledge of food. If we agree that food contributes to the taste properties of something, and that tastes are not entirely in our minds, can we agree on what something tastes like? If we can be mistaken, then there is something out there we can get right: the way food really tastes. If we can't be mistaken about tastes, then we are infallible tasters—and that can't be right.

Food aesthetics. The question of taste in food is both an epistemological and aesthetic problem: epistemological because it involves the kind of knowledge we have about things based on our sense of taste and aesthetic because tasting involves enjoyment, preference, and discernment. There are two important aspects of aesthetic taste: (1) it is a kind of liking and (2) it is a kind of judgment. Food aesthetics is concerned with both enjoying and evaluating what we eat and drink.

Most people would agree that food preferences are idiosyncratic and no one can really say what things taste the best. But, at the same time, most would agree that there is a real difference between at least *some* good and bad foods. We can safely say that rotten fruit, spoiled milk, and rancid meat are worse than their fresh counterparts, that children tend to prefer sweeter things than adults, and that regional preferences point to a degree of local consensus about taste. But beyond that it gets tricky. Likes and dislikes vary from person to person; genes and ambient background conditions play a role, as does social class and context. How can we really say what good and bad tasting food is, even though we do it all the time? Food aesthetics tries to figure out what tasty food is and what it means to have good taste in it.

It also examines the kinds of pleasures we get from food and drink. In some ways, food is similar to other enjoyable experiences, such as sex or laughter. These are good things unless you do them too much (or inappropriately) and it turns into some kind of displeasure either for you or for others. Food is similar: we crave it, discuss it, and relish it so much it plays a huge role in the quality of our lives. But in other ways, food is different because of the unique bodily pleasures it affords and the unique social norms of enjoyment.

There is also a unique kind of displeasure from eating things like rotten or poorly prepared food, or gorging until stuffed. As soon as food enters the body it crosses over into disgusting territory. It doesn't matter how wholesome it is, once chewed into a bolus, spit out, or belched up, the same object of pleasure can become an object of displeasure. How is it that food can be so enjoyable and so disgusting?

Another question in aesthetics (gustatory or otherwise) is the relationship between beauty and morality. It is not clear whether we can separate the descriptive and evaluative aspects of taste judgments. If we can, then aesthetics is independent from morality—food for food's sake. But is it really beyond good and evil? Don't we color our aesthetic judgments with moral judgments so that good tasting food is also seen as good (and appropriate) to eat? Don't we prefer the taste of wholesome things more than those that are unwholesome—homemade and farm-fresh rather than mass-produced and artificial? If so, then there seems to be a connection between good food and good actions. Then again, everyone knows that eating an animal isn't the nicest thing to do, yet we do it anyway because we love the taste of meat, so maybe taste is amoral. Or we are immoral.

Food ethics. Food ethics is about why we *should* produce and consume food in certain ways even though we may do otherwise. There is a well-established literature on food consequentialism and food virtue ethics that examines (respectively) the outcomes and character traits in various food-related activities. But another way to think about food ethics is in terms of our food responsibilities to ourselves, to each other, and to animals. What kinds of food activities should we do simply because they are the right things to do?

Our obligations to ourselves might include the responsibility we all have to self-care. We should all eat the kinds of diets that will not only keep us alive but also keep us healthy, happy, and satisfied. We should eat good foods not bad foods, not too much and not too little. (You don't need philosophy to tell you that.) Our obligations to others might include hospitality and feeding guests, giving aid to people in need, and considering the effects of food production on future generations. We also shouldn't eat other people or feed ourselves to them. Finally, our obligations to animals consist primarily of treating them humanely and slaughtering them painlessly. Or not eating them at all.

Meat eating is a complicated, emotionally charged issue. People are unusually defensive about the foods they eat, which is always a sign that there is something else going on. An obligation-based approach places limits on what we should buy and eat but does not categorically forbid eating animals. It depends on who eats which animals, why and where. Our food obligations are always shaped by the situations we find ourselves in, which means that city dwellers in North America have different obligations than people who live in livestock-dependent societies. Most of us eat meat because we like to, not because we have no other choices. Given that, are tastes and traditions good enough reasons to raise and kill animals for food? People really resist the idea that they should give up eating meat: are they right or are they selfish?

Another important issue in food ethics is the proper role of science and technology. No one questions the role of science in preventing food-borne illness or in food microbiology, but some are wary when food science is used to create new food additives or artificial flavors. The same with food technologies. Unless we scavenge for food, we need at least some kind of technology to farm, process, and cook. City dwellers in particular, who make up over half of the world's population, would literally starve to death without more advanced technologies—yet many people balk at genetically engineered crops or food irradiation.

The question is, what kinds of science and technology are acceptable and what kinds are problematic? Which should we endorse and which should we oppose? And what exactly is wrong with techno-food? Is it health risks, food safety, and environmental issues, or something less determinate and more visceral—maybe nothing harmful or unjust, but something unwholesome and mildly disturbing?

Food political philosophy. Food political philosophy is the application of concepts in ordinary political philosophy to food issues. Usually, philosophers begin with a particular food injustice and then assess it in light of one or more general political theories, for example, why we have the right to food or why agricultural subsidies are good or bad public policy. A food political philosophy examines what food justice and injustice look like from the perspective of a particular theory, or it uses a theory to argue why something that seems intuitively wrong is wrong for this or that philosophical reason. We may not need philosophy to tell us what is wrong in the world, but it is sometimes important to identify the reasons why something is wrong in order to know where to assign blame and what to do about it.

The two most prominent food political philosophies are food justice and food sovereignty, which are either very similar or crucially different depending on whom you ask. Both maintain that our food system is inseparable from our political, economic, and cultural institutions—and that they all influence each other. For example, food injustices, such as lack of safe, adequate, and culturally appropriate food manifests itself in injustices in other spheres of life, for example, in housing and employment. In turn, seemingly non-food-related injustices, such as poverty and discrimination, are manifested in what and how we eat. The food justice response is to argue for better laws; the food sovereignty response is to argue for more democratic participation in food systems. They both argue for changes in the current food system but differ in how to achieve them: by regulations and reforms or by civic engagement and alternative food systems.

There are, however, two intractable challenges to any food political philosophy: one economic, the other cultural. The first challenge is the role of money in food and agriculture. Powerful international corporations and financial institutions have increasing control over food production, distribution, and consumption. Wealth and power in the food and financial industries continues to be consolidated in ways that ripple through the economy and the environment. It's not all bad, but it is a force to reckon with. The political question is, how *should* a globalized food system be governed—and how *could* it be?

The second challenge is the role of food animals in our diets and traditions. The environmental costs of factory farming are inarguable, yet good reasons rarely change the way people eat. Meat is too deeply ingrained in our cultures (maybe our anthropology) to reason away. But that does not mean we can do whatever we want to domesticated animals. If anything, we have extra obligations to care for vulnerable creatures. The challenge to food political philosophy is how to govern the billions of domesticated animals that live among us (and the wild fish we hunt). There are already animal laws on the books but perhaps we need new ones—or maybe less rational means to nudge people to change how they treat animals.

Food existentialism. To say that food is a basic need (or even a right) doesn't even begin to do justice to how it affects our lives. It is a fundamental part of everyday existence, or as Heidegger says, our *facticity*: the situations we are always in (that are often difficult to accept). Each of us deals with food in some way, whether or not we want to. Sometimes we get to choose what and how to eat; other times we are influenced by urges, cultures, and situations that are largely out of our control. We have a "bounded-freedom," as Paul Ricoeur says. Food affects the needs and values that shape our decisions, the emotions and habits that shape our actions, and the most enigmatic parts of our lives: one's character and unconscious. Food influences both our voluntary actions and our involuntary nature.

In addition, it also affects what kind of people we are, or what existentialists call "authenticity"—what it is to be a self in (better and worse) relation to oneself and to others. Usually, the foods crucial to one's experiences are the cuisines of our cultures. The smells and tastes from childhood that stay with us for the rest of our lives are parts of our identities. We come to identify *our* foods with *our* people, or worse, we identify ourselves in terms of what we would never eat. *Those people* sip lattes or eat weird animals. *Our people* eat normal food. The existential question is, how do we respond to our social attitudes towards food? Do we go along with the crowd or do we do own up to our choices?

Furthermore, there is very little that is rational about food. Granted, there is reason to how we procure and process it, but a lot of what we do is pretty arbitrary. Some food choices are inexplicable—what Kierkegaard calls a "leap of faith." There is no apparent reason why, for example, we drink the milk of some but not all mammals, revile cannibalism, and enjoy snails but refuse other insects. Maybe there is no accounting for our most basic attitudes about food—we simply have them for no apparent reason. If that is the case, then why does food matter so much to us? If our lives have no intrinsic meaning and we have enough to eat, then why do we take food so seriously? If the only reason is taste, then we are either a very shallow species or food is really important for a meaningful life.

The three philosophical convictions of this book are that food is always open to interpretation, persons and animals deserve respect, and food is about eating. If we leave out interpretation, we cannot make sense of reasonable disagreements among people, "reasonable pluralism," as John Rawls calls it. Food isn't always the same thing for everyone, nor should it be. If we leave out respect, we cannot rule out forms of treatment that might sacrifice people and animals for the good of the many. We should take a stand against sharecropping, land-grabbing, and factory farming among other injustices. And if we leave out eating, we leave out the very thing that distinguishes food philosophy from ordinary philosophy. There is nothing wrong with treating food as an issue of agricultural ethics, political philosophy, or aesthetics, but what makes food *food* is that we eat it (and sometimes drink it). Food is its own thing that deserves its own subfield of philosophy. Hopefully these philosophical investigations will help contribute to the philosophy of food.

Chapter One

FOOD METAPHYSICS

It is hard to find a common thread among all of the different things people eat. We eat such a wide variety of prepared plants and animals that it is not clear if these things are alike in any meaningful way. Parsley, pigs, salt, and cheese? Ketchup, tuna, vinegar, and cake? Other than the fact that they are eaten, they don't seem to have much in common. If we include artificial ingredients, processed foods, and nutrients, the inventory of things we eat is even more motley. Imagine a grocery store that contains everything people eat: every dish, every animal, and every ingredient. Imagine bringing a group of visiting space aliens there to explain what Earth-humans eat. Would they understand what counts as food for us? Would we have to explain what eating is? What if they didn't have mouths and stomachs? How much do even we have to know about plants, animals, and eating to know what the essence of food is?

We might be tempted to define food in terms of organisms and energy. It is any substance made up of nutrients metabolized to sustain vital life processes. Or shorter: food is anything humans ingest to maintain life. Or shorter still: food is what we eat. Problem solved.

Unfortunately, it is not so simple. Food can plausibly be seen as any number of different things, from a seed we plant, to an animal we shepherd, to a bowl of soup we slurp. But if we leave the seed alone, cuddle the animal like a pet, or spill the soup on the floor, then none of these are exactly what we would call food. Maybe something only becomes food when we frame it the right way and set it in the right context. Maybe *we* determine what is and isn't food because its essence depends more on our conceptualizations than anything in the organisms themselves.

Yet food also has real properties that are independent of what we think or do. Although everything is open to interpretation, food is not whatever we say it is. A bean is a bean, not a brick, donut, or potato. It has a mass, volume, and chemistry. These are not things that people get to make up but are real properties of things themselves.

One way to understand the nature of food is to situate it in between two traditionally opposing metaphysical theories: realism and idealism. Realists hold that there is a ready-made world of clouds, rocks, and fish, one not constructed by human cognitive activity. Idealists deny this, holding that this world is in some sense dependent on human cognition. Food falls somewhere in the middle. It is substantial, more or less natural, and real, but it is also the result of our doing and, therefore, a social construction, like an artifact. Yet, unlike social constructions, food is limited by nature and by our bodies. We can't eat just anything, so we can't completely construct an edible reality. Nor can we understand it however we please in the face of a scientific discourse that also tells us true things.

We might say that food is a partially socially constructed reality. It occupies a unique ontological niche as something that is both objectively real and culturally constructed. One way to steer a course between realism and idealism is to take an interpretive approach to food metaphysics. Any good interpretation is neither entirely objective nor subjective, but rather a point of view that may or may not square with what is really there as well as what other people think. An interpretation should be defensible, open to debate, and potentially agreeable to everyone (maybe even the space aliens).

This chapter attempts to find not one, but a set of interpretations that could plausibly belong to the essence of food. Like *being*, food can be understood in many ways. It is not simply one thing for everyone, at all times. Rather, it can be many things depending on how you look at it. I argue that there are about a dozen important conceptions of food. What food is depends on how we conceptualize it.

Another important topic in food metaphysics is the difference between real and artificial food—not fake in the sense of illusory or plastic, but rather not up to standard or inauthentic. When we say that food is "real," we typically mean that it contrasts favorably to something with a lot of artificial ingredients. For example, "real food" can mean the food is heartier and more substantial than a light snack, it is more pure and natural than junk food, or it is more traditional than a popularized version. Real food is the real deal, usually whole food, or at least made up of natural ingredients. We might say that real food is always time-honored and authentic, not highly processed or an imitation. Then again, maybe the very idea of authenticity limits our ideas of what something should taste like—and cost. Is authentic food the real thing or anthropological dogmatism?

This chapter concludes with several marginal cases where it is not clear how to classify certain foods and drinks. We consume drugs and alcohol, but are they food? We eat vegan mayonnaise and pineapple pizza, but how real are these things? It may not be possible to determine the essence of ambiguous foods once and for all, but we can always explain ourselves better and try to understand where we are coming from.

IS FOOD REAL OR RELATIVE?

The idea that physical things have both objective properties and subjective appearances is a classic issue in metaphysics, well-worn in the history of philosophy. Realists argue that natural things exist independently of us, while idealists argue that our minds play a role in determining what things are. A realist would say that a wooden table is ultimately made of molecules that cause it to appear brown and solid, while an idealist would say that all we can know about the table is how it appears to us. The same with a tomato. For a realist, it is made of an objective set of micronutrients; for an idealist, not only do the tastes and smells of the tomato depend on us, but also its molecular make-up.

The twentieth-century versions of eighteenth-century realism-idealism debates tend to be reframed as realism versus anti-realism or *relativism*—a polemical term that few use to identify themselves. The crux of the contrast is whether we can know how things really are in themselves or if the very truth and existence of things depends on our conceptual schemes. Both sides have an argument. On one hand, we can indeed know the nature of things, otherwise what is science getting at if not the truth? On the other hand, we have different worldviews and perspectives, otherwise how can we account for how things appear different to different people?

The premise of food realism is that food really exists "out there" in the world, independent of our minds. It exists whether or not we think about it, and it arguably existed as food even before we did. Eggs were always eggs, deer were always deer, and berries were always berries. They did not magically transform themselves into something that could be eaten the moment hungry humans appeared on the scene, because food is food regardless of how or what we think about it.

If food is independent of our perception, then there are truths about it we can discover. We can state facts, disagree, and be mistaken about it. Whether our beliefs about it are true or false depends on whether or not they accurately represent how things really are. The idea that things in the world are independent of what we think about them is fairly noncontroversial. No one seriously believes the world would cease to exist if we went extinct because no one really believes the existence of the world depends on our perception. We don't invent facts about the world, but rather they are true because the reflect reality.

Food metaphysics then poses no vexing questions that would call realism into question. Unlike thorny issues about morality (are right and wrong objective?), the self (are thoughts real?), the past (is it real if it no longer exists?), or fictional characters (no Batman, Scrooge, or Santa?), food is indisputably real, its properties are objective, and its facts are true.

On the other hand, the idea that something can be food in itself is a bit odd. Normally we think about food as a source of nutrition for another. Fruits, leaves, and insects become food for an animal only when it takes them as something to eat. Until then, they are simply fruits, leaves, and insects. Organic matter can be seen as food by others but is not food in and of itself. Or to put it another way, the predicates "edible" and "is eaten" are not properties of objects but characteristics of relationships. To be food implies a relationship to something that eats. Food is always food-for-someone (or something). Yet, if something can be food for one creature and not food for another, then the nature of food depends on others and, therefore, is not an intrinsic but an extrinsic (relational) property.

Lisa Heldke makes a similar point about the "tangle of relationships" that "bring foodstuffs into existence." Edible things are fundamentally relational, so much so that it makes no sense to think they are independent substances with unique sets of food properties. Rather, to be food is to be something eaten by another. The very definition of it is relational. As Heldke explains:

To *become* food—to be rendered edible, palatable, delicious—means that a living thing has been part of scores of relationships, both natural and cultural: with the soil in which a plant is grown and the sun and rain that enable its growth; with the factory workers who process a raw material for market; with the heat and the metal pan that turn an ingredient into a "dish" in someone's home. In industrialized society, foods are the products of extremely long and complex sets of relationships.[1]

Ray Boisvert describes this relational character as the "withness" of food, "a veritable carnival of conjunctions" make food what it is.[2] In other words, it makes little sense to think of food as if it were ontologically distinct from the web of relations that make it what it is. Nothing is intrinsically food, rather, things are food in relation to others. Leon Kass makes the same point: all organisms seek out others and assimilate them as food (with a little waste left behind).[3]

Now, of course, there are many truths about the world that are relational, for example, moons that orbit around planets, legs that are longer than arms, and mice that are food for owls. These are relational-mind-independent truths. But what distinguishes "is food" from other relational properties is that it has no existence *as food* apart from us. (I really don't know what happens when owls see mice as food, or when a well-fed owl has no interest in a nearby rodent—but *we* certainly determine what counts as food for us.) Food is relational-mind-dependent. Obviously, the existence of croissants and Cheerios depends on us, but so do hunted and gathered foods that are just animals and plants until we decide to make them food.

Or, to use John Searle's terms, food is ontologically subjective but epistemologically objective.[4] It would not exist apart from human social life but has real properties that can be known objectively. I would add to Searle's definition that food is also open to interpretation. Some aspects of food are properties that can be known by everyone; other aspects can only be known by those who share the same conceptual scheme. Either way, our only access to something as food is through the constructive activities of the mind. We can know things objectively but not independently of us. That means realism is out—but so is relativism. This Kantian approach squares with the main intuition about how we typically understand what food is: part natural, part social.

Most philosophy since the 1950s maintains that our minds contribute something essential to our ability to experience the existence of things. As the phenomenologists say, all experience is an experience of something. It always refers to the world, not to representations in the mind; yet our world experiences are always colored by our perspectives. Experiences are really about things in the world and are also meaningful to us at the same time. When it comes to food, we not only experience what something is, or that it exists, but also how it exists and what it is like. Metaphysical realists have a hard time making sense of the different meanings that foods have for different people. And metaphysical anti-realists have a hard time making sense of the limiting conditions of edibility and digestibility, as if there were no facts of the matter beyond a conceptual scheme.

W. V. O. Quine, for example, argues that if language structures experience, we can never really be sure what a sentence means because words are often ambiguous.[5] That makes it impossible to know what things are actually like apart from us. For example, the simple utterance "this coffee" can mean "this cup of coffee," "this brand of coffee," or "this kind of bean." Quine says we cannot be certain because meanings are always indeterminate. Yet, if there is no way to get beyond language to experience the world as it is in itself, beyond the structuring activities of our minds, then food metaphysics is like chasing ghosts. It is impossible to know what food truly is.

Donald Davidson, on the other hand, argues that the *linguistic structuring* of experience does not confine us to *linguistic ambiguity* but instead provides the basis for reaching agreement about how things are in reality.[6] He agrees with Quine that our only access to facts is through the concepts we unavoidably bring to experience, and that we never have access to an uninterpreted reality. But unlike versions of relativism that claim that conceptual schemes are incommensurable, Davidson argues that they can always be translated and understood by others.[7] We may not be able to transcend the world as it is conceptualized to perceive a mind-independent reality, but we can always communicate and compare our experiences. Therefore, regardless of whether we agree or disagree about something, we can be assured we are talking about the same thing. That might give little comfort to realists, but it should at least assure them that we can conceive of food as intelligible and meaningful without worries about either incommensurability or relativism.

Hans-Georg Gadamer makes a similar claim about the relationship between language and translation in his hermeneutic philosophy. He argues that everything we know and do is always nontrivially influenced by what precedes us. That means we can never reflect on our experience from a perspective that is entirely free from the effects of history. If Descartes famously tried to take stock of everything he knew in order to eliminate all prejudices and establish truth on the self-evidence of the *cogito*, Gadamer argues for the opposite: certainty cannot be found in the cogito because we can never be entirely free of prejudice. Whatever we know, say, and do is always based on prior understandings that did not originate in us.[8] Plenty of other midcentury philosophies make the same case about the mediating role of theories and contexts, but there are three distinctive features of hermeneutics that are not only unique but pertinent to food metaphysics: dialogue, practical reason, and creativity.

Understanding for Gadamer is like a dialogue, modeled after the Platonic dialectic. We understand things in response to implicit questions by testing our interpretations in an open-ended dialogue with others. Gadamer calls interpretation a "play of question and answer.[9] Everything we understand is the result of questioning things based on prejudices and being open to revising our interpretations when they don't square with what others think. When interpretations conflict, it might be because they assume different things, or one person is mistaken or argues from bad faith. (There are a lot of reasons we disagree.) Yet, by examining our prejudices, and by keeping the dialogue going, we can make progress toward understanding each other's perspectives. We can try to figure out where someone is coming from and perhaps learn why we see things differently if we cannot reach agreement. Or, in the absence of another person, we can call ourselves into question to sort through our prejudices to figure out why we believe what we do.

For example, Americans are usually mystified by why Australians like Vegemite, even though the reason is obviously our different upbringing. Some people gradually acquired a taste for something that the rest of us did not. The same for American foods that others might find awful, such as processed cheese, red licorice, and watery beer. It may not be particularly earth-shattering to claim that the reasons people disagree about food is because of their underlying prejudices, but it does explain a lot. When we say "it depends on where you're coming from," it indicates that our understanding is always influenced by what precedes us. It also indicates that we can share and compare our perspectives, and maybe learn to see things from another's point of view. Engaging in dialogue and sharing experiences with an Australian may not be enough to develop a taste for Vegemite, but it can be enough to at least understand why *they* like it.

Another key feature of hermeneutics is its similarity to theories of practical reason. Every interpretation, according to Gadamer, is a new *application* of understanding. We apply prejudices (and test them) by relating them to the present situation. Like Aristotle's ethics, it is about knowing what to do in particular situations. Our understanding is learned and cultivated, closer to *techne* than *episteme*; more like *phronesis* than *sophia*. It takes practice and requires social tact to know how to do it.[10] Hermeneutics *is* a practice with both theoretical and practical dimensions. The two ideas come together when we say we "don't know what to make of something." The expression conveys both knowledge and action: we cannot decide what something is, we are uncertain about whether something is good or bad, or we do not know how to understand something.

This practical and historical character of interpretation is crucial for making sense of food. So much of what we know about it—how to make it, prepare it, and relate to it—is more like a *know-how* than a *know-that*. We inherit our ideas of what food is, what it should be, and what we should do with it. We are never in a position, like Descartes was, to act as if we know nothing about what food is, as if we were entirely free from the influence of others. Instead, we acquire interpretive skills through practice and with the help of others. An important difference between hermeneutics other anti-realist theories of truth is the role of our background experience (not just knowledge) in knowing how to understand and what to do. The know-how we inherit helps us figure out "what to make of things," which, in the case of food, is a fairly apt way to put it.

The third key feature of hermeneutics is creativity. Sometimes imaginative and creative language can tell us more about something than a straightforward description can. It may not be literally true but it can be revealing and, in a strange way, truer than non-fiction. Wine tasters, for example, are known for their use of metaphors. They use words like velvety, buttery, and delicate to describe features that are not merely perceived but are actually there in the wine. Creative language lets us say more when ordinary descriptive language falls shorts.

Frank Sibley, for example, argues that metaphors help us see what is there in food:

> There are of course no limits to the flights into those wildly exotic, exuberant, and flamboyant descriptions possible, and so often and easily ridiculed as pretentious, in the lucubrations[11] of some who talk about food, wines, and perfumes. . . . When in ordinary discourse people bother, as specialists on wine, tea, food, and perfumes have to, to describe tastes and smells fully and carefully, what they say can sound as normal and unpretentious, and as appropriate, vivid, and accurate, as does the language of poets, novelists, or critics describing nature or artefacts.[12]

In summary, the nature of food cannot be known apart from its relationships and how it is experienced. It depends on how you look at it, what you make of it, and what kind of language you use. That said, what does that really tell us about what food is, other than that we know it interpretively? It is one thing to compare the virtues of a hermeneutic theory with food realism and relativism; it is another, more difficult, matter to explain what the essence of food is other than to banally assert that it can be many things depending on your point of view. If Aristotle did more than just assert that being is understood in many ways, but also argued that there are specific categories of being, can we say, in the spirit of the Stagirite, that there are categories of the being of food? Not just any interpretations, but fundamental ways of conceiving of the nature of food?

WHAT IS THE ESSENCE OF FOOD?

There are thirteen main concepts of the essence of food. There could be more, maybe fewer. Either way, so long as there is more than a single Platonic form then the interpretive claim of multiple essences is correct. Yet, there are only so many fundamental ways to conceive what it basically is. Although there are countless things we consider to be food, and countless more things we can say about food, there are not countless things that could plausibly *be* food.

The thirteen conceptions of food are nature, nutrition, fuel, medicine, diet, pleasure, taboo, commodity, goods, meaning, spirituality, recipe, and art. Food can be said to be any of these things. The conceptions are arranged starting with the most natural and ending with the most social, with several that straddle both worlds.

Food as nature. Food is anything that can be turned into energy by a living thing. It is part of a food chain, or a trophic level where species eat and are eaten by others. Food is whatever living things feed on.

The three main groups of life forms are producers, consumers, and decomposers.[13] Producers, such as plants, plankton, and moss, rely on sunlight for energy and draw their nutrients from the soil or water. Primary consumers, such as insects and herbivores, eat producers. Secondary consumers eat primary consumers, tertiary consumers eat other carnivores, and apex predators, such as tigers, eagles, and polar bears, are at the very top of the food chain. (It's not clear where on this schema to place omnivores.)

Food on this biological model is part of the web of life, where creatures feed on each other and transfer energy between trophic levels. There are other models of the way food fits into an ecosystem, but they are also naturalistic conceptions that treat it as a part of the environment.

Sometimes when food is seen as a part of nature, we attribute moral qualities to it. When it comes from nature it is said to be good; when it comes from a factory it is bad. Eating natural foods supposedly brings us closer to a natural, moral order; eating processed junk food tears us away from nature. Sometimes eating natural foods is equated with balance. Ostensibly, the closer we are to our place in the food chain, the healthier and more balanced our lives will be.[14]

Food as nutrition. On another biological model, food consists of organic chemicals essential for living things: carbohydrates, proteins, fats, fibers, vitamins, and minerals. Food is whatever living things metabolize to stay alive, grow, and repair their vital life processes. It consists of the nutrients that organisms and cells need to live.

Most dietary advice treats food as nutrition: the U.S. Department of Agriculture, the United Kingdom's Food Standards Agency, and the European Union's European Commission all conceive of food as nutrition.[15] The idea is that we should all eat enough of the good nutrients and avoid too many of the bad ones, depending on our specific nutritional needs. For example, dietary advice is different for children, pregnant women, and the aged. Food is whatever provides nutrition, regardless of whether ingested orally or administered intravenously. It is simply the biochemicals living things need.

Food as fuel. Another biochemical conception of food is an energy source, like fuel for a machine. We get energy from calories in protein, carbohydrates, and fats. When we are hungry, we need to fuel up; we eat and reenergize.

The American Heart Association (AHA) takes the fuel metaphor even further and describes the body as a vehicle and the heart as the motor. Food is the fuel that goes into your tank; water is the fluid that goes into your radiator. You need to be sure you have enough food and water to run your engine. The AHA warns that not fueling up "is like driving a car on empty." During exercise, it recommends adding water to keep the body hydrated, so it won't overheat. And after a workout, you are told to refuel with carbohydrates, proteins, and fluids, and that you need the right balance to "keep your engine performing at its best."[16]

The idea that food is fuel captures what happens when we eat just to make the hunger pangs go away. It is the reason for energy bars.

Food as medicine. Another common conception of food is to see it as medicine. You might eat oatmeal to lower your cholesterol, drink orange juice when you have a cold, or have yogurt when you are on an antibiotic. People eat specific foods for weight loss, diabetes control, lowering blood pressure, and a host of other health reasons. In some Hindu and Buddhist practices, the differences between food and medicine are trivial, if not nonexistent. Ayurvedic medicine, for example, is widespread through the Indian subcontinent. Traditional Chinese medicine uses foods and drinks therapeutically. And recently in the United States, there is a renewed interest in the health benefits of fermented foods. People eat specific foods to fall asleep, treat depression, boost fertility, train for events, and to increase libido. In each case, food is consumed like medicine to improve health and well-being.

There are, however, important differences in how food is conceptualized as medicine. In the West, the reason a food doubles as medicine is either because of tradition or nutrition: it is either conventionally understood to be healthy or we explain its healthy properties in terms of its nutrients. In Chinese medicine, foods are considered healthy in terms of a very different understanding of existence. The health properties of food are related to the five phases, or the *Wuxing* (wood, fire, earth, metal, water), and the five flavors (sour, bitter, sweet, spicy, and salty).[17]

The medicinal use of food in Ayurveda is based on a humoral classification, where foods are considered to be essentially hot or cold, moist or dry, and prescribed according to an individual's health or psychological state. The Ayurvedic humoral system divides the world, people, and food into five elements (earth, water, fire, air, and ether) combined to create three *dhatus* (bodily parts), corresponding to three *doshas* (humors), corresponding to three *gunas* (personality attributes), and three food types: *tamasic* (cold, stale, spiced), *sattva* (savory, nutritive), and *rajasic* (hot, bitter, sour, dry). Different combinations of foods can be used to restore health, broadly construed as harmony of body, mind, and spirit.[18]

In the West, the traditional humoral qualities of food were related to the four elements (earth, air, fire, and water) and the body's humors: blood (hot and moist), yellow bile (hot and dry), phlegm (cold and moist), and black bile (cold and dry).[19] Different foods, such as cinnamon, garlic, oranges, and coffee, have different curative properties depending on one's humoral constitution. Eastern and Western humoral classifications can be seen as part of the larger conception of food as medicine, although they are so metaphysically different they might warrant their own categories.

Food as diet. Food can also be seen as the totality of what we eat. The relationship is one of parts and wholes: a particular food (or meal) is a part, a diet is the whole. In that way, we can speak of the differences in diets across class or nationality, or between a prehistoric and a contemporary diet. When the space aliens inquire into what Earth-humans consider to be food, they will want to know what we generally eat.

Another sense of a diet is a regimen of food eaten for health reasons, weight loss, or religious beliefs. A diet in this sense is something chosen with desirable good foods and undesirable bad foods, for example, low-fat, gluten-free, or kosher. Diets are always about both foods and lifestyles, geographies and choices.

Food as pleasure. Food can also be seen as simply a source of pleasure, as something to savor and enjoy. People (and probably animals) like the feeling of eating tasty foods. We all dislike the feeling of hunger and thirst and like to feel satisfied and quenched. Food not only satisfies and relieves the sensation of hunger, but it is also enjoyable to taste. Obviously. But that means that food can be seen as primarily something desired and delicious—more aesthetic than practical. (Tastiness, as we will see in chapter 3, is part of the food itself, not added window dressing.)

Food as taboo. Food can also be seen as something off-limits and forbidden. We still recognize it as food but consider it to be impermissible for various cultural or religious reasons, or for ethical reasons for the vegan who considers animal products off-limits. Everyone finds at least some things off-putting, or at least hard to fathom eating. It might be a certain kind of animal or animal part; it might be something that has fallen on the floor, come into contact with a contaminant, or handled improperly. Somehow, when foods cross a line, they become undesirable, if not repellent. They are still food but just barely. Even worse are truly taboo foods that are only eaten by "morally suspect" people, and maybe are not even considered to be food at all. Forbidden foods make sharp distinctions between what is acceptable and unacceptable, often dividing people.

Food as commodity. Food can be seen as an economic object—something primarily for investors and traders to buy and sell. There are approximately five hundred different foods bought and sold on global commodity markets, primarily fish, soybeans, wheat, cooking oil, sugar, beef, and poultry. Food commodities may or may not be eaten; what matters is the economic role they play on the global market: mass quantities that are publicly traded, not small amounts eaten individually. There is little to distinguish a commodity from one producer to another. There might be different grades or quality standards, but there is no product differentiation within a commodity. One Grade-A mackerel is as good as any other. A food commodity is like a gigantic amount of bulk food that is traded many times before it is eaten.

Food as goods. Food can also be seen as a basic good like shelter, security, and freedom: basic things that people want and need in order to live together. It is like any commodity that people are entitled to have (or at least free to pursue), like money or property. We are free to have it, buy and sell it, or give it as gifts. It is regulated by the same principles of justice as other economic goods.[20] For example, when we address malnourishment or hunger, we treat food as a social good that should be distributed more fairly and effectively. When people who need it are not getting the food they deserve, then justice demands a different distribution of goods. The same is true for other food justice issues about availability, access, and sovereignty. What is at issue is distributive justice of a basic good crucial to our health and welfare. It is like bulk food we are entitled to.

Food can also be seen as a *commons*, something not privately owned but a shared resource for the benefit of everyone in a community. Food on this model is like water, air, and sunlight: open-access resources and public goods. Food-commons were wide-spread in antiquity before they fell out of fashion in the Middle Ages. In the late-twentieth century, the ideas of knowledge-commons[21] and environmental-commons[22] resurfaced and now, at the start of the twenty-first century, there is a renewed interest in food-commons as a way to meet the needs unmet by markets or institutions.[23]

The role of food and drink in *hospitality* deserves special mention (and, arguably, its own conception). Hospitality is a form of generosity that used to involve taking in travelers and making sure their needs were met and now typically involves inviting others into one's home, giving food and drink, and making sure guests are comfortable. A good host might also want to make friendly conversation, pour beverages, take coats, and other small actions that are not easy to enumerate. Generally speaking, a host should ensure the happiness of a guest—willingly, not begrudgingly. Motives matter. The role of food and drink in hospitality is unique: we have no right to it, nor is it an act of charity over and above what is required. Instead, it is like a gift that should be given—a little gesture of courtesy for your guests. And it can't just be any food or drink. It should be appropriate for the occasion and, ideally, something nice or special.

Food as meaning. Food is always a particular kind of food that has meaning and significance within a context. It can express values and norms, it can signify special events, and it can symbolize something else. Food can be about something other than itself; it can be read as well as eaten. Carolyn Korsmeyer distinguishes three forms of meaning: representation, exemplification, and expression.

Food that represents is made to look like something other than itself, for example, goldfish crackers, radish roses, candy canes, and gummy bears. Pretzels depict arms folded in prayer, croissants depict the crescent moon of the Ottoman flag, and hot cross buns depict the cross of the crucifixion.[24]

Food that exemplifies has aesthetic properties or tastes that at the same time convey meaning. Chicken soup, for example, is what it means. Korsmeyer says chicken soup "*is* a home remedy that *means* that one is being taken care of."[25] In the United States, cold cereal, oatmeal, and pancakes exemplify breakfast; mimosas, French toast, and eggs Benedict exemplify brunch. Sandwiches, and maybe leftovers, exemplify lunch; desserts are cookies, cakes, and ice cream, with no savory flavors. Of course, differences in cuisines have different meanings embodied in the foods, but every place has foods that taste like their meaning.

Foods that express are those that exemplify more metaphorically in relation to the traditions and circumstances of their consumption. Turkey means Thanksgiving, king cake means Mardi Gras, and dates mean the breaking of the fast at Ramadan. Beer is lowbrow, wine is highbrow; whiskey is a man's drink, a Cosmopolitan is a woman's drink (stereotypically, of course). In a traditional Chinese New Year celebration, shrimp means happiness, fish means prosperity, and peaches mean a long healthy life. And, in pretty much every society, meat expresses prosperity, masculinity, and power.[26] These symbolic meanings are neither extrinsic nor superfluous but rather are seen as properties of the foods themselves, at least among those who share the same conceptualization. Food is always some kind of food relative to a society.

When people say that food is *love*, they mean that it expresses affection and devotion, usually of a parent for a child. It is like a gift given unconditionally to another, but it communicates more than that. The acts of cooking, feeding, and sharing food express intimacy, while the memory of being cared for and fed can create lasting associations of food and love—and the often-complicated relationships we have to both of them. In these cases, food stands for, and substitutes for, love (which is not always a good thing).

Food as spirituality. Food not only forms a bond between intimates but can also form a bridge to a sacred or spiritual realm. Food and drink in religious practices have intangible properties that are part of a righteous life. We may not actually be transformed in the act of eating, but we can commune with our communities and, in that way, realize something special by consuming (or abstaining from) certain foods and drinks. Or, for those who believe in a Christian doctrine of transubstantiation (or consubstantiation), there is a real (or metaphoric) presence of the divine in consecrated bread and wine that transforms the recipient of the Eucharist.[27] Another religious practice is sacrifice, where consumption and self-transformation is less important than the symbolic offering. This sacrificial function is not just one symbolic meaning among others but a uniquely religious meaning apparent only to believers.

Food as recipe. Food (or at least a dish) can be identified in terms of a recipe, or a set of ingredients and preparation techniques. A recipe patterns a dish similar to how a score organizes music or a script structures a play. In each case, the object (dish, song, play) has something like a blueprint that formalizes its material components and rules of organization. Some kind of a pattern or form exists before, and persists after, it is instantiated into matter. In music, the score tells the musicians what notes to play; in a play (or in theatre), the script provides the actors with words to say; in food, the recipe tells us how to make the dish correctly.

Dave Monroe likens food to performed arts and argues that we might define a dish "as the unique combination of a set of material ingredients with a formalized method of preparation."[28] And, like a performance, there is usually some flexibility in definition so that a dish can be considered to be what it recognizably is even if some of the ingredients or preparation methods are different. The exception are dishes that claim authenticity. If there is too much creativity, it can no longer be considered whatever it is supposed to be. Then again, dishes change over time, so it is hard to know which recipe defines it and how much variation there can be before it becomes unrecognizable.

The notion of a recipe raises other metaphysical questions about identity: is each instance of a dish the same thing or is it something different each time? Can I order the same thing I had at the restaurant last week or will it be different because it is physically different? Can I make the same thing I had in a restaurant at home or is that not even possible? Recipes are like adjustable structures or provisional blueprints.[29]

Food as art. Food is aesthetic in two senses. First, it appeals to the senses. It has aesthetic qualities that can be described with adjectives like delicious, fresh, or crunchy. Second, food can be artful. We can describe its appearance, sensual elements, and composition as, for example, elegant, balanced, or simple. When we focus on aesthetic qualities, we treat food more like something we would see in a museum than prepare in a kitchen. It should be appreciated for no other reason than how it appears.

Granted, what makes something art is open to debate. It could be the intentions of the artist, the reception by the viewer, participants in the artworld, or something else. But regardless of the criteria, food can sometimes be more like art than a comestible. Arguably, the only difference between traditional artwork and food art is that only food art can be eaten.

Up until that point, food is as much a work of art as any painting, sculpture, or piece of music.

What, then, is food ultimately? Is it one thing that can be conceptualized in thirteen different ways? Are there more conceptualizations, such as food as power (when used to control others), as status (fancy cheese to impress the guests), or as a paperweight (a watermelon to keep the napkins from blowing away)? Or is there only one conception, food as meaning, and the rest are derivative? Or maybe the dictionary is right and food is fundamentally about nourishment and nothing else really matters.

Regardless of how many conceptions there are, one thing is certain: food is oddly mutable. Things transform into food when we decide they can be eaten. It may not be as magical as turning water into wine or cheap chuck into a choice cut, but we can actually transform things by virtue of our thoughts and actions. We create food, give it objectivity, and it takes on different senses, sometimes with alarming ease. The physical characteristics might remain the same and yet we can make it into something different. And, when cooked, even the physical characteristics change and it actually does become something else.

The challenge of food metaphysics is to know which conception of food to apply to a given case. Sometimes it makes sense to see it as fuel (when quickly eating breakfast); other times it makes more sense to see it as pleasure (when enjoying birthday cake). That does not mean that all interpretations are equally true or that there is no way to tell if some are better than others. It simply means that there are many true things we can say about the nature of food, and some interpretations are more fitting than others depending on the situation.

WHAT ARE QUESTIONABLE FOODS?

Sometimes it is not clear how a food item or dish should be conceptualized. There are always borderline cases that raise questions about what kind of food something is or whether or not it should even be considered food.

Are beverages food? Usually there is no confusing food and drinks. One is more solid, the other more liquid; one satisfies hunger, the other satisfies thirst. We eat food and we drink drinks. But there are marginal cases where some foods (like soups) are sipped and some drinks (like smoothies) can act as meal replacements. There are some beverages, such as beer and wine, that are not food in any conventional sense and some dietary supplements and medicines that are drunk but are not really beverages in any conventional sense. Breast milk and formulas are the only things that infants can ingest, so all food is liquid for them.

Beverages fit most of the thirteen conceptions food, which either means food and drink are fundamentally alike or the conceptions need to be refined. (There's not really a recipe for milk, is there?—unless you count pasteurization and fortification.) Breast milk, infant formulas, and liquid meal replacements can pass as food by virtue of their nutritive functions. The most important differences (other than water content and differences in the acts of eating and drinking) are in their respective meanings. Food and beverages signify different things and are consumed at different times and for different reasons. They belong to related but different social practices. Beverages usually accompany food but are often drunk independently in a dedicated act of drinking, for example, water, coffee, tea, alcohol, and so on. Having a drink while eating is different from having a bite while drinking. They are often either allowed or prohibited together, although there are some times when it is okay to drink but not eat (for example, water during sports or coffee at the office) but not the other way around. From the perspective of the law, beverages are considered to be food under the 1938 U.S. Federal Food, Drug, and Cosmetics Act.

Alcoholic drinks are somewhat different. The presence of ethanol in a beverage gives it different meanings and subjects it to different social and legal regulations. For example, according to the United States Department of Agriculture's Supplemental Nutrition Assistance Program (SNAP) (better known as food stamps), beer, wine, and spirits are not considered food and are, therefore, not SNAP-eligible. It is a legal judgment, not a metaphysical claim, meaning that, with respect to the law, alcohol can never be considered food. That makes some sense: the government probably should not subsidize the consumption of controlled substances.

Another difference between food and beverages is in their aesthetic dimensions. Drinks are less nourishing and take longer to fill us up. We can drink more, and for longer, than we can eat. Plus, there are the social practices that allow it, such as nursing a drink or hanging out at a café. We don't really nibble on food in the same way for as long a time. The deliberate, focused consumption of drinks lets us treat them as purely aesthetic objects, apart from whatever nutritive or social role they might play. I would hazard to say that one reason it is easier to focus more on the taste of drinks than on food is that there is less to look at and less to distract. The absence of visual and more obvious tactile cues allows a taster to focus more acutely on the smells and tastes. Maybe.

Can drugs be food? If food can be considered medicine, can drugs that we eat be considered food? At first glance, they seem to belong to a different set of social practices: we ingest drugs privately, not publicly; we purchase them from different stores; and they sometimes require a prescription if not an illicit transaction. Drugs are more functional than food and provide little, if any, nourishment. Basically, anything we gulp without chewing and savoring is not like anything we do with food.

However, some drugs are chewed and savored, such as special foods for diabetics or dietary supplements that resembles energy bars. And as cannabis is legalized, chefs are becoming more and more ingenious at infusing it into all kinds of edible things. A new eating practice is starting to form—more like drinking alcohol than either eating or doing drugs. One can eat edible cannabis to get high, to relish the experience, or to fill up, however dumb that would be. The eating practices surrounding drug-infused foods are different than ordinary eating, which could change in the future but for now there are still important differences.

The Food and Drug Administration (FDA) has guidelines to help distinguish between food and drugs, specifically guidelines about medical foods and dietary supplements. The guidelines are nonbinding recommendations that carry no legal responsibilities. Worse, they are inconsistent and confusing. According to the agency, medical foods are "intended to meet distinctive nutritional requirements of a disease or condition, used under medical supervision, and intended for the specific dietary management of a disease or condition." They are not ordinary foods recommended by a physician to manage symptoms or reduce the risk of disease. Instead, they are foods that are "specially formulated and processed" for patients as part of a medical dietary regimen, as opposed to a "naturally occurring foodstuff used in a natural state."[30] They may resemble ordinary foods, but they are produced and consumed to be both food and medicine at the same time.

Dietary supplements are similar to medical food but take the form of pills, powders, or bars. By law, they must not represent an item as a conventional food or a stand-alone part of a meal.[31] Liquid dietary supplements, however, are not easily distinguishable from ordinary beverages. Sometimes the only difference is in their labeling. For example, highly caffeinated energy drinks fit the definition of either a dietary supplement or beverage. Some are marketed as supplements (5-Hour Energy, Monster Energy, Rockstar), while others are marketed as conventional foods (Red Bull, Amp Energy).[32] Java Monster Loca Moca Coffee + Energy is a supplement but the virtually identical Starbucks Doubleshot Energy + Coffee is a drink.

The FDA issued guidelines to distinguish between liquid dietary supplements and beverages, but they are not particularly helpful. The difference hinges on how something is labeled and advertised. Whether or not something is a drink or a supplement depends on "a product's name, packaging, serving size, recommended daily intake and other recommended conditions of use, and composition, as well as marketing practices and representations about the product."[33] Legally, the difference between types of drinks has to do with neither ingredients nor social practices but how a company decides to market their product. A caffeine drink can be either a drug, a dietary supplement, or a beverage depending on how it is marketed.[34]

Is frozen pizza real pizza? It is round, has mozzarella cheese, tomato sauce, and a chewy baked dough with a raised crust around the circumference. It appears to be pizza. It says "pizza" on the box. And, to most people, it tastes like pizza: the right ingredients, textures, and tastes.

But it looks and tastes different from what's served in a pizzeria in Italy. The cheese is different, the crust is different, and it isn't made to order and cooked in a wood-fired oven. Is it pizza? Or rather, is it authentic pizza? If it is not, then it needs to be qualified with an adjective like frozen, fast food, or deep dish.

A number of things determine what makes a pizza authentic: the ingredients, the oven, the recipe, and the place of origin. Although we look to Italy for authenticity, there are differences in the pizzas in Naples, Sicily, and Rome. American pizzas are modeled on Italian (probably Neapolitan) pizzas but evolved into something unique. They range from those that would be unrecognizable to an Italian to those that look and taste just as good (if that is even possible).

Is there such thing as authentic pizza, or is the best we can do is to find a pizza true to the style of a region? Authentic is relative to Naples, Sicily, and New York. Some claim that New Haven has its own style. Some claim that Chicago-style even counts as pizza. But it is debatable whether even a regional standard would be useful or unhelpfully broad. Maybe it could set a standard for pizza preparation and appearance, but taste, as well? Don't we already have these standards in the form of the basic categories we use to understand not only what pizza is, but how it should be made, how it should be eaten, and what it should taste like? If we did not have any preconceptions, then how would we know something was pizza and that it is supposed to taste crusty and cheesy and not sugary sweet? If we already have standards, then why is there disagreement?

Food authenticity is a very tricky concept with murky criteria and unclear points of reference. How far back do we have to go before we arrive at the original? And what if the original was barely recognizable to us today, as I imagine the original pizzas would be? There are no lists of necessary and sufficient conditions for determining what counts as an authentic food item, only general categories. It might be like software design where "look and feel" is the key to a copyright. Maybe something has to have the right look and feel to be an authentic dish.

That goes for any food, not just something as contentiously debated as pizza. It also goes for bagels and burritos, sushi and barbecue—anything perceived to be traditional or originally from somewhere else. Although everyone can participate in food authenticity debates, we might want to lend more credence to those who have the most experience with a dish, for example, someone who grew up eating it or a food historian. Maybe the best we can hope for is a "traditional" dish. Maybe authenticity is impossible to pin down, especially when a cuisine is made and eaten outside of its place of origin.

There is a growing backlash to the entire discourse of food authenticity.[35] Some say it is a futile ghost chase,[36] some say it is elitist,[37] and some proudly say they like inauthentic foods better.[38] Too often terms like authentic are more about marketing than anything substantial—or worse, a fetishized version of a culture for visitors seeking exotic experiences. The idea of authenticity can hang like a weight on immigrant cooks and restaurants trapped by the expectations of diners, who want inexpensive dishes in (what they perceive to be) another culture's traditional style.[39]

Then again, doesn't there have to be at least the perception of authentic foods if there are so many counterfeits? The global market in things like counterfeit olive oil, coffee, and caviar costs the industry approximately fifteen billion dollars annually.[40] People really want authentic and traditional foods even if the very notions are suspect. One hallmark of authenticity is sometimes regionality, or *terroir*—a real geographic location, related to the climate, soil, and other physical things. Perhaps geographical indications can settle at least some disputes. Traditional, authentic dishes resemble those from a particular region or place within a country.

Of course, you can have it both ways and agree that some dishes are more in a traditional-style than others and yet still prefer the taste of the untraditional dish. Authentic isn't necessarily better. For example, you visit Naples, try Napolitan pizza, and understand the difference between that and what you grew up with, but you still think the pepperoni pizza at your local place is better. It takes another argument to claim that traditional foods taste better than their untraditional versions. As for frozen pizza, which has been around since the early 1960s, it is so entrenched in American households that it has its own traditions and standards of excellence. Maybe in one hundred years there will be debates about what is authentic frozen pizza.

Is in vitro meat really meat? In 2012, the *New York Times* held a contest for the best short essay in defense of eating meat. The readers (not the official judges) voted for an essay titled "I'm About to Eat Meat for the First Time in 40 years" by Ingrid Newkirk, president and founder of People for the Ethical Treatment of Animals.[41] She announces that she is going to start eating meat again after a forty-year break because there is now a healthier, more humane, more environmentally responsible kind of meat available: in vitro meat made from stem cells taken from animal tissue and placed in nutrient-filled petri dishes that grow into muscle tissue. Newkirk believes it is real meat that comes from a real animal but without causing any suffering, waste, or pollution. It is, therefore, okay to eat.

Is laboratory-grown meat real meat or is it *schmeat*, possibly Franken-meat? Forget whether or not it is feasible, or if people will overcome their wariness and eat it. The metaphysical question is, what is it? Is it meat or lab-grown meat tissue? What do we assume if we say they are the same or different?

I admit, when I read Newkirk's essay, I thought she was side-stepping the issue. The question of the morality of eating meat is about eating animals, not meat tissue cells. It seems like she is dodging the question by taking a narrow nutritionist view of what makes something meat. On a broader view that takes social meanings into account, meat is not only its cells but also its tastes and significance in the lives of the people who eat it, not to mention the animal it comes from.

The standing of in vitro meat as an animal product has consequence for religious peoples. For example, Jewish law prohibits eating the limb off of a live animal, or even eating any part that was separated from a live animal.[42] It basically means do not eat animals while they are alive, and animals should always be properly and humanely slaughtered. But that would rule out laboratory meat unless the stem cells were taken after an animal was slaughtered according to kosher law. It is, however, possible that rabbis could rule that in vitro meat is a novel product that comes from an animal, and not an animal, per se. That would make it more like milk or cheese than meat. Or, it could be considered *pareve*—foods containing neither meat nor dairy. Arguably, an in vitro cheeseburger would be kosher.

Islamic law similarly states that the product cannot be halal unless the source is. If cells were taken from a halal source and grown in a halal medium, then the final product would be acceptable. In that case, in vitro meat could be considered to be meat. However, a recent ruling from the International Islamic Fiqh Academy stated that laboratory-grown meat would not be considered meat from an animal but "cultured meat." Because the animal was not slaughtered, the product is vegetative and "similar to yogurt and fermented pickles."[43] If it is not considered meat, then it is not subject to either Islamic dietary or animal welfare laws.

According to Hindu law, laboratory meat would be considered meat even if no animals were harmed; however, there is no consensus about what it is exactly or even if it would be strictly off limits.[44] A secular vegetarian might balk at eating it, if for no other reason than that it looks and tastes like real meat and, therefore, condones the culture of eating animals, although, arguably, you could make the same case for eating any hamburger substitute, even if it's entirely plant-based. It is not clear how to classify in vitro meat even though it originates from an animal—and that has moral and religious consequences.

Is egg-free mayonnaise still mayonnaise? Sometimes questions about the identity of food hinge on legal decisions. For example, Unilever, maker of Best Foods and Hellman's mayonnaise filed a lawsuit against Hampton Creek, a start-up that makes an egg-free product called Just Mayo. Unilever claimed that Just Mayo did not meet the legal definition of mayonnaise because it did not contain eggs. They also accused them of false advertising for having an image of an egg on their label. The lawsuit was dropped a few months later.

But, strictly speaking, they were right. The FDA's definition of mayonnaise is the "emulsified semisolid food prepared from vegetable oil(s), one or both of the acidifying ingredients specified in paragraph (b) of this section, and one or more of the egg yolk-containing ingredients specified in paragraph (c) of this section." Paragraph C mentions liquid egg yolks, frozen egg yolks, dried egg yolks, or liquid, frozen, or dried whole eggs.[45] The idea of egg-free mayonnaise makes no sense.

The FDA issued a warning letter to Hampton Creek that their product did not conform to standards and asked that they change or clarify some of the wording on the label.[46] As a compromise, they were allowed to keep their name and their logo (of an egg around a silhouette of a plant shoot) but made the words "egg free" larger and added the words "spread and dressing." They also had to including wording that explained that the word "just" did not mean "only" but referred to social justice. Their product isn't *simply* mayo but *righteous* mayo.

But is it really mayonnaise? From the perspective of the law, it is not clear. The FDA determined that it did not meet their standards, so it would seem it is not; but they made an exception and allowed them to keep their name so long as they changed the label to make it clear that it was an egg-free spread, not actually mayonnaise. Just Mayo is somehow considered to be mayonnaise even though it does not contain one of the main ingredients in the FDA's legal definition.

However, the product looks, smells, and tastes like real mayonnaise. You can cook and bake with it and do all of the usual things one does with mayonnaise. I imagine a connoisseur would be able to tell the difference, or even a layperson tasting the two condiments side by side. But when it is spread on a sandwich or mixed into something else as an ingredient—the way mayonnaise is typically used—it passes for the real thing.

The ingredients are one way to determine if vegan mayo is real, the law another, and conventional usage still another. It depends on what the criteria are and who decides: a consumer, a cook, or a lawyer—and even then, it is ambiguous. Common sense (usually not a reliable way to do metaphysics) would say that mayonnaise has to be gelatinous, spreadable, and taste like it is supposed to otherwise it is something else. It is mayo with respect to its social meanings but not mayo with respect to its chemistry.

Is dirt food? People around the world have eaten dirt going back thousands of years. Usually the dirt is soft, crumbly, and clay rather than dry, dusty, and dirty. Some kinds of dirt are more comestible than others. Geophagy is rare, and probably not a good idea, but not uncommon and, arguably, time-tested. Various health benefits have been linked to geophagy, including nutrient supplementation and pathogen protection. Of course, various health risks have also been linked to it, because dirt is not really that good for you if you eat too much or eat the wrong kind.[47]

But what makes a nonfood craving (or pica) reasonable depends more on the intentions of the eater than on the nature of the dirt. There are wholesome and pathological forms of pica. The wholesome ones are the ancient, ongoing, and time-tested practices of geophagy for medicinal, religious, or nutritive purposes. Some people even boil their clay before eating it—essentially cooking dirt to make it more palatable.

But for some, pica is simply an eating disorder motivated by unhealthy desires for self-control or self-destruction. It often occurs with other mental health disorders and impaired functioning. It is not considered pathological when toddlers eat dirt but when adults do, and when it is not part of a culturally supported practice, then it is diagnosable. According to the *Diagnostic and Statistical Manual of Mental Disorders*, the criteria for pica are: a person must display the persistent eating of nonnutritive substances for at least one month; the behavior must not be socially condoned; and the behavior must occur alongside another mental disorder.[48] Then it warrants clinical attention. Pica has less to do with a desire for food than some other not well-understood root causes.

The interpretive answer to whether or not dirt counts as food is that it depends on why someone is eating it. The meaning changes depending on the intentions of the eater. The same dirt can either be food or the object of a pathological desire. That in itself has interesting consequences for food metaphysics, if the nature of something depends on how it is perceived (or intended in consciousness, as a phenomenologist would say), then the status of dirt as food has less to do with the object and more to do with how we perceive it.

When does food become garbage? At what point does something become food and at what point does it transform into something you would rather discard than eat? Fruit ripens, then rots; animals are butchered into portions of meat that eventually decompose; flour, water, salt, and yeast can be baked into bread that stales and grows mold. Pretty much everything we eat is transformed by some kind of processing, and everything has a shelf life and turns into something inedible, if not revolting. When does the changeover happen? Is there a line or is it a judgment call?

In a *Seinfeld* episode, George Costanza took a discarded éclair out of the trash and ate it. He explained to Jerry why he believed it was still food: it was protected by a doily, it was sitting on top of the trash (not mixed in with it), and it only had one bite taken from it. Jerry claimed that if something is in a trash bin, it is trash; if it is adjacent to trash, then it's trash; and if it was partially eaten and discarded, then you shouldn't eat it because it's trash.

The transformation from food to garbage is vexing. Something that is acceptable to eat in one context can be unacceptable to eat when placed in a slightly different setting—or after someone else eats a part of it. Clearly, social norms govern rules of appropriate food eating. That does not mean that the answers are easy, even within an established framework, otherwise George and Jerry would agree whether or not the éclair was trash. But it does mean that we can turn to social conventions to try to answer questions about what and when something is acceptable to eat. We can have a conversation about it, learn more about different perspectives, and maybe even reach an understanding.

There might be general agreement about when something is ripe and ready or rotten and unfit for human consumption. Food judgments are not only based on social precedents but also on taste, smell, and instinct—molded by socialization, for sure, but only up to a point. Our bodies sometimes override our minds and tell to us whether or not something is okay to eat. We are wired for self-protection against disgusting and inedible things. Somehow, we know to avoid anything overly bitter, stringent, or pungent in favor or what is sweet, salty, and familiar—away from what is foreign and potentially dangerous, toward what is familiar and safe. We are probably wired for comfort foods rather than anything exotic.[49] Then again, sometimes our minds override our bodies when we acquire tastes for counterintuitive things like alcohol, moldy cheeses, and hot peppers. Anything aged and fermented has decomposed a bit and yet that very process of decay is what makes the pickle delicious.

The answer to the question "what is food?" is complicated. There are several good answers and many true things we can say about what food ultimately is. Borderline cases, where it is unclear how to conceptualize something, or even if something counts as food, point to the difficultly in trying to nail down what exactly food is. The best we can do in these judgment calls is to defend our claims and be open to the interpretations of others. An interpretive approach to these in-between cases may not resolve the issue once and for all, but it can help to clarify where someone is coming from and what reasons back our claims. People may not agree about what kind of food something is, or whether something is food, but we can at least try to figure out why we disagree.

Chapter Two

FOOD EPISTEMOLOGY

Food epistemology is somewhat different than ordinary epistemology simply because we experience food differently. We not only perceive, know, and judge it, we also smell, taste, and feel it. We crave it, savor it, and indulge in it. We stress about it, have regrets about it, and hate ourselves because of it. There really is nothing else like it. We also do a lot of things with it, such as farming, processing, and cooking. We have practical, not just empirical, knowledge about it. Chapter 1 argued that there are several different conceptions of the nature of food and that marginal cases are open to interpretation. This chapter examines some of the other ways we experience food beyond questioning its essence.

Although we know a lot of different things about food, and we do a lot of different things with it, there are patterns in our experience that underlie the countless interpretations we make about it. One might view things as a Christian, vegetarian, or libertarian; one might see things as a safety inspector, connoisseur, or consumer on a budget. These interpretations not only explain how the world is but also map out what we could and should do. Rawls calls them "comprehensive doctrines," the belief systems we all have and which often clash in pluralistic societies.[1] Food interpretations put things into context, organize complex information, and help us gain perspective.

This chapter examines how a particular kind of interpretation, "narrative knowledge," can help us make sense of the complex world of food—not just essences but food actions, events, and identities. A narrative (or story) is like an interpretation but broader, more comprehensive, and geared toward representing things that have a historical dimension. Narratives can tell us more than descriptions or explanations simply because they can take a longer view, incorporate more perspectives, and cover more details. They can help us make sense of what would otherwise be a vast range of unrelated things, and they can also guide our actions.

This chapter examines some of the common stories we tell about food in the United States.[2] Not all of them are very good. Some are slanted and oversimplify; others are tired, clichéd, or at best, banally true. But others are genuinely insightful and help shed light on how we make and eat food. The trick is to read food narratives critically and always hold them lightly.

Another issue food poses to epistemology is the unique kind of knowledge we get by smelling and tasting. We have knowledge of it from our eyes and ears but also (and crucially) from our mouths and noses. On one hand, it doesn't really matter how we know it. Food is a matter of interpretation, like any other empirical knowledge, known by the senses in relation to backgrounds, presuppositions, and expectations. It does not seem to pose any difficulties either to traditional epistemology or to narrative knowledge. The source of knowledge might be different, but the kinds of judgments we make are no more or less interpretive and defeasible than anything else we experience.

On the other hand, smelling and tasting are such bodily activities—and eating such a primal act—that we have to stretch epistemology to make sense of something so visceral. The kind of knowledge we get from eating and drinking is more bodily than ordinary knowledge (inside of the mouth, with the help of the tongue, nose, and stomach). How something tastes is a very different kind of perception than how something looks, sounds, and feels. Knowledge acquired by the mouth is less reliable in some ways, more sensitive in others, and uniquely capable of tasting.

To further complicate matters, our food experiences are often motivated by unconscious biases and beliefs. We all are inexplicably drawn to some things and repelled by others. Sometimes it is harmless; other times advertisers and marketers deliberately manipulate us. It can be hard to understand our own likes and dislikes when their causes are often beyond our ken. An interpretive theory of food knowledge has to contend with the effects of both external manipulation and unconscious desires that make it hard to know even the most basic things, like when we are hungry and when we are full.

Yet, in spite of the influences on food experience, it is important to remember that food epistemology is always about the things we eat, not just what happens in our minds. The way something tastes depends on what is actually in it. We may not agree whether or not something tastes good, but we can often agree on what the taste profile is. Does that mean that tastes are objective? Can we determine what something really tastes like even though people have different, even conflicting, interpretations? The objectivity of taste is the subject of the final part of this chapter.

WHAT KIND OF KNOWLEDGE DO WE HAVE ABOUT FOOD?

Chapter 1 claimed that the knowledge we have about food is interpretive. It is always based on presuppositions and background conditions in dialogue with others and our societies. Anything empirically known is based on one's perspective—or where someone is coming from. But we are all products of our times and we could never know all of the ways we are affected by our historical contexts even if we tried. Instead, the best we can do is to make interpretations in light of our limited points of view and to engage with others to find common ground. To put it differently, our histories are not something to be overcome but conditions for arriving at the truth—a fallible, defeasible, and interpretive conception of truth.

When an interpretation takes a broad view of human affairs that unfolds over time, it has an implicit narrative form. For example, we tell stories whenever we recount events, connect agents to situations, and sketch out scenarios. The premise of narrative knowledge is that stories answer basic journalistic questions: who, what, where, when, why, and how.

The case for the philosophical function of narratives is not new. In the last forty years, we've seen the importance of narratives for epistemology,[3] ethical theory,[4] bioethics,[5] personal identity,[6] and philosophy of mind.[7] Narratives have become a part of the methodological diet of the social sciences, education, and psychotherapy. Their role is well established.

There are five things stories do well that are important to understanding food.

1. *Stories interpret events.* Stories are always told from someone's perspective, which means that any account of what happened is interpretive, not objective. This is not to say that all interpretations are equally valid but, rather, alternate interpretations are always possible. Unlike simple propositions about natural events or logical necessity, human affairs and historical events are essentially interpretive. Because they are temporal, they have a narrative form: unfolding over time, occurring in episodes, and always understood in a partial and limited manner. Stories give meaning to what would otherwise be an endless series of occurrences.
2. *Stories portray characters.* Stories answer the question "who?" by explaining the experiences, relationships, and events that make up our lives. The identity of a person unfolds over time (even a lifetime) and includes whatever details round out a character. A narrative creates a portrait of who someone is by cobbling together parts of a life into a whole. The same goes for the identities of groups, cultures, and nations. We are all embedded in the stories we tell about ourselves and the stories others tell about us: about who we are, where we come from, and how we are similar to and different from others.
3. *Stories depict scenarios.* Stories not only recount the past but also forecast the future. They are inventive as well as interpretive. Scenario planning (or predictions that try to take as many social variables into account as possible) have become a standard practice in fields that require strategic forecasts.[8] Businesses, farmers, and the military, among others, use story scenarios to test possible situations by imagining how events might play out. Sometimes moral deliberation, particularly consequentialism, involves telling stories in order to test the ethical outcomes of possible decisions. Scenarios can help us figure out what could happen and how we might best respond.
4. *Stories make arguments.* Stories can supplement and even stand in for arguments. A narrative framework depicts situations, portrays characters, and imagines consequences in defense of truth and normative claims. In turn, defeasible claims sometimes rely on stories for illustration and support. For example, President Reagan used to tell stories of "real people" in his speeches in defense of his policy agendas, such as the "welfare queens" who leeched off the system at taxpayer expense or the earnest small businessman hampered by government regulations. The stories justify policy proposals, and the policy

proposals promise better endings to the stories. As Reagan knew, reasons and evidence are not enough to persuade people about politics. Stories can be more persuasive because they employ a wider range of rhetorical devices to make even weak cases appear strong, and strong cases even stronger.[9]

5. *Stories humanize characters and make events relatable.* Perhaps the greatest virtue of stories is that they can engage us in ways that theories cannot. They bring us into their world and let us see things from the perspectives of others. They can draw us in and make us care about persons and things we otherwise might never have considered. And they can do so in ways that are relatable and accessible, especially for those lacking expertise. Stories help us to identify with others and to understand where they are coming from.[10] They have the unique ability not only to connect us, but also to provide models for resolving moral problems to help restore relationships in ways that are acceptable to everyone. Stories help us navigate our relationships.[11]

There are a number of narratives that shape the way we interpret food, agriculture, animals, and eating. These narratives do more than the conceptualizations of the essence of food in chapter 1; they also account for the many things we do with food. Narratives are about food actions and events, not just food essences. Here are some of the most common ones we tell in the United States about food affairs.

Freedom narratives. The freedom story is the bedrock of American ideology. It is about how we are a free country, how governments shouldn't interfere in our lives, and how nowhere else in the world is as free (or as great) as the United States. It is the core story of the founding of this country. It is also about how economic markets work best if we have the freedom to produce and consume without interference from others. And it's not entirely implausible: most of us believe we are free to choose how to live our lives and that no one has the right to tell us what to do.

According to this story, food choices are up to individuals who should be free from government meddling in making, selling, or eating food. The food industry is free to produce what it wants and you are free to buy it or not buy it. It's up to you. For example, poor and hungry people may be unfortunate, but unless there was a specific injustice done, each of us is responsible for ourselves. The same for migrant farmworkers. So long as no one forced anyone to emigrate and work on farms, their situation can be explained by a series of free choices that might result in hardship but not injustice. For any food issue, freedom to choose is always good and restrictions on choice are always bad. The freedom narrative has a libertarian answer for everything: no government spending, let the market figure it out, and if regulations are needed it should be handled at the local, not national, level. Food stamps, soda taxes, and mandatory food labeling? No. School lunch standards and no antibiotics in farm animals? Only if that's what people want. Reduce hunger, raise animals humanely, and reduce food-borne illness? It's up to you, not the government.

Utopian narratives. The utopian narrative is not only about freedom, but also about faith in progress and endless optimism in our ability to improve our lives. This story paints a rosy picture of human nature and the technologies that will make everything cleaner, healthier, and better. The future promises abundant food, booming economies, and the end to hunger. Governments, private industry, and pro-business interests typically invoke some form of utopianism, as do the advocates for laboratory meat, nanotechnology, and sustainable agriculture. The websites of Monsanto (www.monsanto.com) and General Electric (www.ge.com) are filled with optimistic assessments of what new technologies can do to feed the hungry and clean the environment. All modernization narratives are essentially utopian: free markets plus new technologies equal abundance for everyone. Whatever is currently bad about food and agriculture will have an innovative solution in the near future.

Dystopian narratives. By contrast, dystopian narratives are usually about the dangers of science and technologies run amok. They portray a bleak, dehumanized future with despotic rulers, environmental catastrophes, and dreary food, among other bad things. In the science fiction dystopias in *Alien*, *Brazil*, and *The Matrix*, people eat "oppressive mush" in highly controlled future worlds.[12] Closer to home, we find dystopian narratives in cautionary tales of modernization gone awry, for example, in the alarmism that colors the debates surrounding genetically engineered foods.[13]

The reason food technology debates are so charged might be because people often feel helpless in the face of the industrial juggernaut and blame technologies for their problems. A lot of us believe, for example, that factory farming, water pollution, and food contamination are inevitable.[14] We seem to be gripped by a dystopian story about how we are destined for disaster. The 1970s were filled with grim projections about overpopulation, shrinking resources, and global famine.[15] Those stories are still out there—and, obviously, famine and ecological disaster should be taken seriously—but the fear of a blighted world without food is a well-worn story with a long history. Warren Belasco describes the ongoing debates around the future of food as a contrast between "gloomy Malthusians" and "optimistic cornucopians." There have always been, and probably always will be, food dystopians and utopians.[16]

Romantic narratives. The typical Romantic narrative does two things: it criticizes the status quo and promises to restore lost harmony with nature. Like dystopianism, Romantic narratives blame science and technology for corrupting our food and the environment; like utopianism, they propose a better future if we take a holistic worldview and create an emotional connection with nature.

Michael Pollan's food writing follows a Romantic narrative when he tells us to avoid processed food in favor of the kinds of things our grandparents ate back in a simpler time. The story he tells warns of the dangers of taking a narrow, reductivist view on food and suggests we see it as connected to cultures and traditions. The more acquainted we are with food production and preparation, the better our lives will be.[17] In other words, alienation from our food is bad and connection with it is good. Pollan's version of Romanticism helped lend support for farmer's markets, community supported agriculture, and do-it-yourself foods. The story is mixed with reasons, arguments, and empirical evidence, but it found an audience (probably) because the story of Romanticism is familiar.

American agrarianism is a homespun version of Romanticism that celebrates the virtues of rural life before industrialization ruined communities and commodified agriculture. The heroes are farmers and ranchers, small towns and traditions; the villains are capitalists and industrialists, alienation and mechanization. At its worst, agrarianism is an "us versus them" story of noble country folk standing up to corrupt (possibly Jewish) eastern elites, merchants, and financiers. Nineteenth century rural American anti-bankism was colored by anti-Semitism[18] and its echoes continue today.[19] But, at best, agrarianism can be a radical critique of the corporate takeover of agriculture and an argument for alternative food systems.[20]

Political narratives. These narratives frame food and agriculture as a political affair among producers, consumers, and governments. The freedom narrative may be the dominant story, but there are others out there in the op-ed pages, the advocacy literature,[21] and documentaries, such as *Cowspiracy* (2014) and *That Sugar Film* (2014). The Marxist version of the narrative centers on capitalist accumulation at the expense of workers, food quality, and the environment.[22] Marion Nestle's liberal narrative tells of understaffed regulatory agencies, food industry lobbyists, and co-opted nutritionists.[23] Similarly, anti-colonialist narratives tell of resource extraction, transformed diets, and domination of locals.[24] What they have in common is the way they frame food and agriculture into a coherent view that explains how ordinary foods have an ugly backstory. Facts are woven into narratives to make compelling arguments.

These stories are like travelogues that take us to farms and factories to reveal unsavory secrets about our food. For example, Upton Sinclair's book *The Jungle* brought readers to hideous slaughterhouses and spurred political action; *Omnivore's Dilemma*, by Michael Pollan, and *Fast Food Nation*, by Eric Schlosser, bring readers to industrial food facilities and encourage ethical consumerism.[25] These narratives attempt to empower people to effect change over the entire food system with every purchase. In some stories, the ethical plea is explicit, for example, the Academy Award nominated documentary *Food Inc.*[26] urges us to vote with our dollars, giving shoppers the power to determine the nature of their food.[27] The film uses jarring images of factory farms and humanizing stories to drive home how the food system makes everyone and everything worse off—except corporate profits.

Of course, conservative political narratives tell very different stories from the same set of facts. On an alternate telling, the villains are lazy, immoral people and the national government; the heroes are self-disciplined people and traditional values. Bad people and too many regulations are the problem, not the food system. Clearly, which political narrative is evoked makes all the difference. The same thing can appear entirely differently depending on the framing: Michelle Obama's healthy school lunch program can be seen as either a progressive policy to improve public health or government intrusion into our private affairs; genetically modified food as either corporate control over nature or technological solutions to practical problems; and veganism as either ethical consumerism or liberal elites dictating other people's diets. Food politics is always bound up with political narratives and we tend to believe sources we already trust and people we perceive to be like us.[28]

Eating narratives. The simple act of eating also has a narrative form. It goes like this: I was hungry so I ate. The beginning is an appetite, the middle is the act of eating, and the end is satisfaction. It is not much of a story, but a story nonetheless. Usually it is not worth telling, but there are a few noteworthy eating narratives.

One is about how food brings people together: they were strangers or enemies before the meal, then became friends or allies after eating together; they were able to bridge differences by dining together and sharing a pleasant experience. This eating story is about peace, harmony, and reconciliation.

Another eating story is about conflict. The dinner table is the place where we air our grievances and confirm our differences: Thanksgiving was ruined by my daughter, who returned from college a vegetarian. We are reminded about how unlike we are, how differently we see things, and how we dislike each other's food choices. Eating together can heighten generational or social differences. This eating story is about disagreement, division, and difference.

Another eating story is about savagery, revenge, and violence, or what Korsmeyer calls "terrible eating."[29] Fairy tales and folk stories are filled with savage eating: ogres who eat human flesh, vampires who suck blood, and monsters who eat things alive. Stories of poisoning are about how food can be used to betray and harm. These stories speak to the level of trust and vulnerability we share when we eat. Worst of all are stories of cannibalism, perhaps the most transgressive kind of eating.[30] Terrible eating narratives are about the treachery, violence, and destruction of life.

Another eating story is about weigh loss: I was thin, I gained weight, and I lost weight. Or another version: something happened and I gained weight, I decided to act, and I succeeded—so can you. The narrative is part confessional, part self-help guide, and part motivational. It plays two roles for readers: we learn about the lives of others and we are inspired to model ourselves after them. Weight loss narratives are stories of salvation: I was lost, I changed, and now I am saved. They follow a basic Judeo-Christian narrative of life after death, mediated by trials of temptation, suffering, and ultimately redemption.

In reality, weight loss is complicated, diets almost always fail, and not all bodies respond the same way. The more realistic story would be about an unsuccessful weight loss attempt—less inspiring but more true to life.

Then again, the purpose of these stories is to motivate, not dissuade, and they are readily available at the supermarket checkout line, cynically used to sell things to insecure dieters.

Other noteworthy eating narratives include hunger strikes, fasting, forced feeding, picky eating, and food cravings. Each has its main actors, setting, and a plot. Each puts the reasons people have for eating into a context that explains their choices and their fate.

Traditional narratives. There are several kinds of traditional narratives that recount how our food should be made and what it should taste like. These narratives appeal to the authority of tradition to explain the way things are and how we should act. For example, food preparation, eating ethics, and dining customs are usually explained on the basis of the past. Even though, in logic, we are told that arguments from authority are weak, in most of our daily lives the authority of the past is all we have to go on. The fact is that traditions are not senseless or irrational, nor are they impervious to change. Instead, they are made up of the beliefs, practices, and institutions that form the basis for most of our everyday activities. We have to contend with traditions regardless of whether we agree with them or criticize them. Gadamer describes the role of tradition in our experience as "effective-history."[31] We are always affected by the past whether we like it or not.

The three main forms of traditional narratives are about culture, religion, and gender. The cultural narratives explain how "we" do things, or how things are done "around here." In academic food studies, the relationship between food and culture is known as "foodways" and refers to what and how members of a group eat, the meanings they assign to foods, and how cuisines relate to cultural identities. Foodways recount how things should be in terms of cultural norms and traditions, for example, why Texans typically use forks and eat chicken but not chicken feet. (Why? Because that's how people have always done things around here.)

Religious narratives do many of the same things as cultural narratives with added elements of sacredness, communion with the supernatural, and various rewards and sanctions that are compelling to believers. They are older and more established than cultural (and especially national) identities.[32] Gendered narratives overlap with both cultures and religions by dividing up a wide range of activities, beliefs, and tastes along gender lines. Stereotypically, men eat meat, spicy and unhealthy foods, and consume large portions. Women eat fruits and vegetables, sweet and healthy foods, and consume modest portions. Men eat first and eat the most; women feed others and eat less. The particulars of who eats what may vary across cultures, but all cultures divide food activities by gender.[33]

Othering narratives. Sometimes traditional narratives portray outsiders unkindly by othering the foodways of those who are different from us. These stories might romanticize the eating habits of others (healthy Mediterraneans or respectful Native Americans), demean others (as cannibals or lovers of animal innards), or simply misrepresent others (their food is too spicy). Othering narratives range from naïve, to exoticizing, to dehumanizing. It is not clear if a story can be othering in a positive sense—respectfully appreciating differences. Usually, the act of othering generalizes and fetishizes differences based on imaginary or exaggerated representations.

Sometimes culinary authenticity is used as a test of group membership, for example, when presidential candidates are seen chowing down on some regional treat at a local joint in order to prove they are regular slobs like us—except when they fail and order the wrong food (Senator Kerry, Swiss cheese on a cheesesteak) or eat it the wrong way (Major DeBlasio, pizza with a fork). Fox News pilloried President Obama for ordering a hamburger with spicy mustard (that phony!). After the culinary faux pas, the story writes itself: the candidate is clearly an elite snob who is out of touch ordinary people.

Othering narratives can also be told within a group about each other, for example, by fat-shaming overweight people. Weight discrimination relies on a narrative that blames people for their appearance and justifies harsh judgment. It overlaps with a freedom narrative but it contains additional information about who overweight people are presumed to be, how they are responsible for overeating, and (through a series of explanations about how the health care system works) how they cause others to bear their medical expenses. It others on the basis of body type through narratives that link food, complex social relations, and institutions—in ways that a space alien would have a hard time understanding unless it understood both the narrative and a lot of details about life on Earth.

Meat narratives. Eating meat figures into each of the other major stories of food in one way or another, but it also has its own narratives that justify or criticize killing animals for their taste. Both marshal facts, recount the past, and trace out a range of consequences for humans, animals, and the environment. Meat-eating narratives recount who eaters are, what a good life for an animal is, and what the fate of the planet might be. No other food, except maybe alcohol, has such elaborate justifications or endures such ongoing criticism.

One common meat-eating defense is a naturalistic story about human evolution (with special attention to the shape of our teeth). The story follows an inevitable arc of life: all creatures are born, eat, reproduce, and die. It's futile to think that we are different from any other animal, so we should eat our natural, dentally appropriate, omnivorous diet. The naturalistic defense is basically the circle of life song from the *Lion King*. It combines Darwinian evolution theory, Romantic longing for unity with nature, and religious conceptions of redemption after death. In short, it is natural for us to eat meat because everything fits together perfectly in a food chain and it would be unnatural to disrupt it.[34]

Critics of meat eating connect the dots between industrial food-animal production and consumers to show the bad consequences, usually for our health or the environment. Like a travelogue, these stories follow the lifecycle of food-animal production and consumption to make the case that it is shot through with injustices to everyone involved. The best of these stories includes the lives of meat packers, who have dangerous jobs that take a terrible physical and psychological toll. Slaughterhouses around the world are usually staffed by the poor and vulnerable, often undocumented immigrants and refugees.[35] When framed as more than a dietary choice, the pro-meat-eating narrative affirms human superiority over animals while the anti-meat-eating narrative is a generally depressing story.

The main point I'd like to affirm is that narratives are a distinct form of knowledge geared toward human affairs that affect public perceptions about food, agriculture, eating, and animals. Unlike the conceptions of food from chapter 1, which only concern metaphysical questions about essences, narratives do much more. They frame food actions and events, assign roles to humans and animals, add detail to situations and characters, and help make arguments more compelling.

HOW RELIABLE IS OUR FOOD KNOWLEDGE?

Food (and drink) can be conceptualized and narrated in a number of different ways to shed light on what they are and how we relate to them. But the one thing that sets them apart from everything else we experience is the source of knowledge about them. We not only see, hear, and touch food and drink, we also sniff and taste them. Furthermore, we only know how things taste by actually tasting them in the mouth. Or, more precisely, we know the flavors of food and drink by tasting, smelling, and mouthfeel.[36] The key differences between ordinary and food epistemology are that experiences of tasting and savoring are appreciably different from our experiences of seeing and hearing. The kind of information we have is different, what we can know is different, and the way we make and verify truth claims is different. Yet experiences of tasting and savoring are crucial to the central questions of a food epistemology: How can we tell what X tastes like? Does X taste the same to everyone? What is belief, truth, and justification in food perception?

Another reason food knowledge is different from ordinary knowledge is the extent of what can be known. Tastes perception is limited by our physiology somewhat differently than vision and hearing are. The range of what we can detect, the background conditions that affect it, and the role of our bodies are all relevantly different. Tasting is a proximal sense that requires we come into contact with something; it is almost more chemical than cognitive. That means that our bodies play a far greater role than they do in the distal senses. Our experiences are affected by things that are beyond the reach of our awareness—not just our brains but also our guts.

For example, consider what it feels like to be hungry. Our bodies let us know when we need calories: the absence of food is felt in the stomach and experienced as a craving. Yet hunger is more than just a physiological state; it is a complex mix of neurological, social, and economic causes. Although its origins are knowable (albeit debatable), the cause of an individual's experience of hunger is often mysterious. Hunger comes and goes, sometimes at predictable times, other times not. The sensation itself is susceptible to peripheral factors that make us feel more or less hungry or make us crave certain foods. We don't really know why it starts and stops or how we can be mistaken about our own feelings of it. It is odd that our central experience of food can be so enigmatic.

Granted, for many people in the world, there is nothing mysterious about it. One in eight go to sleep hungry every night. One in nine suffer from chronic hunger, without enough food each day to live a healthy active life. Nearly half (45 percent) of the deaths of children under the age of five are caused by malnutrition: 3.1 million children every year.[37] The causes of world hunger are well understood. They include poverty, lack of agricultural development, wars and displacement, and the whims of the market.

Most of us, however, are neither undernourished nor malnourished. Nor are we wasting, stunted, or underweight. Still, we all experience discomfort when there is a lack of food: pangs of pain and a mild, crampy sensation; growling and contracting of the stomach; and feelings of lightheadedness and weakness. The hormone ghrelin is gradually released in the gastrointestinal tract and triggers the brain to cause pain. Ghrelin also increases the secretion of gastric acid and readies the body for food intake.[38]

Other brain chemicals seem to be involved in the feeling of hunger, including neurotransmitters dopamine and serotonin. There does not appear to be a single hunger center within the brain but rather an anatomy that includes the hypothalamus, amygdala, and frontal cortex. The precise physiology cannot be reduced to a single mechanism, nor is there one that tells us when we are full. The brain and brain chemicals interact with the stomach, intestines, and central nervous system in ways that are not very well known.[39]

It is, however, beyond a doubt that the feeling of hunger and satiety are largely involuntary processes tied to the biological need for the right amount of food. Likewise, the craving for fluids is also largely involuntary, albeit with different neurophysiology, hormones, and organs. Our brains regulate, hunger, thirst, and satiety to impel us to start and stop consuming. That means that our main experiences of need and satisfaction are not in our control. We can tell when we are hungry, thirsty, or full, but these experiences emerge from beyond the reach of possible experience.

Pathological eating is another matter. People eat from anxiety, depression, addiction, or self-criticism; they eat after they stop smoking cigarettes, finish smoking cannabis, or suffer trauma. We overeat, under-eat, and binge eat. Food can be the object of obsession, the trigger of strong emotions, and the source of shame and despair. Hunger is only one of many reasons we eat.[40]

In addition, we can be made to feel hungry by external cues, for example, the smell or sight of food, the sound of someone cooking, or the mere mention of food. The pancreas is triggered to produce insulin, which lowers blood sugar and makes us feel hungry. We're like Pavlov's dog, conditioned to respond to anything previously associated with eating. Hunger and thirst can also be influenced by how active we are, how much sleep we had the night before, and the surrounding air temperature. (If it is hot, you'll eat less than if it's cold.) It is often hard to tell when we really need to eat and drink or when the need has been induced by something external.[41]

The same is true of satiety. There is a complex interplay of physiological causes and psychological influences that make it difficult to know why we start and stop eating and drinking. Like hunger, satiety can be triggered or delayed. There no clear signal or feeling we have that indicates when we have had enough to eat, short of feeling so stuffed that we literally couldn't take another bite. The feeling of satiety is not only elastic but alarmingly out of our control.

There is a vast literature on the psychology of food that analyzes how susceptible we are to prompts and nudges that affect how much we eat. For example, studies show that people will eat more when food is served in a large container and eat less when it is served in a small container—and yet each group reports feeling satisfied. Other studies show that subjects who think they have eaten a lot will claim to feel full, while subjects who think they have not eaten a lot will claim to feel hungry, even when they have eaten the same amount. The perception of the amount of food matters more for feeling sated than the actual amount consumed.[42]

We seem to rely on visual cues more than how we feel to tell us how much we have eaten. We usually stop eating when we finish a portion, not because of the neurophysiology of satiation, but because we believe our eyes more than our stomach, even though visual cues can be deceptive. Studies show that people eat more when distracted, for example, by talking or watching TV.[43] We also eat more when served a variety of foods. Psychologists call it "sensory specific satiety." We grow numb to the experience of the same stimuli. We eat less when our senses (not our stomachs) are sated and eat more when more tastes are available, hence the danger of the buffet.[44]

Social influences affect our appetites and food choices, especially our friends and families, but also strangers in our vicinity.[45] We eat more when those around us eat more; we eat less when those around us eat less, yet test groups that eat vastly different amounts will both say they were satisfied.[46] Families, in particular, have an effect on the foods eaten in and out of the household. If parents eat fruits and vegetables, so will their children;[47] if they drink soft drinks, so will their children.[48] Yet even adults will eat more fruit and vegetables if those nearby are eating them.[49]

These and the thousands of other experiments on the psychology of consumption show our vulnerability to external influences. If our understanding about our own food intake is so unreliable, we cannot really know for sure when we are hungry, how much we have eaten, or when we have eaten enough. It's amazing to think about how well we know all kinds of complicated things, but how terrible we are at gauging our own appetites. The knowledge we have about the central experience of food is dubious.

The perceptions we have about the flavors of food and drink are equally suspect. Like appetite, tasting and smelling have a physiology and a psychology. The former is centered on the mouth and brain. Tasting, or gustation, occurs when oral sensors detect minute amounts of molecules in liquids; smelling, or olfaction, occurs when nasal sensors detect molecules in air. They operate in tandem to produce tastes. Molecules are released into the mouth and nasal cavities to produce retronasal scents. It's not outside of you, like smelling a flower. Tasting and retronasal smelling only happen inside of you in the acts of eating or drinking.

Gustation and olfaction are considered to be chemical senses primarily because they require physical contact with their objects. They are largely involuntary, tied to bodily reactions, and often resistant to interpretation. These senses are primitive survival mechanisms that help us seek out things that are good to eat and avoid the things that are bad to eat, if not poisonous. Humans are especially able to detect foul, fetid, and bitter tastes and scents. We turn our heads away in disgust, or we immediately spit things out. These gag reactions are good defenses for keeping unwanted things out of the body. Our bodies don't even give us a chance to try out something that strikes us as initially offensive. Tasting and smelling can override our will, for example, to protect us from ourselves when it comes to beautiful but inedible berries or poison look-alikes.

But, assuming something gets past our involuntary defenses, the primary ways we know what food and drink tastes like is by gustation and olfaction. We also get information about food and drink by vision, hearing, touch, and temperature, but nothing is as sensitive to flavors as the tasting-smelling tandem. When chemicals come into contact with taste cells in the mouth, neurons on the chorda tympani nerve lead to the parts of the brain that detect tastes. When chemicals in the air contact the odor receptors in the nasal cavity, receptor cells transmit neurons into the olfactory bulb in the brain. However, the precise mechanism that explains how we register any particular flavor is not well known.[50]

The physiology of taste involves the tongue and also the lips, teeth, roof of the mouth, and salivary glands. The brain is involved, including the medial temporal lobes, limbic system, cerebral cortex, medulla oblongata, and the pons for eating, chewing, and swallowing. Digestion has its organs and relevant cerebral activities. Stomach microbes seem to play a role in everything from appetite, digestion, satiety, and, somehow, cognition. No one knows exactly how or why.[51]

And there is still more to tasting physiology, including the role of genes and inherited preferences, the effects in utero of the mother's diet on adult tastes, and the curious case of supertasters, who have an innate capacity to experience flavors more intensely and who are more sensitive to bitterness than most people. All of these factors shape, limit, and affect how we taste food and drink.

However, psychology is just as fundamental as physiology to taste perceptions. One's upbringing, memory, and expectations color the way we taste things, as do our bad experiences and traumatic events. It can be hard to recognize, much less overcome, the positive or negative associations we have to particular things. We often have little to no choice in how we taste something, for example, our age is entirely out of our control and yet plays a key role in how we perceive flavors. Children cannot help but favor sweet over spicy and bitter foods. Older people cannot help but lose much of their ability to taste. Health, illness, and time of day can influence tasting. And everyone knows that nothing tastes like much when you're congested. It seems that our bodies, our histories, and our ages delimit our ability to taste.

Other influences that are beyond our control include the ambient conditions of eating, such as the lighting, noise, and smells. As we saw, people eat more when distracted, but their food also tastes better—and tastes worse when we're on airplanes. Food psychologists routinely run experiments to test the role of external influences on our sense of taste. It is striking how vulnerable we are to biases and external manipulation. We taste what we expect we will taste, and we like and dislike what we expect to like and dislike.

Experiments show that if people are told what they are eating, that's what they will taste, even if what they are told is false. Somehow knowledge overrides and supersedes perception. For example, in one experiment when people were given a lemon-flavored beverage with red food coloring, they believed they were drinking a cherry-flavored drink.[52] We seem to taste with our minds and our eyes. In another experiment, when subjects were given the same dessert served on different colored plates, researchers found that the color and quality of the plate (somehow) affected the taste of the food.[53]

Restauranteurs know that lighting, music, décor, and table settings can create positive expectations. They know that the more descriptive and tasty-sounding menu items are, the more likely customers will find the food tasty. Experiments show that the same food items described differently will actually taste different to test groups. Foods with more enticing descriptions are perceived to be tastier than the identical foods with less appealing descriptions. Maybe the easiest way to make food taste better is to call it something different.[54]

Other studies show that the use of vivid adjectives can trigger our expectations and favorably incline us to like what we eat. Call it menu psychology. It tends to draw on some basic themes: geographic labels (to associate a place with the food), nostalgic labels (to associate happy feelings toward family or traditions), sensory labels (to associate the food with a taste, smell, or texture), and brand labels (to confirm expectations that brand names are better than generics).[55] Psychologists call it "confirmation bias," or "expectation assimilation."

Studies that compare brand names and generics find that, almost without exception, people cannot tell the difference once the food is out of the package. But, when labeled, brand-named foods taste better because we expect them to. We also expect more expensive food and drink to taste better than their cheap counterparts—and they do. Wine tasting is particularly susceptible to manipulation. People always prefer the taste of wines when their expectations are set for high quality. They like cheap wine when told it is from California and dislike the same wine when told it is from North Dakota. The same effect can be induced by fancy or plain labels. Interestingly, people who have high expectations of their wine also find their *food* tastes better—and they eat more—than people who eat the same thing but have low expectations of their wine.[56]

Our experience of food is bound to the body, the unconscious, memory, prejudices, and social influences. Granted, all experience has involuntary origins and suffers from implicit biases, but food experience is different. Tasting alone gives us knowledge of flavors, and hunger and satiety alone tell us when to start and when to stop eating.

Yet the unreliability of tasting and appetite makes us susceptible to manipulation by a food and restaurant industry that is dedicated to getting us to eat more than we need. We have to be vigilant: pay attention to our appetites, be aware of our eating environments, and try to see through hidden biases. We should also pay attention to tastes to try to figure out which are genuinely our own and which are the result of deliberate manipulation. Food epistemology can help by calling attention to the biases and distortions that manipulate our appetites and alter our tastes against our will. Maybe "taste for yourself!" is the enlightenment ideal for food and drink—with the recognition that neither appetite nor taste are ever entirely under our control.

CAN WE TASTE OBJECTIVELY?

If food perception is influenced by expectations and social settings, can we know what anything really tastes like, or is tasting so unreliable that we can never know for certain? Is the taste of something always relative to the perspective of a taster, or is taste something we can all know and get right in spite of our different points of view? In other words, are tastes objective, subjective, or somewhere in between?

If tastes are objective, there is a flavor to the food or drink that can be detected by tasting it. We can recognize, know, and articulate it. Moreover, we can evaluate how things taste and argue that some things are better than others. But if they are subjective, there is nothing knowable there in food that can resolve disputes about tastes. Each of us might taste the same thing differently, and there is no way we can step outside of ourselves to taste it in a neutral and impartial fashion.

A third option is that tastes are interpretive, which means there are better and worse, and more and less creative, ways to understand tastes. We may not be able to detect mind-independent flavors, but we can make defeasible claims about how something tastes that others can potentially agree with. Or, if we disagree, we can look to our presuppositions and background experience to figure out why. Yet the question that always lingers over interpretation theories is about the basis for agreement. Does a taste claim have validity because it is accurate and true, or does it have validity merely because enough (of the right) people make the claim? And what are we to make of wildly different experiences of something, when people make contradictory claims about how something tastes? Interpretive pluralism is one thing (when there are many true things that can be said), conflicting interpretations are another (when we fundamentally disagree).

The gustatory aesthetics literature is divided over how accurately and objectively we can taste food and drink. For example, Michael Shaffer challenges the objectivity of tasting by questioning the authority of gastronomes, who supposedly have a more refined sense of taste than the rest of us. If gastronomes have no special tasting abilities, then there is no reason to accept their judgments about how things supposedly taste. That also goes for food critics, restaurant reviewers, and wine snobs—all of whom might be better at describing food and drink only because they are better describers, not better tasters. Shaffer claims we all have fundamentally the same abilities to taste, just as we all have more or less the same abilities to see and hear (marginal cases notwithstanding). No one thinks that art critics have better vision or music critics better hearing. Why would we think that food critics have better tasting?[57]

Shaffer distinguishes between *direct* and *reflective* tasting. Direct tasting is our immediate, uninterpreted experience of basic flavors: sweet, salty, sour, bitter, and umami. These are the taste equivalents of basic particulars or simple impressions: the building blocks to more complex flavors. No concepts or creative language are needed to identify them. However, reflective tasting requires interpretation and higher cognitive functioning in order to make sophisticated judgments about flavors, for example, when we describe a dish as hearty or well-balanced. We need concepts and knowledge in order describe anything more than basic flavors. Shaffer argues that gastronomes and connoisseurs are no better at direct tasting than you or I; they are, however, much better at reflective tasting. They can more eloquently articulate the taste experiences we all have.

Shaffer claims that disagreements about taste properties "can only really be disagreements about how the direct taste experience is to be conceptually interpreted or described and not about the objective experience itself."[58] The only reason we might disagree about how something tastes is because we use different concepts to describe the same thing. So-called gastronomes simply have a greater vocabulary to apply to the same direct experiences we all have. For Shaffer, anything we taste in food beyond the most basic flavor elements is interpretative and, therefore, completely subjective.

Some of the scientific literature is even more subjective. Scientists can be surprisingly anti-realist in the way they attribute taste perceptions entirely to brain activity. You would think they would argue that our brains accurately register and detect the objective properties of things. You would think they assume that the tasted objects themselves have at least some bearing on how things are perceived. But, instead, scientific explanations of experience solely in terms of brain function omit reference to the external world—secondary without primary qualities.

For example, Jamie Goode, a biologist and wine writer analyzes how the brain represents the experiences we have drinking wine and explains that the "higher-order processing" that occurs whenever we detect and identify flavors is a complex neuronal activity that gathers and organizes information. But he also argues that when critics rate a wine, they are mistaken to assume that they are rating the wine itself. In reality, they are only rating their perception of it. He says that wine critics are "actually describing a conscious representation of their interaction with the wine . . . and not the wine itself."[59] A wine critic is actually a perception critic.

Gordon Shepherd, a well-regarded neuroscientist, makes a similar case. He believes we should focus less on the features of a wine, such as the grape, the region, and the winemaker, but instead the experience of the drinker, in particular, what happens in the brain. He argues that food and drink are made up of molecules but flavors are created by our brains. What is external to us in the world is less important than what is internal to us, namely retronasal smells and the activities of the brain's flavor-center. Flavors come from our brains, not from flavorful foods.[60]

As I philosopher, I have no reason to cavil with either a biological or neurological analysis of what happens when we taste. In fact, I think both are right to emphasize the constitutive role of the mind in processing information. That squares with our modern, post-Kantian sensibilities that our minds contribute to the way we experience things. But my concern is with the way these scientific analyses both separate the perception of flavor from the composition of food. Isn't it common sense that something tastes the way it does because of what's in it? Doesn't tasting tell us what something tastes like—which means it is always about something external to us? When I complain that the turkey is dry, I am referring to properties anyone could also detect (in the turkey). I am not saying "yuck, turkey!" or "my brain makes this turkey seem dry to me." I am saying it tastes dry because it actually is dry. Maybe it was overcooked or the cut of meat has low fat content. Who knows? But the reason I say it is dry is because I detected the dryness of the turkey with my sense of taste.

It is a mistake to conflate the experiences a subject has with the properties an object has, however they are connected. The sensory experience of tasting is not the same as the flavors of something. We detect flavors by using our sense of taste (and smell) in the same way we detect sounds by using our sense of hearing and see things by using our sense of sight. In each case, there has to be a gap between the act and the object of experience, how things appear and how they actually are—between appearance and reality—otherwise our perceptions would always be right. We would all be infallible tasters. Granted, tasting is the only way to experience tastes, but we assume others can taste the same thing, don't we? If we didn't, there would be no food criticism, no comparisons, and no invitations to enjoy the same things. If we truly believed tastes were subjective and entirely in our minds, we wouldn't bother to communicate our experiences to others. We would assume no one could possibly experience the same thing, like describing a dream.

By contrast, Barry Smith argues for the objectivity of tastes by noting the parallels with sight and hearing.[61] There is always a gap between the perceptual act and the object perceived: between seeing and what is seen, hearing and what is heard, and tasting and what is tasted. It might be more difficult to separate the experience of tasting from the flavors that we taste but it is not impossible—certainly no more difficult than distinguishing between touching (the sensation of the keyboard on my fingertips) and the object touched (the keyboard). This difference between perception and reality is crucial. It means we can be right and wrong about tastes, and we can share and compare them. Tastes "extend beyond experience."[62] We detect them in the things we eat and drink because they are actually there, not merely in our minds.

Wine tasting is instructive. A good wine can be enjoyed by anyone, even beginners who can quickly learn how to appreciate the difference between a good and a bad wine. But experienced tasters do more than detect differences; they also know how to discern qualities, how to compare them, and even how to taste *properly* to get the most flavor from something. The experienced taster can actually taste more in a wine than the beginner. His or her knowledge of wines adds to the experience by helping to focus, analyze, and even to improve the drinking experience. Smith believes that knowledge adds to the pleasure or displeasure in drinking. With knowledge and practice we can not only describe but also evaluate the wines accurately. We can learn to tell if a wine actually is fruity, silky, bright, and bold.[63]

Curiously, Smith's case for the objectivity of taste hinges on how something is perceived. *What* is perceived depends on *how* it is perceived: accurately or inaccurately, with or without knowledge, and with attention or indifference. If Smith is right that the right kind of knowledge is required to taste objectively, then truth in gustatory judgments depends on bringing the right things to experience: the right expectations and background knowledge. That means we can change the way something tastes by changing something in the tasting conditions, for example, after brushing our teeth or eating a habanero pepper, or even by having mistaken assumptions. ("This yogurt is awful! Oh, it's sour cream?") We can even cover up the way something tastes if we approach it with the wrong kind of knowledge, as in the case of the red-colored lemon-drink.

If it is true that knowledge matters to tasting, then what are the right kinds of knowledge to have? What helps us appreciate the qualities of food and drink and what prevents it? Kendall Walton argues that proper aesthetic experience depends on having the proper interpretive categories. Speaking of artworks, he says that in order to identify the aesthetic properties of something, you need to have not only facts about it but also what category the artwork belongs to: what kind of work it is supposed to be. If you approach a work with the wrong category in mind, you will misinterpret its aesthetic properties. ("That artist can't paint!" "Oh, it's supposed to be abstract?")

Walton examines how categorization affects our perception of artworks and attempts to distinguish better and worse ways to apply categories. If aesthetic judgments are category-relative, then we need to know how to determine in which category a work should be perceived. Is it a painting, sculpture, song, or installation? What style, what time period, what genre does it fall under, and so on. If Walton is right, the objectivity of aesthetic and non-aesthetic properties of artworks are category-dependent, and there is a proper way to understand and evaluate them.[64]

Can the same case be made for food? Is food also category-dependent, and therefore, is there a proper way to understand and to taste things? Cain Todd applies Walton's notion of interpretive categories to the perception of wine and lists some of the wine-relevant categories that can help in assessments and comparisons. These include: grape varieties, geography, intentions, the age/maturity/vintage, the type of wine, and the quality (premium or regular). These categories are not arbitrary or merely social but depend "in large part on the existence of certain physical properties of wine types and our physical propensities and thresholds involved in experiencing them."[65] Other food and drink have their categories, as well: steaks, cakes, sodas, and pies. It depends on what something is supposed to be.

An immediate question to any discussion of categorization is about authority. Who is to say what the right and wrong categories are? Well, obviously, we do: societies, traditions, and people with experience. Just because our interpretive categories are social and possibly relative to groups of experienced tasters does not mean they are arbitrary or incommensurable. We can always communicate and compare our experiences with others, who may or may not agree. Furthermore, food categories often include nonsubjective things such as ingredients, geography, and preparation techniques. As with wine, these additional categories help to anchor our understanding of what something is and how to taste it.

Of course, even when people employ the right categories, they can still disagree. One way to make sense of different tastes is to acknowledge "taste pluralism." It is possible that when people taste the same thing differently that everyone is right and no one is wrong. For example, people taste the same flavor but disagree about how to describe it. Maybe their different descriptions mask their underlying agreement. Or they describe the flavor in the same way but disagree about how to evaluate it. For example, we agree that the bread is sweet, but I think it's great and you think it's terrible.

There are, however, times when we deeply and fundamentally disagree about the most basic tastes and categorizations. Unlike taste pluralism, where many true things can be said about something, sometimes our judgments flatly contradict one another. That pizza that you describe as fresh, crispy, and delicious is none of those things, as far I can tell. It is reheated, chewy, and so bad it shouldn't even be considered pizza. Both of us cannot be right, unless we assume tastes are completely subjective, or maybe interpretive but radically incommensurable.

Todd takes deep disagreements more seriously than Smith and does not try to explain them away. Instead, he tries to reconcile conflicting judgments with the objectivity of taste by, ironically, defending a "limited relativist position," which is essentially what we called interpretation in chapter 1. Differences in taste experience do not necessarily mean we are unable to understand each other, and we can understand each other without agreeing with each other. Instead, our disagreements can be seen as the start of a conversation, not the end of it. Todd calls for a "defeasible account of the justification of aesthetic judgments."[66] We can always try to see things from the perspectives of others to explain why we disagree. The reasons always lie in our presuppositions and expectations—what Walton calls categories, or what we have been calling conceptualizations and frameworks.

Meanwhile, as philosophers dispute how and by what authority we might evaluate tastes, every day food scientists, flavorists, and professional tasters use "descriptors" to describe flavors and scent profiles without giving it a second thought. People who taste for a living assume a common vocabulary about a common object, that everyone working on a flavor has a common understanding of what they are tasting, and, if they are trying to create something new, what the desired flavor should be. They recognize that, even though perceptions and expectations are different, there are taste and aroma descriptors that we can all agree on. Descriptors are more like heuristics to help us describe than an exact terminology.

One food consulting company says that its lists of flavor profiles are not meant to be all-inclusive, but rather they can "help jumpstart your mind to think of other words for what you are tasting."[67] Another company describes its descriptors as a "useful tool that can be used to communicate" flavors and scents. In addition to the established descriptors it routinely uses, the company wants to "encourage clients to come up with their own and get inspired by the profiles of other ingredients."[68] These companies take what I would call an interpretive approach to taste perception: shared experiences, mindful of different presuppositions, that can accurately and creatively describe aesthetic properties.

In summary, the interpretive theory I've endorsed emphasizes the role of narrative frameworks that create common understandings of things and help make sense of a wide range of actors, objects, and events. In addition to narratives, we have knowledge about food by tasting and by appetite, that is, the food-specific ways we know flavors and know that we desire to eat and stop eating. Both tasting and appetite are, however, subject to influences that challenge our agency. The body, the brain, and the unconscious affect us, as do external influences and visual cues—the kinds of the things that marketers and food psychologists know how to manipulate. Food knowledge has to contend with all of these influences that mediate our experience, right down to how hungry we feel.

An interpretive theory of taste maintains that we can describe and evaluate flavors in light of the litany of influences on experience. We can actually get it right—or at least make claims that others can understand and maybe even agree with. Chapter 3 continues to examine food judgments by considering some of the aesthetic dimensions of taste, including how we acquire it, what kind of pleasures are involved, and what the relationship is between aesthetic and moral judgments about food. Roughly, what is the difference between tasting and having good taste, and if there is a proper way of tasting, is there also a proper way of liking?

Chapter Three

FOOD AESTHETICS

Taste can refer to the sense that perceives flavors, the act of tasting food or drink, the qualities perceived by it, a personal preference for something, a critical appreciation of quality in the arts, the sense of what is fitting and appropriate, or a tiny morsel. Chapter 2 focused on literal tasting and the kind of knowledge we get from eating and drinking. This chapter focuses on metaphorical tasting as preference and discernment of the best things, as when we say "everyone has their own taste" or "their house is decorated tastefully." Food aesthetics is about both the act of tasting flavors and the aesthetic discrimination that Enlightenment philosophers called taste.[1]

Food (or gustatory) aesthetics has shadowed art aesthetics since the eighteenth century when taste became the lead metaphor for art appreciation. Modern philosophers try to balance the subjective way we experience likes and dislikes with the expectation that any judgment about quality should apply to everyone. The Moderns want to affirm critical standards in artworks in the face of the subjective pleasures that underlie our tastes. Kant, for example, tries to reconcile the subjectivity of preferences with the universality of taste standards by distinguishing between literal and aesthetic taste—between tasting and having good taste. Art appreciation for Kant is like tasting food, only more rational and disinterested. Similarly, Hume maintains that having good taste is like being really good at tasting, even if that means that the standards for taste in art are based on a subjective experience. A person who has good taste knows how to enjoy the right things in the right way.

One key difference between the pleasures of food and artworks has to do with the kind of displeasure that can come from putting something in your mouth. We dislike food and drink with more intensity, I would wager, than we dislike art, film, or music. Bad food ranges from the mildly distasteful (this apple is mealy), to strongly distasteful (this coffee is undrinkable), to disgusting (this meat is rotten). The feeling of disgust is especially acute. Our bodies protect us from truly awful tastes. We recoil, spit things out, and even vomit. There is nothing quite like that in art aesthetics. We might find a picture, song, or film really bad, but not so bad that it's physically repellent—a visual or audio analogue to spitting food out. The only thing in the artworld remotely similar to eating disgusting food is watching horror movies, but it's not quite the same. Distaste and disgust deserve attention not only because they are aesthetic but also for what they tell us about food and eating.

Specifically, is there any connection between the way something tastes and the moral judgments we make about it? It is possible that ethically produced foods actually taste better and unethical foods taste worse? If something tastes disgusting, should it be avoided on ethical grounds—and should we seek out morally wholesome foods? Then again, there is something to the conventional idea that aesthetics and morality are completely independent of one another: food for food's sake. The classic issue of the relationship between beauty and morality is worth revisiting in light of the aesthetics of food.

It might appear dated (if not worse) to continue to use the language of taste in food aesthetics after it has been so roundly criticized for the last hundred years. In the 1920s, Western Marxists argued that taste is a class-based concept that reflects nothing more than one's social station. There are no standards that can cut across social class.[2] In the 1980s, Pierre Bourdieu argued that taste is relative to a "habitus," the social and economic factors that organize how we experience the world. Patterns of taste serve power structures by making minute distinctions to separate individuals and groups according to elaborate aesthetic rules that define status and prestige.[3] The very notion of taste serves to reinforce classism.

Given the devastating critiques of taste, you would think that it should be left in the eighteenth century along with other historic relics, like chastity belts and thumbscrews. But gustatory aesthetics is, for better or worse, wedded to the language of taste in spite of whatever other connotations it has. The term describes what happens whenever we eat and drink and there is, quite simply, no way around it.

WHAT IS GOOD TASTE IN FOOD?

The problem of taste for eighteenth-century philosophers was to reconcile how the subjective experience of enjoyment in an artwork could possibly provide an impartial basis for judging something's merits. If we each have our own preferences and tastes, then there is no way to determine if something really is beautiful or if it just appears that way to someone. The very notion of taste seems to lead to aesthetic relativism, where judgments are based on nothing but pleasurable feelings. Yet we make aesthetic judgments all of the time, and they do not seem arbitrary. We believe there really is a difference between good and bad food, or a great and a forgettable movie. The Moderns wanted to know how exactly we can make judgments of quality if they are based on nothing but subjective feelings.[4]

Hume's answer to the problem of taste largely squares with common sense: we all have our preferences and there's no accounting for why we like some things more than others. He describes our tastes in terms of pleasurable feelings of "approbation" (of the beautiful and agreeable) and unpleasurable feelings of "disapprobation" (of the ugly and disagreeable). The experience of beauty is a subjective feeling in our minds, not an objective quality in things. It exists "merely in the mind that contemplates them; and each mind perceives a different beauty."[5] Any pleasurable or unpleasurable feeling is correct because "it has a reference to nothing beyond itself."[6] But Hume also says no one really believes that all tastes are equal or that great works of art are equal to crummy works. Instead, he argues that a good work is one that is preferred, enjoyed, and approved by a good judge—someone who has good taste. The standards of good taste are set by experienced critics, who have refined palates and experience judging and comparing things like art, music, food, and drinks.

Hume then undoes his case for critics as the standard bearers of taste by noting that different preferences and different cultures can get in the way reaching agreement. There are no standards for deciding among "harmless, unavoidable preferences." (You like coffee, I like tea. There you go.)

Nor is there any way around the fact that we tend to like things that we grew up with. We tend to like things that resonate with us more than unusual things that we aren't as familiar with. But if there are no standards for deciding among personal and cultural preferences, then only like-minded people from within a specific place and time can reach agreement over the things they already like. It would be futile, for example, to discuss jazz, minimalism, or cheese with someone who doesn't particularly care for these things—or with someone with radically different sensibilities. Hume claims to have found standards of taste that are based on our natural, human abilities but then concludes that they do not apply to cases where preferences and cultures are different.[7]

Jerrold Levinson finds an even deeper problem with Hume: are the good judges the best at resolving disputes or are they the best at detecting beauty? Do they referee the critics (like a meta-critic) or do they detect beauty (like a Geiger counter)? Sometimes Hume says the latter but ultimately says the former: taste is the verdicts of the best judges. But Levinson asks why should you care what someone else likes. If they're not like you, why should you want to perceive the world like they do? An ideal critic, according to Hume, has "strong sense, united to delicate sentiment, improved by practice, perfected by comparison, and cleared of all prejudice."[8] But why is that better than an *izeal* critic, who is introverted, zany, larger than average, arrogant, and left-handed? If you are unlike both the ideal and izeal critics, why should you care what either of them likes?[9]

Furthermore, we have no way of knowing if ideal critics are aesthetically better off than we are, or if they enjoy things more than the rest of us do. If we already have aesthetic pleasures, we don't really have any reason to want to trade them for what a critic experiences. Assuming the judges are right, why does it even matter what things are *really* beautiful if I already experience things that are good enough for me? What motivation would someone have to give up their aesthetic preferences to take on those of another? There are no obviously clear reasons why someone should make the trade off to enjoy new things ideal critics love but then hate the old things he or she currently loves. Levinson asks why we should aspire to beautiful works when we already enjoy *meautiful* works: those gratifying to middle-brow people like us. It is not clear why Hume wants to draw such a sharp distinction between critics and regular people.[10]

There is another problem with Hume's standards of taste: liking something and assessing something are not the same thing. As Noël Carroll notes, everyone has enjoyable experiences and we all have our preferences, but that is different from thoughtfully assessing and judging something. I can like something that I know is not very good (my guilty pleasures), and there are things I know are good that I do not particularly like (for me it's blue cheese). A critic's pleasurable experiences might be more refined and informed than mine, but there is no necessary connection between feelings and judgments of quality.[11] Besides, just because you are partial to something you grew up with, that should not prevent you from at least trying to judge it impartially.

Hume provides a good starting point for making sense of taste even if he's not entirely right. His emphasis on literal tasting, discerning, and practicing still rings true today. Of course, his excessive subjectivism go against the commonsense belief that food tastes are caused, at least in part, by the food itself. But, to his credit, Hume wrestles with hard questions about the roles of preferences and culture. And while his concepts of "good sense" and "freedom from prejudice" strike our twenty-first-century ears as a bit quaint, the idea is simply that a good critic should be fair and impartial. And that makes sense: wouldn't anyone be skeptical of a restaurant review written by the owner or a taste test that isn't blind? The Enlightenment ideals of objectivity and impartiality are not unreasonable and are hard to shake.

The other important starting point for gustatory aesthetics is Kant, who also compares aesthetic discernment to tasting and enjoying food, and, like Hume, believes that beauty is a subjective experience, not a quality in objects. But, unlike Hume, Kant claims that we can decide for ourselves whether or not to experience beauty in the world. We can either view things practically and scientifically or we can view things aesthetically. When we view aesthetically, we experience pleasure (or displeasure) as a free, detached contemplation of the sensual qualities of things. It is as if our minds go blank as we let a beautiful experience wash over us. He calls the special ability to perceive and judge beauty a "judgment of taste." When we all have similar aesthetic experiences, under the same conditions, we can potentially agree whether or not something is beautiful.[12] Furthermore, Kant says that aesthetic experience is a "propaedeutic" for morality. The more aesthetic experiences we have, the more practice we get at communicating with others, seeing people as equals, and appreciating things unconditionally. Aesthetics attunes our moral feelings and prepares us to have a good will.

The fateful distinction Kant makes that (supposedly) excludes food and drink from aesthetic judgments is between what is *beautiful* and *agreeable*. We enjoy what is beautiful for the sake of itself, free of any interests, desires, or intentions. We enjoy what is agreeable because it satisfies, gratifies, and arouses us. It is always bound up with our inclinations and desires. We cannot be *disinterested* (or unbiased) about the agreeable because we always have some *interest* (or bias) in the qualities of something when it satisfies our desires.[13] Any feeling that is bound to the satisfaction of personal interests and desires is too bound up with contingencies to be the basis for a truly universal standard of taste. Kant argues that everyone has their own preferences about what is pleasant or agreeable to them, but beauty is for everyone and cannot be dependent on a private condition peculiar only to an individual.[14]

A number of philosophers claim that Kant's distinction between the beautiful and the agreeable is fatal for a gustatory aesthetics. Compared to a judgment of taste, actual tasting is too biased to be applicable to others. We know too much about it (with concepts), we care too much about it (interests), we feel satisfaction from it (desires), and we know what food is supposed to do and supposed to be (purpose). Philosophers today tend to view Kant's aesthetics as an impediment to food aesthetics; anyone concerned with food aesthetics should repudiate Kant and affirm the very senses and experiences he deems to be defective and inadequate.[15]

I read Kant more generously. I find his aspirations to connect aesthetic experience to universality, communicability, and morality both admirable and worth redeeming. In fact, we assume each of these things in food criticism. We assume that a judgment is universalizable, that others can experience it; we assume that we can communicate and maybe reach agreement with each other; and we assume that there is something vitally important about enjoying good food and drink that is part of a rich and full life that everyone deserves to have. Not surprisingly, Kant relates aesthetics to both reason and freedom—a cosmopolitan ideal of a peaceful world community. Food criticism shares the same universalizing aspirations to persuade us to overcome narrow provincialism, to appreciate the foods of others, and to share in common experiences. The idea that food connects us and helps us appreciate one another is thoroughly Kantian.

Gadamer's gustatory aesthetics builds on Hume and Kant but without any eighteenth-century baggage that doesn't really hold up today. Like Hume, he agrees that the best guide for taste is the judgment of history: the classics, traditions, and things that stand the test of time. He also believes that taste is measured by those who already have developed it through experience, but anyone can be a good critic with enough practice. From a hermeneutic perspective, Hume's aesthetics is too subjective and ignores the universalist aspirations of a good critic, whose attributes are not merely good traits for tasting food but also for having knowledge, for developing ourselves, and for acting morally—the keys to cosmopolitanism. And where good judgment and taste for Hume refer to one's feelings, for Gadamer, they refer to properties in things that anyone can enjoy.

Like Kant, Gadamer sees taste as an inherently public and communicable truth claim that presumes universality in the sense that we expect agreement (or at least recognition) when we make aesthetic judgments. We assume others can know what we are talking about whenever we communicate about our tastes. But, unlike Kant, taste for Gadamer is always affected by interests, prejudices, and presuppositions. As a result, our judgments can legitimately express different perspectives, each coming from some place valid. Aesthetic judgments can also aspire to disinterestedness, albeit in the eighteenth-century British sense of civic virtue—rising above private profit and advantage to be unbiased where personal interests might be present.[16] We can always try to be reasonable and fair-minded about our prejudices and our tastes. That would not satisfy Kant, but maybe the best we can do is to try to find consensus over what is agreeable, to use his term.[17]

The hermeneutic answer about where good taste comes from is history, understood as the shared context and background of our experience. Unlike Enlightenment judgements of taste, *interpretive* judgments of taste are always bound up with prejudices and expectations, yet potentially everyone can find common ground. Like any interpretive claim, food judgments are dialogical, practical, and creative. They pose no unusual challenges to hermeneutics, except for the ones we have already identified from our bodies, the unconscious, and external influences. That is a lot but nothing insurmountable for an interpretive theory. Judging food is a piece of cake, so to speak.

The bigger challenge in gustatory aesthetics is to expand the eighteenth-century concerns with beauty and good taste to include the kind of concepts we commonly use to describe and evaluate food and drink. Our gustatory vocabulary includes words like elegant, rich, flavorful, and well-composed. Sibley calls them "aesthetic qualities" (that require concepts to perceive) as opposed to "non-aesthetic qualities" (that do not), like Shaffer's reflective and direct experiences. There are a lot of ways to describe the aesthetic qualities of something—far more than merely identifying beautiful art and delicious food. Sibley says that critics are particularly good at recognizing aesthetic qualities and distinguishing them from the non-aesthetic. They know how to create new interpretations by drawing contrasts, making comparisons, and explaining how the non-aesthetic and aesthetic work together often with the help of metaphors and descriptors, like professional tasters do. The key is to know what to look for and how to describe it.[18]

In food and drink, that might involve understanding how the non-aesthetic components such as ingredients and preparation techniques give rise to aesthetic qualities depending on what we are tasting and what the specific standards are for each dish. For example, baked goods, fermented beverages, and fish dishes have different aesthetic qualities because of their non-aesthetic parts, as well as the particular categories that inform what we are tasting for. You need the right category for traditional foods, homemade foods, high-end restaurant food, and so on. You need to know about the right combinations of categories for fusions cuisines and how to use creative language for really novel dishes. You have to have the right concepts and categories (even narratives) about something in order to be able to appreciate it fully. If we don't have the right preconceptions, we're like the sour cream eater who expected yogurt.

An interpretive theory of food criticism is about detecting flavors and communicating qualities in ways that resonate with others. It is about saying true things about food and creating new interpretations that let us experience things in new ways. You can see these qualities in the works of Jonathan Gold, the long-time food critic for the *Los Angeles Times*. Gold had years of experience tasting and writing about food (Hume),[19] he believed that food can bring people together and help us learn to see each other

(Kant), and he was really good at putting food in the context of its culinary history, the neighborhood setting, and the backstory of the restauranteurs (Gadamer).[20] Food criticism for Gold is also cultural criticism. (His style is dialogical. Notice the use of the second-person.)

Here is his review of a small hamburger stand in Pasadena, California:

As with all good hamburgers, a Pie 'N Burger burger is about texture, the crunchy sheaf of lettuce, the charred . . . surface of the meat, the outer rim of the bun crisped to almost the consistency of toast. When compressed by the act of eating, the hamburger leaks thick, pink dressing that is somewhat more tart than it may look; soft, grilled onions, available upon request, add both a certain squishiness and a caramelly sweetness.

The slice of American cheese, if you have ordered a cheeseburger, does not melt into the patty, but stands glossily aloof from it, as if it were mocking the richness of the sandwich rather than adding to the general effect. The burgers here come jacketed in white paper, and are compact enough to generally remain intact through three-quarters of their life—it's kind of a genteel thing, a Pie 'N Burger burger.[21]

Here's his review of a donut shop in Glendora, California:

Have you ever seen a strawberry doughnut from the Donut Man? It is an iceberg of a doughnut, a flattened demisphere big enough to use as a Pilates cushion, split in two and filled to order with what must be an entire basket of fresh strawberries, and only in season. The fruit is moistened with a translucent gel that lubricates even the occasional white-shouldered berry with a mantle of slippery sweetness, oozing from the sides, turning the bottom of the pasteboard box into a sugary miasma in the unlikely event that the doughnuts actually make it home. The tawny pastry itself is only lightly sweetened, dense and slightly crunchy at the outside, like most good doughnuts, with a vaguely oily nuttiness and an almost substantial chew. It is the only doughnut I have ever seen that is routinely served with a plastic knife and fork. It is worth every penny of the $2.50 it costs.[22]

Gold had good taste in food. He's thoughtful, credible, insightful, and really interesting to read. That does not mean everyone would like the same things he likes or agree with him about every food review. It just means that he's a good model for how to appreciate and talk about food.

WHAT ARE THE PLEASURES OF FOOD?

That fact that food is pleasurable is a given. Everyone savors and delights in it. Sometimes we go to great lengths to have it, overspending, or making unhealthy choices all for the sake of taste—and most of us don't have a problem with that. So long as we don't routinely over-do it, we usually consider the pleasures of eating and drinking to be among the best things in life. However, it is not clear what kind of pleasure it is, how worthwhile it is, or how much is too much. When philosophers acknowledge the importance of pleasures, they usually rank food lower than other ostensibly more worthwhile pursuits, such as friendship and love. Eating is said to be a lowly animal pleasure; human pleasures should be more refined. But that doesn't begin to do justice to the role food plays in our lives.

Elizabeth Telfer takes on the traditional ranking of pleasures and argues that tasty foods are an underrated part of a full life. First, she rejects the usual *quantitative* arguments against food pleasures, that the amount of pleasure we get from food is not as great as we tend to think it is.

(1) Seeking food pleasures is said to bring about more unhappiness than happiness. The aftereffects of eating include such unpleasant things as bloating, aftertastes, and poor health. Telfer says, not always. If we take care, we can avoid unpleasant consequences, although for some people the risk of misery is worth it.[23]

(2) The pleasures of eating are said to be fragile and vulnerable. People lose their teeth, have reflux, get sick of the taste of their favorite foods, waste their money, and so on. Should the quality of our lives really hinge on something as vulnerable as our mouths, teeth, and appetites? No, says Telfer, but this is not an argument against food pleasures but against any pleasure. Tasting might be vulnerable but so is hearing and seeing, or really anything that involves our bodies. We all lose our capabilities at some point, either by injury, illness, or aging. The claim that the sensorial pleasures are more vulnerable to incapacitation than cognitive pleasures is not necessarily true.[24]

(3) Food pleasures are said to be more temporary, fleeting, and insatiable than other more refined pleasures. Plato said that eating pleasures are like an addiction: we can never be fully satisfied and are often even less satisfied the more we eat and drink.[25] Telfer is skeptical. Is the argument that we never enjoy our food that much, or that we feel like we've never had enough? A food addict

(who cannot control the urge to eat) or an epicure (who has unusually high standards of taste) may never truly enjoy food, but that is different from claiming that the pleasures of food are temporary and that we will always desire to eat again. For most of us, the pleasures of eating are something we get to satisfy more than once every day. Far from providing less pleasure than other experiences, food provides a renewable source of it that anyone can enjoy.[26]

(4) The pleasures of food are said to be not worth the effort. They sometimes require a great deal of time, money, and work, and then they are gone forever. Think of how much work it is to produce a Thanksgiving meal and how quickly it's devoured. Then think of the kind of lasting pleasures that can come from learning another language or reading a book. Don't these activities provide more and longer lasting pleasures than food? Maybe, says Telfer, but not necessarily. Some meals are intensely deliciously and truly memorable. But more importantly, food pleasures are unique, not commodities that can be exchanged for other kinds of pleasures. The experience of eating cannot be substituted for something else.[27]

Next, Telfer examines the usual *qualitative* arguments against food pleasure—that the kind of pleasure we get from food is less worthwhile and that it is even worse than other kinds of pleasures. Both arguments consider food to be little more than a necessity, as a means to an end, but never an end in itself. Plato privileges reason over feeling, mind over body, and restraint over desires. Physical pleasures are lowly; rational pleasures are the only ones worth pursuing. Mill also says we should devote ourselves to "mental pleasures" that involve intelligence and imagination. They are qualitatively better, "higher," and more worthwhile than "lower," "physical pleasures" that we share with animals. Only the pleasures that use our "higher faculties" employ the "distinctive endowments of a human being."[28]

Telfer argues the opposite: the pleasures of food are an important part of a meaningful life. Without them our lives would be impoverished. For example, it would be terrible to permanently lose the ability to taste. It is crucial not only for enjoying food but for sharing experiences and communicating with others. In fact, she argues that food pleasures are a "vehicle for other kinds of significance," such as religious observance, celebration, and expression of values. Food is bound up with both everyday living and special occasions. It is hard to disentangle food and drink from the pleasures of feasts, holidays, and shared meals. The point is not to elevate food pleasures into a more elevated category but to highlight how entrenched they are in some of the things people enjoy the most.

There are echoes of (this standard reading of) Plato, Mill, and a general disregard for food pleasure in the animal ethics literature. If meat lovers overestimate their need for meat, animal ethicists typically underestimate the importance of taste. The most common arguments against eating meat weigh the trivial human interest in eating meat versus an animal's (serious) interest in staying alive. We do not *need* to eat meat in order to live; we simply prefer to eat it because we enjoy it.

Peter Singer, for example, dismisses "the trivial purpose of pleasing our palates" and urges us to adopt a vegetarian diet.[29] James Rachels says that the basic argument for vegetarianism comes down to "whether our enjoyment of how meat tastes is good enough reason to justify the amount of suffering the animals are made to endure. It seems obvious that it is not."[30] Gary Francione writes that the "only use of animals that is not transparently trivial is biomedical research." He is dismayed that people both recognize that animals deserve ethical treatment yet eat them anyway, merely for the sake of "palate pleasure."[31] The enjoyment of food can never offset harming animals. Maybe research or survival can but not the trivial pleasures of eating.

Some animal ethicists argue that only the interest in eating meat is indefensible, not the general interest in the pleasures of taste. They claim that we cannot justify our desires for the taste of meat when plant-based foods taste just as good. Mylan Engel, for example, says that a plant-based diet is "equally delicious" and "does not require one to forego the pleasures of taste."[32] Tristram McPherson argues that going vegan may require that we give up some enjoyable tastes, but the diet on the whole is "compatible with a richer gustatory life than most omnivores currently experience."[33] And Francione says that, in his experience, people assume vegan food is "boring and tasteless" but are surprised to learn how "delicious, interesting, and varied" it is.[34] In other words, there is nothing wrong with enjoying food, only in seeking the pleasures of eating meat, which are described again and again as trivial.

Is that true? For those who have already decided to eschew meat, a plant-based diet is satisfying enough. But for meat eaters—even those who have qualms about it—it is not so simple. Humans have been eating meat for hundreds of thousands of years. There is something about it we truly enjoy. (I state this as fact, not justification.) It might be in our genes, or in our culture, or in the way it is marketed to us. Whatever the explanation, our taste for it persists and it takes more than a good argument to get us to shake the habit. We are hooked on meat. And in spite of the increasing awareness of the health risks and environmental harms associated with eating animals, the number of meat-eating consumers grows each year. The fact that there are meat substitutes and costly in vitro technologies to simulate the real thing is telling. Most of us like the flavor so much we will seek out something that tastes like it if we cannot have the real thing.

The pleasures of eating meat are far from trivial. They are not lowly, animal desires—mere physical urges that we need to tame for the sake more worthwhile endeavors. (Imagine how unlivable life would be if we actually gave up all of Mill's lower pleasures!) Telfer agrees that it is more complicated than that. Food pleasures are physical, mental, and cultural. Our tastes and enjoyments are about more than bodily urges and impulses but shared experiences and social practices.[35] As we said earlier, how much we like something depends on what our expectations are. Our food pleasures are bound up with a conceptual framing, or in the case of meat, long-standing meat narratives.

To say food is only about (mere) pleasure devalues the importance of it in a full and satisfying life. The same is true of eating meat. Animal ethicists treat our desire for meat like a nicotine addiction that should be treated with a patch if we aren't strong enough to give it up on our own. But who would really opt to have their taste for meat physiologically eliminated? I am sure some vegetarians whose lingering taste for animal products keeps them from a strictly plant-based diet, but for most people, eating meat is bound up with a lifetime of habits and tastes that people truly enjoy. Animals ethics should take the pleasures of eating more seriously and really grapple with the role of meat in a happy and good life. The food industry does; that's why we are starting to see plant-based burgers in fast food restaurants.

Meanwhile, aesthetic philosophers should take bad food and displeasures more seriously. Food is not only about delights and pleasures but also avoiding things and having bad experiences ranging from mild distaste to complete repugnance. Like a judgment of taste, a judgment of distaste is similarly interpretive, bound up with expectations and context, influenced by one's body and unconscious desires. And like good food, bad food is made up of aesthetic qualities in Sibley's sense that can be universally communicated and (potentially) understood by everyone. An experienced taster needs just as large a vocabulary to describe bad aesthetic qualities as good ones.

Like food pleasures, food displeasures are also not trivial. The mild ones may be, but strong food displeasures are just as important as strong pleasures in the quality of our lives. As we said before, science fiction sometimes uses bad food to show how bleak and hopeless the future is when you have nothing to eat but food pills, space insects, or reconstituted people. The meal-replacement beverage Soylent plays on and celebrates the blandness of dystopian foods.[36] Science fiction aside, for the 2.3 million incarcerated in the United States, a bad-tasting diet is very real and very grim. The Marshall Project website details what is in a typical prison meal—and it does not look good.[37]

Disgusting food is even worse than bad food. Paul Rozin defines disgust as a food-related emotion, as "revulsion at the prospect of oral incorporation of an offensive object." He says, "The offensive objects are contaminants; that is, if they even briefly contact an acceptable food, they tend to render that food unacceptable."[38] Disgust reactions reject offensive objects based on taste (or other "negative sensory properties"), harm, and "ideational factors" or preconceptions of something as already repugnant. Disgust is both sensory-affective and cognitive. But where distaste rejects foods that are recognizably edible, disgust rejects foods perceived to be dangerous, inappropriate, or contaminated. It is much worse to put something disgusting in your mouth than something distasteful.

Rozin's test case for the cognitive content of disgust squares with the interpretive theory advanced here. In an experiment, he presented test subjects with two opaque vials, both containing the same decayed odor. They are told that one vile contains cheese, the other contains feces. Those who think they are smelling cheese (and who like cheese) think it smells fine; those who think they are smelling feces think it is disgusting. "It is the subject's conception of the object, rather than the sensory properties of the object, that primarily determines the hedonic value."[39] What we think about an object (including its origins, social history, and who or what touched it) is primarily what makes something disgusting. Rozin surmises that if a ground cockroach tasted as sweet as sugar, people (who do not eat insects) would not want to try it or would claim it tasted disgusting if they did.

In addition to contaminated foods, Rozin and colleagues extend a taste-based theory of contamination to six other kinds of disgust elicitors: (1) bodily products such as vomit, pus, mucus, semen, urine, and feces, (2) violations of hygiene; (3) lowly animals; (4) violations of bodily integrity such as wounds and evisceration; (5) perverse sexual activity; and, above all, (6) death and decay. Disgust is about protection from what is alien—especially oral contact with animals and animal products. Bodily secretions, feces, and decay not only connect us with animals we'd rather not be like but also our own demise and death.[40]

Theorists disagree whether the main function of disgust is to avoid eating bad food, to avoid disease, or to distance ourselves from any kind of animality. William Miller generally agrees with Rozin but emphasizes our vulnerabilities and mortalities as the target of disgust:

> What disgusts, startlingly, is the capacity for life, and not just because life implies its correlative death and decay: for it is decay that seems to engender life.... Death thus horrifies and disgusts not just because it smells revoltingly bad, but because it is not an end to the process of living but part of a cycle of eternal recurrence. The having lived and the living unite to make up the organic world of generative rot—rank, smelling, and upsetting to the touch. The gooey mud, the scummy pond are life soup, fecundity itself: slimy, slippery, wiggling, teeming animal life generating spontaneously from putrefying vegetation.[41]

And so, we recoil from reminders of our mortality and avoid contamination to protect our bodily integrity from itself becoming disgusting.

Yet, as Miller points out, we are also oddly drawn to disgusting things, like automobile accidents and bodily fluids. Martha Nussbaum agrees and asks, "insofar as they are objects of allure or fascination, is this simply because they are forbidden, or is the attraction prior to the prohibition?"[42] Or maybe it's a little bit of both: we might actually be attracted to some things because we are averse to them. There is such thing as pleasurable disgust where we enjoy and even savor unpleasant things.

Korsmeyer, for example, considers how it is that we have come to enjoy such off-putting, even revolting, things like caviar, brains, and chitterlings. Or hot peppers, bleu cheese, and bush meat—and, of course, Vegemite. She argues that disgust has a "hidden aesthetic resonance in food, even in the finest cuisines."[43] Far from repelling us, foods that flirt with disgust are compelling and often delicious. When revulsion is "deliberately approached and overcome," it can "increase the potency of the taste experience."[44]

Korsmeyer offers a provisional list of six categories of disgusting foods—fully understanding the impossibility of transcultural agreement. The first two items on the list focus on taste experiences; the next four on the nature of the object: (1) There are foods with initially repellant tastes (for example, coffee, spirits, bitter greens), including a "residue" of a disgusting substance (such as fermentation and decay in meats and cheeses). (2) There are foods that are delicious in small amounts but sickening in large amounts or after one is satiated (for example, sugary sweets or condiments that should be used sparingly).

Next are repugnant objects: (3) Objects or animals too foreign from us (such as innards or insects in the United States) or that are unpleasant to touch. (4) Objects that are too familiar to us (such as cat, dog, or human). (5) Objects that resemble their natural form too much (whole animals and mammal heads but not fish, for some reason). (6) Objects that have fermented or decomposed too long, which are not unlike the first category of difficult taste experiences. Korsmeyer is aware of her cultural bias and stands by the principle, rather than the specifics, of the list: everywhere there are foods that are initially disgusting but then transform into something delicious. Disgusting foods are not only what other people eat but what we eat as well.[45]

There are three important lessons from Korsmeyer's discussion of delicious disgusting foods. One is that food pleasures are learned and interpretive. We acquire our tastes for not only pleasant but unpleasant (even repugnant) foods. That means how we taste food and how we experience pleasures and displeasures depends on our presuppositions and expectations. Rozin and Fallon say as much when they state that it is "the subject's conception of the object, rather than the sensory properties of the object, that primarily determines the hedonic value."[46] Of course, Korsmeyer (and I) would argue that a subject's conceptions *and* an object's sensory properties are related to one another so that different conceptions reveal different sensory properties. The substance that can be taken either as feces or as cheese *really is smelly*, regardless of your point of view. The foul-smelling object can either be disgusting or alluring depending on the interpretation. That doesn't imply relativism but rather attests to pluralism: there actually is something there that can be interpreted in many different ways.

The second lesson is that death and decay are not things we always avoid but sometimes things we hold onto and savor. Korsmeyer parts ways with Rozin and Miller and follows the lead of Aurel Kolnai and his theory of the "eroticism of disgust" to explain how we are both compelled and repelled by life, death, and organic matter, in general.[47] These unsavory things, somehow, make food taste better. It is like Edmund Burke's theory of the sublime where terror can evoke feelings of ecstatic delight.[48] Some delicious foods remind us of rot, decay, and dead animals. Slaughtering, butchering, and chewing—even picking, peeling, and chopping vegetables evoke the violence and destruction that are an inevitable part of eating. But certain meals go farther and "seem deliberately to harbor an awareness of the fact that to sustain one's own life one takes another."[49] Fish served whole, crawfish heads sucked, and Thanksgiving turkeys solemnly carved at the table. The presence of death in the act of eating transforms disgust to pleasure and aversion to enjoyment.

The third lesson (albeit mine, not hers) is that the transformation of disgust to delight is always an act of shared meaning. Food taste never occurs naturally but rather because of an interpretive act that allows us to see, smell, and taste something as yummy or yucky. We eat these foods not only for pleasure and thrills but also to affirm our membership in a community and our identities as people who eat these foods. Disgusting dishes are acquired tastes that only people like *us* enjoy, not you. We owe a good deal of our identities to the foods we eat—especially the foods that others detest and even we know are a little bit gross.

The short answer to the question "what are the pleasures of food?" is that the sensory experiences are nontrivial and play a huge role in the quality of our lives, the pleasures and displeasures are interpretive yet potentially universalizable, and we have a rather ambivalent relationship to the things that disgust us. We usually avoid them, but certain foods are delicious precisely because they are kind of nasty, at least to outsiders.

WHAT IS THE RELATIONSHIP BETWEEN ETHICS AND TASTE?

Typically, ethics and taste have little to do with one another. Ethics is supposedly based on reason, free from feelings, and aesthetics is based on feelings, free from reason. When ethics is mixed with (or worse, based on) feelings, the result is solipsistic emotivism; and when aesthetics is mixed with reasons, it not only prevents aesthetic experiences but also thwarts creativity. Or, to put it another way, the claim that ethics and tastes have nothing to do with one another presupposes that ethics has no affective component and aesthetics is not normative. While the former has been challenged again and again in the twentieth century, the latter remains widely accepted. We all believe (including Kant) that moral judgments are never entirely rational, but we probably believe that there's no accounting for taste. You either like something or you don't; we all have our preferences, and they can neither be explained nor defended. Tastes are resistant to reason, if not beyond good and evil.

But if the interpretive arguments about taste are correct, and there is a cognitive component to aesthetic experience, then there is an important relationship between the taste of food and the moral judgments we make about it. Perhaps a moral judgment about food affects the way it tastes, or an aesthetic judgment about taste influences a moral judgment we make about it. If we say something is disgusting, for example, does that mean that any self-respecting person should avoid it and that there is something morally wrong with someone who eats it? I'd argue that moral judgments affect tastes and that aesthetic appeals to disgust can be morally significant. Disgust reactions are potent warning signs that something *might* be off about food. Or it might just be a pungent dish that takes some time to get used to.

To make the case that moral judgments precede and influence how food tastes, we assume an interpretive theory of aesthetic experience. Food tasting is never disinterested (in the strict, Kantian sense) but instead effected by the prejudices of the taster, as well as the context of the thing tasted. The former includes things like upbringing, preferences, and expectations; the latter includes things like what foods are served together (ketchup on fries or on a steak), the eating environment (home, restaurant, or picnic), ambient conditions (noisy or quiet, cold or hot), and the actions of those around you (enjoying or criticizing the food). All of these things can affect how food tastes.

As we saw in chapter 2, psychologists have demonstrated the role of external influences on taste perceptions. They tell people, for example, that ground baloney is fine pâté and it will taste as if it were. They pour Walmart wine into a nice bottle and fine wine into a Walmart carton and even sommeliers can be fooled. These tests are not meant to show how little experts know (or how deceptive psychologists are), rather they are to affirm the basic claim that tasting is always mediated by concepts.

The next question is whether knowledge of food ethics can affect how something tastes. Does prior knowledge of the moral qualities of our food improve the taste and immoral qualities worsen it? In other words, can ethics prejudice tasting? Not to give too much authority to psychologists, but they have done experiments that show that people will change their aesthetic evaluation of food if given different moral information about it. Subjects like the taste of something more when they are told that it is wholesome, local, and organic; they like the same thing less when they are told that it is mass-produced with cheap ingredients made by cheap labor. In other words, morally bad things taste bad and morally good things taste good. Knowledge of moral qualities seems to affect aesthetic qualities.[50]

Korsmeyer makes a similar argument but takes it a step farther. She argues that we can actually taste moral qualities in food. "*If* certain kinds of meal preparation are morally dubious and *if* the object and its preparation impart a trace on flavor, *then* this quality is simultaneously aesthetic and moral."[51] Her example is the traditional (and now illegal) French delicacy of ortolan (bird), which is drowned in a regional brandy called Armagnac, roasted, and eaten whole. Anyone who eats an ortolan knows exactly what it is and how it was prepared. You never unwittingly eat it; it is an expensive dish eaten in an unusual, ceremonial fashion. Korsmeyer argues that because the Armagnac can be tasted, the morally dubious nature of the preparation imparts flavors into the bird. The taste has a moral component, and to enjoy the flavor is also to endorse the way it was prepared. If you condemn the dish, then you should not enjoy the way it tastes. If you do enjoy it, you are indifferent to a morally offensive act.

If Korsmeyer is right, then perhaps we should be able to taste other kinds of morally questionable flavors in different dishes. For example, if you know how foie gras is produced, then you can taste the violence visited on the goose. Unlike the ortolan, where you can taste the brandy it was drowned in, with foie gras you can picture the act of force-feeding but cannot actually taste it—unless you want to say that the taste of foie gras is what force-feeding tastes like. Taste two servings of foie gras side by side: in one the goose was force-fed, the other not. If you can taste the difference, and if you know how each was produced, then you can taste the flavor of suffering. If you enjoy the taste of the suffering goose better, then you are either indifferent to goose suffering or you endorse it.[52]

If the foie gras example is right, then an informed eater can taste other morally dubious production and preparation methods. We can taste what pig castration tastes like in the delicate pink flesh of pork. We can taste what calf confinement tastes like in a tender cut of veal. We can taste the disgusting production practice of cooling slaughtered chickens in a massive vat of disgusting water in the water-saturated, flavorless taste of a commercial broiler. We taste pain and suffering in the flavor of shark fins cut from living sharks and served as soup.

Granted, we need background information in order to taste how an animal lived before it became food, but that's all right. We always need at least some background knowledge to know what we are eating and to know whether or not it is a good example of it. For example, we need to know what a dish is supposed to be like before we can evaluate it. That is the only way to know not to say "too sweet" when eating dessert or "too crispy" when eating potato chips. We need a lot of background information to properly set our expectations for challenging foods like stinky cheeses or alcoholic beverages that would otherwise be unpalatable.

However, the ethical information required to affect the taste of something might have to be more direct and intense than ordinary knowledge. It might have to be really jarring, such as a hidden camera video of animal production or a first-hand encounter with the sights, sounds, and scents of slaughter. Everyone knows animals are killed for meat, yet for most it is too unappetizing even to think about, much less witness. The premise of the BBC show *Kill It, Cook It, Eat It* is that people unfamiliar with animal agriculture are brought to the countryside to meet typical food animals, then to an abattoir to see them slaughtered, and then to a kitchen to prepare the fresh meat. The show tests the thesis that it is hard to eat an animal if you see for yourself how it got to your plate. As it turns out, most of the participants have a hard time stomaching the meat they had met a few hours earlier when it was an animal. The implication is that if even first-hand experience with animal slaughter does not move you (and make it hard to enjoy the taste of meat), then you are morally indifferent. Granted, it might be unwise to generalize this claim for everyone, but it seems to hold for the cross-section of United Kingdom participants.

Knowledge of morally dubious practices or shocking experiences of blood and death is one thing; disgust is another. Does it also have a moral valence? Some have argued that strong feelings of revulsion reliably tell us what we should morally oppose. This well-known argument in bioethics is the so-called "yuck factor" or the "wisdom of repugnance."[53] Disgust responses are reasonable reactions to some of the objectionable things we typically call unethical, such as gruesome violence or horrific carnage. Our moral vocabulary is colored with disgust language. Bad people are rotten, slimy, and dirty; bad actions are repulsive, sickening, and offensive. Disgust and morality converge on things, like cannibalism, necrophilia, and bestiality, that feel terribly wrong at a visceral level. There seems to be some kind of connection between what people find repulsive and what they find immoral—or at least what we have an aversion to.

However, many philosophers are wary of basing moral judgments on feelings of repugnance. Nussbaum's work on emotions and the law makes a good case that a lot of moral judgments are post hoc justifications for visceral reactions to violations of social norms. The only reason some people are opposed to homosexuality or transsexuality is that it feels off—hardly a good reason to justify legal discrimination.[54] Daniel Kelly agrees that appeals to emotions are too volatile and irrational to provide reliable moral guidance.[55]

Some psychological studies seem to confirm their concerns. Apparently our moral evaluations (even our deepest convictions) can be manipulated by the presence of disgusting images or scents. For example, subjects seated near a chewed pencil or a food-stained desk viewed moral transgressions more harshly than those seated at clean desks. Foul odors can illicit similarly harsh judgments; they can give harmless acts moral overtones.[56] The reverse is also true: cleanliness reduces the severity of moral judgments, suggesting a connection between physical and moral purity.[57]

Furthermore, our moral and political attitudes seem to shift when we feel susceptible to disease, infestation, or other disgust elicitors that can amplify, and even change, existing prejudices. Sensitivity to disgust seems to reflect our more conservative moral and political convictions. The squeamish tend to be hard on crime, strict with children, deferent to power, and hostile to gay rights. Political conservatives seem to be more moved by fear and revulsion than political liberals. They are also more concerned with bodily and spiritual purity.[58]

That said, it is not clear how much incidental disgust amplifies the severity of moral judgment. Some psychologists say the experiments have not been replicated and that, overall, feelings of disgust only make things appear slightly more wrong.[59] Strong emotions only confirm what people already believe.[60] It takes more than that to get people to change their convictions.

Either way, we should probably be careful about arguments that rely too much on disgust: just because you feel it doesn't mean you should. Isn't a moral action often defined by doing what you ought to do even if you don't want to? (I was brave even though I was really frightened. I volunteered even though it would have been easier not to.) The ethics of disgust slides over this fact and into a naturalistic fallacy.

The one—*and only*—place where revulsion might indicate a legitimate moral concern is about animals. If disgust is about feces, decay, or other gross things, it is amoral. If disgust is about any person or group, then it reflects only bigotry and bias. But if disgust is about eating an animal, it might indicate something we should take seriously. Most city dwellers in industrialized nations (and I suspect in other parts of the world, as well) cannot stomach the sight of the slaughter and processing of an animal. We shut down table talk when it turns to discussions about where the meat came from. People are generally repelled by the sight of blood, guts, and death, and don't like to see animals harmed, especially individual animals: this pet, this cow, this pig. Even the thought of it is upsetting. We would think something is seriously off about someone who didn't just accept the reality of animal slaughter but actually enjoyed it.

Yet, even without concern for animals, meat is more likely to disgust than vegetables. It is bloody, slimy, and uncanny before it is cooked; it can cause indigestion and food poisoning when eaten; it reminds us about death, perhaps even cannibalism. Strong feelings of revulsion could be a sign that something is afoul. Robert Fischer calls it a "heuristic" that can provide evidence of a moral wrongdoing.[61] If you already believe something is wrong, the experience of disgust can serve as a reminder of your prior moral judgment. Yet unlike the feelings of revulsion that conservatives have about gay sex and human cloning, it is pretty noncontroversial to maintain that we should not harm domesticated animals. If you feel disgust by animal agriculture or slaughterhouses, then it might be a clue that something is wrong with it. The initial feeling of disgust can lead to feelings of sympathy—a less questionable, more noble emotion.

Then again, for many people reminders of the animal origins of meat make eating more pleasurable. Whole seafood and meat on the bone are more enjoyable—and praised by experts—than meat and fish in patties, burgers, or balls. Makers of meat substitutes and in vitro meat strive to make their products as lifelike as possible, such as the plant-based *Impossible Burger* that appears to bleed meat juices when eaten. In these cases, the same thing that might elicit disgust and moral condemnation for someone who believes it is wrong to eat meat has the opposite effect on someone who believes it is not wrong. Disgust, as Fischer notes, is only a heuristic for what we already believe is wrong.

We should, however, be careful how we use raw, emotional appeals to raise moral concerns. Gory details and shocking images can shut down a discussion. I'm thinking of the images of aborted fetuses that show up on pro-life posters. Those pictures are stand-ins and shortcuts for arguments. Even worse, those images tend to shut down rather than start a conversation. Speaking from my own experiences, I never engage those people. I think it's telling that they appeal to shock and horror instead of discourse: it's a weak form of argumentation that should be used sparingly. We never saw Martin Luther King Jr. or Nelson Mandela "dabbling in disgust."[62] Maybe we shouldn't either.

Then again, when is it ever a good time to talk about where the meat came from—and is that discussion even possible without recounting something upsetting and possibly disgusting?

Let me finish with three wishy-washy conclusions.

(1) Ethical evaluations about food are among the prejudices we bring to the experience of eating. Prior moral approval can improve the taste of something; moral disapproval can worsen it. Knowledge (or experience) of the often-horrific treatment of animals should make something distasteful, particularly to urbanites.

(2) Strong aesthetic judgments are not in themselves enough to support moral judgments about food, but they can be a sign that there is something ethically suspect it. If the object of disgust is feces or a rotten plant, the feeling indicates nothing immoral. If the object of disgust is a person, the feeling indicates bigotry and bias; you might want to reflect on your prejudices. But if the object of disgust is an animal, then it could indicate that the animal was harmed. Or it could indicate an acquired taste and make the food appear tastier.

(3) The conventional view that moral and aesthetic judgments are independent from one another is not entirely false. Although ethics and taste are related in principle, in practice it might be wise to keep them apart. There is something to be said for the eighteenth-century ideal of detached aesthetic experience—enjoying food for the sake of enjoying food, free from the buzzkill of stern moralizing.

Chapter Four

FOOD ETHICS

The ethics of eating is about what to eat, how to eat, and how to procure food for ourselves and others. What exactly we should eat and who exactly we should feed is an open question—but it is clear that we have food-specific obligations for ourselves and for others. Eating and feeding are not optional. Closely related are questions concerning animals. Most people eat meat, which means either there is nothing wrong with it or most of us are doing something we should not. So, which is it? Is it okay to eat animals? The answer hinges on both an interpretation of animal lives and a judgment about when, if ever, we can rightfully kill them for food.

Closely related to eating and animals are questions concerning technologies. All agriculture and food production require devices, some require machines, some require vast technological systems. Yet some man-made things are also morally controversial, such as genetic engineering and food irradiation. If it is wrong to produce food in certain ways, then it is wrong to purchase and (arguably) to eat it. Food technologies also raise questions about animals, for example, if we should grow meat in laboratories or engineer barely sentient farm animals that wouldn't care if they're slaughtered. By focusing on eating, animals, and technology, we get a nice overview of a range of ethical issues concerning food and agriculture.

The connection between an interpretation of what food is and a judgment about what we ought to do is not always apparent. It seems that we can experience food without judging it (like we do most of the time) and make judgments about it without much interpretation (don't we already know it is wrong to eat babies?). I will leave it to others to sort through the thorny meta-ethical issues of how facts relate to values. I will assume that our perceptions and our moral judgments about food are somehow related. We should be clear on what is at issue before we evaluate it, and our evaluations should be sensitive to plural and conflicting interpretations about the facts.

It is, however, debatable as to which morality, desires, and values are appropriate for food. Most of the food and agricultural ethics literature relies on either utilitarian or virtue ethics; but I want to press a Kantian, deontological theory of obligation into service to evaluate ethical issues concerning eating, animals, and technology. At the heart of Kant's ethics is the idea that all sentient creatures deserve to be treated with respect because their experiences matter to them. In fact, Kantian ethics recognizes the dignity of *all* living creatures. Humans may have more dignity than animals but not so much more that it allows us to disregard them and treat them however we please. It is not, however, clear how much more dignity we possess, nor if dignity is even the kind of thing we can measure and compare. Nor is it clear what exactly our obligations are to animals and how they differ from our obligations to humans—as if our obligations to each other are a settled matter.

This chapter starts by considering our food-related obligations to ourselves and to others. We each have a responsibility to eat a healthy and nourishing diet and not to deprive or disrespect oneself or others in eating or feeding. That might seem vague but in fact says a lot about what we should do. Minimally, neither to starve nor to endanger oneself by food deprivation. Ideally, you should aim to realize your capabilities as you feed yourself. The same is true about our responsibilities to others. We should neither eat other people nor deprive them of food (obviously). Instead, we have obligations to feed the people we are responsible for and to be hospitable to our guests.

Next, in light of our discussion about how to eat and to feed, is the question about eating animals. It is not a simple question. If it is okay to eat them, can we eat any of them or are there some we should leave alone? And does it matter who the eater is and what his or her reasons are? If we argue that it is not okay to eat animals, then what do we say about the majority of the population who disagree? Are they all doing something wrong, or are they right and it's worth it for a good meal? After reviewing arguments for and against eating animals, I will argue for a dignity-based theory of respect for both the human eaters and food animals.

Finally, there are a number of questions about the appropriate reach of science and technology into food and agriculture. There are legitimate concerns about health and food safety, pesticides and fertilizers, bioengineered animals and food additives, to name just some of the things people find problematic. Of course, few have qualms about science and technology when it makes food safer, healthier, and tastier. Some technological interventions raise moral issues, others solve them. This chapter tries to figure out what exactly is troublesome about combining machinery and chemicals with food and agriculture.

WHAT ARE OUR FOOD OBLIGATIONS?

Let's assume that an ethical theory prescribes obligations for ethical agents. That means that there are certain things we ought to do, that there are certain things we should not do, and that we can provide reasons why we are compelled to act. The reasons can include the resulting consequences, caring for others, the authority of traditions, or the obligation to treat people with respect, as Kant maintains. Most philosophers treat food issues in relation to either consequentialist or virtue ethics theories: as questions concerning either outcomes or character traits. For example, ethical issues about animals and agriculture are about why we should avoid bad consequences (for example, pollution, health problems, and climate change) and seek out good consequences (for example, productivity, employment, and enjoyment). Or, ethical issues can be framed in terms of how virtuous people should live together and care for others. Morally upright people do the right thing for themselves and for others because good actions flow from their good characters.

By contrast, deontological (duty-based) theories maintain that there are some things people have to do simply because it is the right thing to do. As Kant argues, actions motivated by self-interest, love, or anticipated consequences are fine, but they are too contingent to provide reasons why everyone has the same obligations. Quite simply, not everyone has the same interests, or lives in the same circumstances, so none of these things can reliably apply to everyone. The only thing that we all share is our common humanity, and the only thing we all have to do is to respect and help each other. The reason we should respect and help is because it's the right thing to do. You should be a *mensch* for no other reason than to be a mensch. Moreover, sometimes the right thing to do is opposed to what we want to do, or what our societies tell us to do. The true test of menschiness is when what you *should* do conflicts with what you *want* to do but you do the right thing anyway. Kant believes that good actions only come from a *good will*, the only thing that is necessarily (and unconditionally) good regardless of our circumstances. Everything else is conditional on our desires, goals, and other things that do not always apply to everyone.

Kant's *Groundwork of the Metaphysics of Morals* (1785) presents a rather severe account of moral life, easily dismissed as too strict and unfeeling.[1] But in *The Metaphysics of Morals* (1797), Kant presents a much more nuanced account of obligation that is inseparably related to our desires, our goals, and our purposes.[2] Simply put, we owe each other respect. Kant's famous formulation, in the *Groundwork*, of the categorical imperative to "act only according to that maxim through which you can at the same time will that it should become a universal law" all but disappears in *The Metaphysics of Morals*. Instead, the focus shifts to the principle of humanity as an end-in-itself: "act so that you treat humanity, whether in your own person or that of another, always as an end, never merely as a means." In other words, always respect the dignity and humanity of others—the qualities that deserve to be protected no matter what and for no other reason than it's right to do. We may fall short, but we should always try to be respectful.

Kant distinguishes between *perfect duties* that are always required of us (and failure to perform them is blameworthy) and *imperfect duties* that are contingent and only sometimes required of us (and are praiseworthy).[3] We have to respect and help. For the former, we have an obligation not to harm, deceive, or coerce. For the latter, we have an obligation to set ends for ourselves (to do something), but there is latitude about which actions to take to realize those ends, and their fulfillment is meritorious, not obligatory. In others words, we have a strict (perfect) obligation to treat ourselves and others as capable of making decisions and choosing our own ends, and because we have an obligation to protect ourselves and others, we have loose (imperfect) obligations to further our lives as best we can.

Kant is unusually lax about our ethical duties. He prefers to speak about the "moral strength" required to fulfill our obligations: the quality of character to counter our worst inclinations, self-conceit, and social settings that can prevent us from doing to the right thing. He explains that there are "certain moral endowments such that anyone lacking them could have no duty to acquire them. They are moral feeling, conscience, love of one's neighbor, and respect for oneself (self-esteem). There is no obligation to have these because they lie at the basis of morality, as *subjective* conditions of receptiveness to the concept of duty, not as objective conditions of morality."[4] We do not have a duty to virtue in the same way we have a duty not to harm others, but rather we can only feel bound by morality if we are virtuous. Moral feelings are at the heart of our moral obligations. (It might sound like virtue ethics but it is a little different. For Aristotle, the virtues are always present in a good person; for Kant, we only need them when the time comes to do the right thing. And the only virtue that is always and unconditionally good is a good will. Other virtues could serve bad ends, such as the evil genius or brave burglar.)

Food and drink appear a few times in *The Metaphysics of Morals* in the context of our perfect duties to ourselves as "animal beings." Each of us has a positive obligation to preserve ourselves in our "animal nature," our basic, bodily integrity. The negative obligation is not to kill, mutilate, or deprive oneself "permanently or temporarily" of one's capacities for the ordinary use of our abilities. That includes no "defiling oneself by lust" or "stupefying oneself by excessive use of food or drink." No sex for pleasure, no masturbation, no overeating, no intoxication. The intuition behind his sexual moralizing is to always treat your body with respect (although I'm not sure what the difference between respectful and disrespectful autoeroticism might be).

The claim that we should avoid excessive eating and drinking of alcohol is not that unreasonable, even if Kant's language is a bit drastic. He says a drunk person is "like a mere animal, not to be treated like a human being." (That's a bit harsh.) Gluttony is even worse. Not only are we "incapacitated" when stuffed with food, but our senses are lulled into a "passive condition" that "approaches more closely the enjoyment of cattle." (That's not very nice, either.) Furthermore, unlike intoxication, gluttony "does not even arouse imagination to an *active* play of representation."[5] (It's worse to be stuffed than drunk?)

He says that moderate use of wine "bordering on intoxication" is okay because it "enlivens the company's conversation and in so doing makes them speak more freely." But only wine: spirits and opium "make the user silent, reticent, and withdrawn by the dreamy euphoria they induce," so those things are out. (Is cocaine okay if it livens up the party?) A banquet poses a bit of a moral conundrum. On one hand, it is a "formal invitation to excess in both food and drink." But on the other hand, it "aims for a moral end" beyond mere physical enjoyment and it "brings a number of people together for a long time to converse with one another." Nevertheless, it depends on how many guests attend. If there are too many "it allows for only a little conversation" because the seating arrangement is "at variance with that end," while the banquet itself—the food and drink—remain there as a temptation to intemperance.[6] (Kant complicates party planning.)

The problem with both gluttony and intoxication, as he sees it, is that we lose our dignity and self-respect when we lose control of ourselves. Or to use his language, we fail to respect our humanity. Now, clearly Kant's concerns with intemperance strike us as stodgy and dated. He sounds like Plato only worse: there is always a chance that Plato is being ironic. (Kant doesn't exactly have a light touch.)

Then again, although he himself might have been mistaken, a *Kantian* approach to our eating and drinking obligations remains promising. There are other ways we can be respectful (or disrespectful) by what and how we eat and drink beyond eighteenth-century moralizing about moderation. Namely, if we have an obligation not to kill, maim, or deprive ourselves (either permanently or temporarily), doesn't that mean we have a positive obligation to protect, care, and provide for ourselves? We should not only refrain from making ourselves worse by overeating and drinking, but we should also protect our bodily integrity with food and water. Eating sufficiently is a necessary condition to be capable of thinking, choosing, and acting for oneself. No food, no life, much less autonomy.

Following Kant, we could say that we have perfect and imperfect *food obligations* to ourselves and to others. They are not commandments, fixed in stone, but rather eating- and feeding-specific responsibilities that we should all do our best to live up to in light of the conditions that limit our experience. Kant also recognizes that we all have responsibilities that arise from our particular relationships and social institutions and that they are important, but they do not apply to everyone. He means only to specify the obligations we all have to ourselves and to others simply as human beings above and beyond the obligations we all have in relation to contingent social circumstances. In that spirit, what eating and feeding obligations do we all have?

Perfect food obligations to oneself. We all have an obligation to eat enough to live a healthy life. That says nothing about what food, how much, how often, or any other specifics. The diet does not have to be particularly good or even healthy; it just has to be sufficient to allow us to think and to pursue ends. Put negatively, we have an obligation not to starve or deny ourselves food.

Self-denial is, however, a difficult concept with murky boundaries. There are healthy forms of it (such as self-restraint and self-discipline), unhealthy forms (such as excessive concern for one's appearance, a desire for an unrealistic body type, or as a self-punishment), pathological forms (such as eating disorders that stem from depression, anxiety, or trauma), and forms motivated by self-respect or respect for others (such as religious fasting and hunger strikes).

Other examples of reasonably respectful abstinence could be a cutting back on food after a terrible day of eating, or dieting before your high-school reunion. We might frown on social pressures to lose weight, but is there really anything wrong with eating less to try to feel good about yourself? Is nonmedical dieting nothing but conformity to indefensible social norms, or is there a less judgmental way to understand dieting for the sake of appearance? It is hard to know whether someone's self-denial stems from a lack of self-regard, an eating disorder, or a harmless abstention from eating.

Imperfect food obligations to oneself. We also have the obligation to eat in a way that makes our lives better and helps us realize our ends—not all of the time, for every meal, but it would be wrong if we never tried to improve ourselves by eating well. (Or at least "disconcerting," if "wrong" sounds overly critical.) If our imperfect duties to virtue are a matter of degree, and we have a wide range of discretion in what we can do to fulfill them, we should choose healthy foods, moderate portions, and not eat too often. Of course, we all know this and fall short sometimes, if not routinely.

Eating is never a simple matter of choice and will power. Obviously we are each responsible for what we eat, but we never have complete control over our diet. As we've said, we are driven by hunger, motivated by the unconscious, nudged by society, manipulated by marketers, and fooled by flavor scientists who design foods to be irresistible. The urban environment itself inclines us to eat in ways that may not be the best for us. You might be surrounded by fast food restaurants, with no grocery stores nearby, and routinely have to stave off impulse items at checkout lines. Dietary self-care is a moral issue inseparable from economics, geography, brain chemistry, and other things beyond one's scope of responsibility. But nothing should stop us from trying our best to do the right thing by eating well. As Kant puts it, our obligations are to humanity, so we all benefit when everyone takes care of themselves.

Perfect food obligations to others. Our food obligations to others are somewhat easier to put a finger on. First, we should not eat people. There is rarely, if ever, good reason to consume human flesh. When people resort to cannibalism it is usually because their only other option is starvation—hardly a choice. Emergency cannibalism is usually viewed as regrettable and repugnant yet not immoral precisely because it is done for survival and, in an important way, without any real freedom to act. It is safe to say that a starving person would not elect to eat human flesh if he or she had other choices. That person is outside of the "circumstances of justice," in Hume's sense, where ordinary rules of conduct no longer apply.

In addition to emergency cannibalism, there are those few existing societies that practice ritualistic cannibalism, where, presumably, everyone there knows and approves of the practice. It might strain Western conceptions of tolerance, but it can be seen as acceptable even from a Kantian perspective so long as practitioners are motivated by the desire to honor the dead and treat them with respect. If it is okay to eat another, it is okay to let yourself be eaten. However, if we say it is wrong to eat another, then it is also wrong to let yourself be eaten. It is safe to say that we should all respect our bodily and moral integrity, both in ourselves and in others whatever that may entail.

It is extremely rare for anyone to consent to be eaten after death outside of a society that ritualistically eats their dead. There was one case of consensual cannibalism in 2001 that received a lot of media attention precisely because it was unusually lurid. The victim not only volunteered to be killed and eaten, but also to be dismembered alive and to consume part of himself. It is hard to imagine how anyone can reasonably consent to being eaten, and there's good reason to suspect the victim's psychological state.[7] The typical response to an attempt to be eaten is to resist, or at least refuse if asked. That said, it is not against the law to offer oneself up to be eaten by another after death. Nor is it implausible to imagine that someone who really does not care about what happens to his or her dead body would agree to be eaten. It seems like an affront to one's dignity to agree to it, but I am not sure there are good reasons to question another's voluntary choice about the fate of their body after death.

Kant would say it fails to respect humanity, unlike survival or ritualistic cannibalism, but he might be wrong.[8] Our society permits and even endorses things like organ donation, the use of corpses for medical training, and body disposal methods like cremation that might strike some people to be as offensive as consuming the dead. If someone can agree to cremation, why not corpse mutilation? Is it because there is something particular cruel—almost mythological—about eating human flesh that places it in a different category? There is something particularly barbaric and heinous about it that goes beyond the grotesque and horrific into a realm of its own. Perhaps it is simply disgusting. That is not what makes it wrong to eat human flesh or feed yourself to others, but that might be what makes the thought of it so troubling, at least to Western minds. The feeling might be a clue that something's wrong. The same is true of feeding oneself to an animal. Although suicide is permissible under certain conditions, I doubt that one can feed oneself to lions in the name of death with dignity. Maybe utilitarians would endorse it if it makes the lions happy.

Then again, in 2016 a man cooked and served his amputated foot to his ten dinner guests. He marinated his foot overnight, sautéed it with onions and peppers, and served it in corn tortillas. All of the guests knew what they were in for and seem to have had a good time. The host described it as "bonding" and a "unique experience together." What is wrong with these people eating that foot under those conditions?[9]

In addition to the general principle to refrain from cannibalism, we have perfect obligations to provide food and not to withhold it from others: to feed and not to starve. The latter is easy. Withholding food from others can cause serious harms. Unless done for medical reasons, it is a form of torture. The more difficult question is about feeding others, specifically who we have to feed. Clearly, not everyone or just anyone. We have no *general* obligation to provide food for another person. We have only a *special* obligation. Parents have an obligation to feed their children. Doctors (and hospitals) have an obligation to feed patients. Prisons have an obligation to feed inmates. Armed forces have an obligation to feed servicemen and women. Governments have an obligation to provide emergency food relief.

In these cases, the special obligations to feed arise from a prior obligation to care for or provide services and assistance to those in need. Restaurants and food services may have a professional and legal obligation to provide food, but these are tied to professional roles. Those to whom the obligation is owed also assume the role of a customer or client. The interaction is voluntary, unlike a patient, refugee, or disaster victim who has not chosen that role and who is dependent on others for food, much like seniors, children, and pets. Perhaps our perfect obligation to feed is for the sake of the vulnerable, not the capable.

We certainly have an obligation not to force-feed. Most of us cannot imagine a scenario where we would force another person to eat against his or her will. Medical feeding is permissible if a doctor follows an advanced directive or has the consent of those charged with responsibility for a patient. Enteral feeding (through a feeding tube) is routinely used on infants and for patients who cannot eat. A doctor's obligation to care for patients may require force-feeding.

However, it is less clear if a doctor should force-feed someone suffering an eating disorder. In 2016, a superior court judge in New Jersey ruled that a twenty-nine-year-old severely anorexic woman could not be force-fed. She had steadfastly made her wish known not to be fed, and the judge stated it would be wrong to disregard her wishes. The state attorney general unsuccessfully argued that the patient was not mentally competent to make the decision. The ruling in this case hinges on the patient's capability to decide for herself.[10] There might be cases where someone's autonomy is less evident and doctors would be right to force-feed, for example, if the person was incapable of making decisions, then either the parents or someone with medical power of attorney could decide against the patient's wishes. Needless to say, it is wrong to use enteral feeding outside of a medical context, for example, as a form of torture or to end a hunger strike.

Although decisions made by governments to force-feed prisoners are often not without reason, the justification cannot be about respecting humanity given how inhumane and degrading it is.

We do not have an obligation to feed anyone who is hungry. By "we" I mean individuals. You and I do not have to feed someone we have no special obligation to, such as a person suffering from famine in another continent or even someone in your city who needs food assistance. Governments, not you and I, have an obligation to feed the hungry. We only have to support those efforts through our taxes and through other government efforts to care for needy citizens and refugees.

Food insecurity is a political matter, not something that can be remedied by individual acts or charitable contributions. Affluent nations and institutions, not individuals, have the responsibility to address global food insecurity and malnutrition. Each of us has a responsibility to do something, sometime, to help provide food for hungry people—or at least to alleviate the underlying causes of hunger, such as poverty and economic injustice. But these are imperfect, not perfect obligations. We all have to help others live dignified lives, but we are never morally responsible for failing to act even if it comes at little cost to us. Rather, we each have an obligation to help others sometimes.[11] And our obligation is to assist others, not necessarily to feed others. It is best to leave it at that before muddling the issue with questions about how many people each person is responsible for, at what cost to oneself, how much and what kind of food is owed. We don't have to know the answers to these questions to know that we are obligated to do something for others but not for everyone all the time.

Imperfect food obligations to others. As for our imperfect food obligations to others (or what Kant calls our "duties of love"), we have to help others eat well. Negatively, that means not interfering in a diet or, perhaps, not tempting others to break theirs. We should also respect those who are trying to remain sober by not making it more difficult for them. Positively, we have to be hospitable when the occasion arises by offering food and drink to those who are not members of our households. Sometimes hospitality involves offering accommodations, sometimes other acts of kindness and generosity, but it always involves offering someone something to eat or drink—at least a glass of water. If no offer of food or drink is given, then someone is not being very hospitable.

Kant treats hospitality as a right, specifically the "right of a stranger not to be treated as an enemy when he arrives in the land of another."[12] But he says nothing about food and drink, only the right to membership in a community and, eventually, world citizenship. Telfer characterizes hospitableness as an "aspirational virtue": we should try not to be inhospitable to strangers but strive to be kind and generous to those outside of our circles. She considers it an "optional virtue" that is contingent on one's circumstances, means, and abilities.[13]

Hospitality is usually seen as a secondary, derived virtue that we only do occasionally. The primary virtue might be something like benevolence or friendship. Telfer's Kantian intuition, however, is right: hospitableness is not something we always have *to be*, but rather something that we always have *to do* when the time comes. If the virtues are supposed to be enduring character traits, it is not clear what it would be like to always be hospitable. You need guests before you can host. How can you be hospitable if there's no one there to take care of? Instead, it is better to see hospitality as more like an imperfect obligation we have to do when the occasion arises. That means we not only have to host our guests when they happen to be in our homes, but we should also seek them out and extend ourselves to them. Not always, but sometimes, simply because it is the right thing to do.

To review what a Kantian-inspired food ethics might look like, we have perfect and imperfect obligations to ourselves and to others.

	To oneself	To others
Perfect food obligations	• Eat and drink enough • Do not starve yourself	• Do not eat others • Do not force-feed • Do not deny food • Feed your dependents • Do not feed yourself to humans or animals
Imperfect food obligations	• Eat well • Do not eat poorly	• Feed your guests • Help others get food • Help others keep their diets

We also have obligations to future generations (to leave them enough to eat and drink), to the environment (not to pollute it too much or endanger the flora and fauna), and to animals (to treat them well or leave them alone, depending on the animal). Future generations, the environment, and animals are huge moral issues but less a matter of individual obligation than public policy. These ethical issues require collective action and political solutions. Each of us individually cannot do much for future generations or for all of the plants and animals across the globe. Instead, we each have imperfect obligations to do the best that can be expected of us given our limited capabilities.

There are also countless little things we do each day regarding eating and feeding that our societies require of us. Our cultures and traditions specify how we should view the world, how we should act, and what we can expect from others. Within a society, our specific roles and relationships determine who and what we are responsible for. Most of the time, we are not even aware of the subtle moral valence of our daily lives until a social rule is violated, and then we recognize the appropriate way to do things. The standards depend on who we are, what we are doing, and what social role we occupy—which is precisely why these countless little things are impossible to universalize.

Table manners are a good example of moral practices that regulate a wide range of eating and drinking behaviors down to the minutiae. The list of dos and don'ts is not trivial. They include the appearance of the table, the cleanliness of the diners, the placement of the hands and feet, the usage of utensils, the manner of eating (including chewing, licking, and swallowing), regulation of the eyes, conversation topics, and belching. All cultures have rules that govern eating practices even if tables and utensils are not used. Different contexts and settings involve different rules (for example, when eating in a restaurant or at home), as do different roles and relationships (for example, food preparation and feeding family, guests, small children, and so on).

It is difficult to characterize the vast range of context-bound perceptions and behaviors other than to describe how they hang together. The way we do things is never isolated and free-floating but rather always bound up with other ideas, actions, and narratives. We will return to this subject in chapter 6 to examine how we should relate to our social web of food practices. The "soft normativity" of our social lives is bound up with our understandings of food situations and the practices of responsibility that constitute our relationships, our options, and our identities—more about food existentialism than food ethics, per se.

IS IT OKAY TO EAT ANIMALS?

It is not even a question whether or not we have moral obligations to animals. We do and everyone knows it. Even hunters and people who slaughter animals for a living recognize that there are some things we should never do, like torture animals for fun or eat our neighbor's pet. We might disagree about killing and eating them, but no one really believes that we can do whatever we want to them. Animals are sentient creatures who can experience pain and fear, pleasure and enjoyment. Some have memories and form lasting relationships. We cannot treat them as if they have no more feelings than rocks and sand, as if their lives count for nothing.

Yet most people also think there is nothing wrong with eating animals raised for food. They like the taste, they enjoy the traditions, and they like to think the animals don't suffer too much. Or, when people find the facts about where the meat comes from unpleasant, the effect is usually short-lived and they eventually return to their carnist way. It is not easy to change our habits, especially when we have to give up something delicious.

The question of whether we should eat animals has been debated for thousands of years and offers no easy solutions. We all agree that animals should be treated well, if not left alone, yet we think it is okay to raise and kill some of them for food. Many of us, I would guess, have qualms about it and hope the animals don't suffer too much, but we are not so troubled by it that we go vegan. We know we should do the right thing and be mindful of animals, maybe even spend more for happy meat, but we enjoy the taste too much to give it up entirely. The animal ethics literature typically frames the issue as a conflict between our (moral) obligation not to harm versus our (selfish) desire for pleasure. What we want to do (and to eat) conflicts with what we should do. Usually the literature criticizes industrial food-animal production but endorses small farms so long as the animals live good lives and meet a swift and painless end. Arguments for vegetarian and vegan diets are more common than defenses of factory farming, which are rarely found anywhere outside of industry public relations.[14]

The most enduring arguments against eating animals raised for food are that they suffer, they have dignity, raising them is bad for the environment, and eating them is bad for your health. Let's briefly recount each argument.

Food animals suffer. One-half of the animals raised for food are in large-scale, confined animal feeding operations (CAFOs), where they suffer from overcrowding, boredom, stress, fear, and sometimes mistreatment. They live in discomfort, often in filthy conditions, and are not able to exhibit their natural tendencies. Cows have their horns removed, pigs have their tails docked, and chickens have their beaks clipped. Pregnant pigs are kept in gestation crates, chickens are forced to molt, and calves are taken away from their mothers and confined to tiny stalls. It's sad—and not worth it just so we can enjoy meat.[15]

Even farms animals that live good lives in good conditions where they can express natural behaviors suffer. Cattle are branded and forcibly inseminated; they have their ears tagged or flesh notches cut into their ears. Pigs have their teeth cut, are forced to wear painful nose-rings, and those with hernias are operated on without anesthetic. Chickens are often debeaked and turkeys have their toes cut off, even on happy farms. Fish might endure the worst pain and stress. Most commercially caught fish either die of asphyxiation awaiting slaughter, are immersed in ice-water, or are gutted alive. Other options include percussive or electrical stunning, or a practice called "spiking," which is as brutal as it sounds but at least quick and preferable to a slow death.[16]

Even if food animals endure no mutilations and are allowed to enjoy happy lives outdoors, where they express all of their natural behaviors free from any human control, they still suffer an early death in our hands. Depriving a living creature's life denies it the opportunity to experience life. Like us, they do everything in their power to avoid death. They cower, they resist, they cry, and they are very afraid when they know it's coming. It is hard to imagine any animal experiences its own death as "humane."

Food animals have dignity. Animals are aware of their experiences and they care about their lives. They have needs, interests, and desires just like we do, and they are capable of acting to achieve their goals. For example, chickens can distinguish among dozens of fellow chicken faces, they teach their young, and they learn from the experiences of other chickens. Pigs are quick to learn, have excellent memories, and can understand symbolic communication. Cows can navigate a maze, grasp causal relations, and mourn the loss of their calves.[17] Food animals are fundamentally like us in that they too are beings for whom things can be good or bad. As such, they deserve moral consideration for the same reasons we do: they possess a fundamental dignity as living beings that care about their experiences and act to realize their chosen ends.[18] If it is wrong to deny an animal the ability to pursue its life, then taking its life away, however quick and painless it might be, significantly harms it. In other words, they have the right to live and we have an obligation to respect them.

Food-animal production is bad for the environment. Food-animal production produces a litany of harms, mostly caused by cattle, which require vast amounts of land, both for grazing and for grain production used for feed. Livestock production accounts for 70 percent of all agricultural land and 30 percent of the arable surface on the planet.[19] The consequences are land degradation, soil erosion, deforestation, desertification, and biodiversity loss. Livestock production contributes to climate change—anywhere between 9 percent and 24 percent of greenhouse gas emissions, depending on who you ask.[20] It also accounts for 80 percent of water usage in the United States, and it contributes to water pollution by animal wastes, antibiotics and hormones, fertilizers and pesticides from feed crops, and sediments from eroded pastures.[21] Food-animal production also compromises air quality from soil particulates, farm chemicals, and odor and manure from CAFOs. In other words, industrialized food-animal production is very bad for the soil, water, air, forests, wetlands, and other animals. We should stop eating CAFO meat for the sake of the environment.

Eating meat is bad for your health. A regular diet of red meat will likely shorten your life. A thirty-year study by the Harvard School of Public Health of 120,000 men and women showed that high red meat consumption increased the risk of mortality. The researchers calculated that one additional serving of red meat per day raised the mortality risk by 13 percent. An extra serving of processed meat (such as bacon, sausage, and salami) raised the risk by 20 percent. They also estimated that by substituting one serving of red meat per day with other proteins, participants could lower the risk of mortality by 7 percent. And if participants had consumed half as much red meat, 9.3 percent of the deaths in men and 7.6 percent of the deaths in women could have been prevented.[22] Another study that tracked the diets of 536,000 men and women ages fifty to seventy-one for sixteen years found that high meat consumption increased the rate of death from cancer, heart disease, respiratory disease, stroke, diabetes, infections, kidney and liver disease.[23] Neither study claims that meat consumption is the direct cause of death and disease but it seems likely. To put the matter in moral terms, it is irresponsible to eat meat and to serve it to others.

The most enduring (and plausible) arguments in defense of eating animals are that meat tastes good, it supports valued traditions, it's not that bad for the animals, it's good for the environment, and it's good for your health.

Meat tastes good. People enjoy the taste of cooked flesh. It might be tied to our genes or evolutionary history, to our dietary needs and brain chemistry, to money and marketing, or to psychology and culture. Meat is eaten at celebrations, festive occasions, and the symbolism is generally positive. Above all, people enjoy the taste and they assume there is nothing wrong with it, although for many the good taste overrides any moral qualms they might have.[24] Meat is simply what we eat. We evolved into humans because we cooked and ate it, and it has formed the lifestyles of people around the world for thousands of years. Granted, this is less of an argument than a statement of fact, but it is important to remember that eating meat is not something that we all could easily stop doing. It is a really big deal, more like an institution than a collection of choices.

Eating meat supports valued traditions. We have been eating animals for so long it is thoroughly embedded in our practices. Any radical change in our traditional diet would ripple through society causing drastic changes. If everyone were to go vegan, the loss would be more than economic. It would not only mean the disappearance of time-honored traditions that revolve around the care of animals, but also a vast range of vocations that center on animal parts: fishing, butchering, tanning and leather crafting, cooking, barbequing, and meat curing, in addition to the loss of countless dishes and cherished cuisines. Granted, people would find new jobs, new traditions would take the place of old ones, and we would all develop new tastes. But that would not lessen the loss of all of the valued meat-centered traditions that people everywhere cherish.

Animal agriculture is not so bad for the animals. Farm animals raised in confinement live reasonably good lives and are slaughtered swiftly and painlessly. In fact, the Humane Slaughter Act (1958) requires that animals are to be sedated or rendered senseless so that they do not experience pain. It is designed to be less terrifying for an animal than the traditional way of capturing and restraining an animal to kill it. So long as we do not make them suffer unnecessarily during their lives and during slaughter, there is nothing wrong with continuing to eat meat. The fact is most food animals are cared for, received medical attention, and are sheltered from extreme temperatures and predators. Temple Grandin has posts on her website that show intensive food-animal production at its best: conscientious farmers, well-designed stockyards and pig sheds, and humane animal transport, handling, and slaughter.[25] For the most part, it is nothing like the scandalous videos we see of downed cattle (that cannot stand on their own), anxious sows in crates, and poultry sitting in filth. Grandin tells us that animals raised in CAFOs can live good lives if they are handled properly. If that is the case, then animal agriculture is not as bad as the critics make it out to be.[26]

Animal agriculture is good for the environment. Small-scale, nonindustrialized agriculture and animal husbandry is actually good for the environment. Well-managed livestock grazing, for example, is crucial for maintaining the balance and biodiversity of grasslands, pastures, and other ecosystems. Cattle, goats, and sheep consume plants that would otherwise overgrow and prevent the regrowth of grasses, flowers, and other flora. They also consume invasive species and help reduce fire hazards. Grazing, when done right, is also good for the soil. Herbivores help to till the soil, release helpful microbes, and spread manure, all of which helps regenerate the land. Better soil quality means less erosion, more plant diversity, and better water retention. Livestock grazing also improves the habitats for a number of wildlife species who depend on native grasses and plants.[27]

Yet none of these environmental benefits would happen unless there was a market for grass-fed meat. We cannot rely on wild bison or de-extinct wooly mammoths to do the job. The best way to properly manage grasslands is to support the companies that raise grazing animals. Arguably, we have an obligation to buy grass-fed meat, although we would not necessarily have an obligation to eat it.

Eating meat is good for you. Meat provides complete protein, B-vitamins (niacin, vitamin B_{12}, vitamin B_6, and riboflavin), vitamin D, vitamin E, choline, selenium, phosphorus, copper, zinc, heme iron, and omega-3 fatty acids. Dairy foods contain calcium, phosphorus, vitamin A, vitamin D, riboflavin, vitamin B_{12}, protein, potassium, zinc, choline, magnesium, and selenium.[28] We need this stuff to be healthy and we can get it all (with fewer calories) from meat better than from a vegetarian diet. For those living in parts of the world where animals and animal products are the only sources of protein, it is unhealthy *not* to eat them. For millions of people, eating meat and fish is necessary to prevent malnutrition.[29]

These are probably the best pro and con arguments (that do not evoke arguments about the shape of our teeth or Disney songs about the circle of life). Setting aside for the moment whether our dietary choices are even motivated by reason, there are a number of questions that have to be answered before we can determine whether or not it's okay to eat meat. The arguments presented above are often at odds with each other. They make conflicting empirical claims about the environment, health, and animal welfare, and conflicting normative claims about the value of an animal's life and the importance of pleasure and tradition. And neither set of arguments really answer the question of whether or not it is morally permissible to *eat* meat. They are really about the ethics of buying it and financially supporting food-animal production.

Take the environmental arguments. On one hand, there are persuasive arguments that animal agriculture is bad for the environment. The often cited UN Food and Agricultural Organization report claims that "the livestock sector emerges as one of the top two or three most significant contributors to the most serious environmental problems, at every scale and from local to global."[30] (The authors of the report later lowered their estimate of the amount of greenhouse gasses caused by food-animal production from 18 percent to 14.5 percent, but they also claimed that farmers could reduce emissions by 30 percent if they adopted better practices.)[31] The authors stand by their 2009 report and the otherwise uncontroversial claims about animal agriculture and the environment.

On the other hand, there are persuasive arguments that animal agriculture is not bad for the environment. It just depends on how it's done. Grass-fed cattle and pigs fed on food waste and crop residues are not only beneficial for the environment but also vastly improve global food security. The food conversion rate is actually quite good, about 1.4 to 1. That means if you divide the amount of food fed to animals by the amount of food we get from animals, the figure is 1.4—far from the usual estimates of ten kilos of grains needed to produce one kilo of meat. When we eat animals that are fed on things humans do not eat anyway, the environmental impacts are much lower than if we all ate lentils, rice, and chickpeas.[32]

So, who should we believe? Is it simply that CAFO-produced meat is bad for the environment and grass-fed and small scale is good for it? Would intensive pig production be okay if it more adequately dealt with the amount of manure produced? Would poultry production be okay if the by-products were properly managed and recycled? Is fishing okay so long as there is no habitat destruction, overfishing, or bycatch? It would be immensely helpful to have a simple answer about whether or not food-animal production is bad for the environment. If the answer is not simple, then it would be helpful to know which animals and which production methods deserve our criticism and which deserve our support. Or, if Simon Fairlie is right and some meat eating is environmentally optimal, then it would be nice to know how much meat each of us can responsibly eat and how much it would cost.

The health arguments are also equivocal. On one hand, the National Institutes of Health (NIH), U.S. Department of Agriculture,[33] and American Dietetic Association[34] claim that vegetarian diets are linked to lower mortality, while regular meat eating is linked with higher mortality and increased risks of diabetes, heart disease, and cancer. It is clearly better for your health not to eat meat, although there does not seem to be anything wrong with eating a little on occasion.[35]

On the other hand, there are one billion or so people who live in livestock-dependent societies and on small mixed-use farms who rely on animal products for their survival. For these mostly poor and low-income people, food from animals plays a key role in improving nutritional status and maintaining food security. Livestock help to increase the total availability of food when they are used in places where crops grow poorly, particularly where the animals use feed sources that are unfit for human consumption.[36] How can eating meat be bad for your health if so many people would be malnourished without it? That goes for not only those in extreme poverty but for an additional three billion people, or half of the world's population, who live on about $2.50 per day.[37]

It seems that the health consequences of eating animals have to be qualified. For most people, it is bad for your health, but for some people it is good for your health. Is it that simple? Is the answer contingent upon region and class? It would be helpful to have an answer to the empirical question about how much meat is bad for you—and what realistic options are available to those who live where vegetarian and vegan diets are impossible.

The unfortunately wishy-washy conclusion is this: food-animal production can both increase and decrease access to food, it can maintain or pollute the environment, it can promote or worsen health, and it can have positive or negative effects on the animals themselves. Any good answer about eating animals depends on what precisely is at issue. What is right for humans, animals, and the environment will be different depending on which diets, which animals, and which environments are at issue. We have to be specific.[38]

Arguments for and against eating meat depend not only on getting the facts right but also on getting the story right. The same set of facts can be set in different narratives that make opposing arguments. When combined with different values about the worth of an animal's life (trivial, significant, or sacred) and conceptions about what meat is (energy, pleasure, or meaning), it is possible to tell very different stories about whether or not it's okay. Anti-meat-eating narratives are about assorted ghastly deeds, but they usually downplay taste pleasures and traditions. Pro-meat-eating narratives paint a nice picture of happy animals on happy farms but tend to gloss over animal mutilation the gruesome reality of slaughter. It depends on how the issues are framed, who the main actors are, and which facts are omitted. It's not a simple yes or no, especially when the story is set in a livestock-dependent society.

However, even for those who maintain that it is wrong to kill and eat animals in countries like the United States where we have choices, there is disagreement about how wrong it is. Is it a major or minor offense to purchase something that was produced under morally dubious conditions? How wrong is that, and how would it compare to purchases and consumption of things that harm humans, like cocoa and tea harvested by child and slave labor? Shouldn't we oppose those products more strenuously than those that harm animals? And what does it matter whether or not we eat something after it has already been purchased: isn't the damage already done?

There are two overlapping issues to sort out in order to determine how wrong it might be for each of us individually to eat meat: (1) consumer complicity in the seemingly harmless acts of purchasing and eating and (2) if or when exceptions are permitted. Let's assume that any food-animal production is bad for the animals, bad for the environment, bad for workers, and unhealthy to eat. No nuance—it's all bad. Some say the answer is to boycott any animal products, particular those that are factory farmed.[39] Ethical consumers should vote with their forks and stop purchasing it from stores and ordering it at restaurants to signal to retailers and producers the lack of demand for their products.

Yet, assuming this is true and a boycott (or even gradual change in consumer preferences) could bring an end to factory farming, is there anything wrong with individual purchases of meat? Does that make one complicit in an unjust industrial food system? The short answer is practically, no, but symbolically, yes. No, because individual behaviors make no difference either way. Obviously, the choices you and I make have no bearing on the market, so, practically speaking our actions are inconsequential. We might be able to have an effect on a small-scale enterprise, such as a restaurant or farm, but not on an entire food system. It is a long way from anyone's individual decision not to eat meat to the ranch or CAFO. There are too many middlemen between the consumer and producer to have a direct effect. Producers are shielded from consumers both by the sheer scale of their industry, as well as the fact that we usually eat parts and not entire animals.[40]

What if someone decides only to buy plant-based foods but still supports grocery stores that buy animal products? Kroger and Walmart profit regardless of what one buys there. If they are complicit in an unjust system, then so are their customers. It seems that if a boycott is to be effective against factory farming, it would require us to stop making purchases anywhere along the supply chain: the ranch, the CAFO, the slaughterhouse, the transportation company, the intermediaries, and the grocery stores. That would make it next to impossible for most people not to be complicit in an unjust food system, especially for city dwellers. Yet it seems wrong to claim that someone shares in the responsibility for a moral offense simply by purchasing anything whatsoever at a grocery store. If there are no discernible consequences and no one disrespected in a purchase, then there is no blame to assign to a consumer.

The same arguments can, of course, be made about eating unethically produced meat. An individual who eats something purchased by someone else neither causes harms nor violates rights. In fact, it is, arguably, more polite for a guest to eat rather than refuse whatever the host serves. No blame should, therefore, be assigned to anyone who eats already purchased food, meals prepared by others, leftovers, free food, or anything in your parents' refrigerator. If you played no enabling role in the life and death of animal, then there is nothing wrong with eating it. Elizabeth Harman calls it a "morally permissible moral mistake." One should not purchase or eat meat because of the many moral reasons against it, but it is not morally wrong to do so. Her proposal squares with the intuition that vegetarians have that meat eating is wrong but also that there is nothing wrong with accommodating meat eaters and tolerating their choices.[41] There does not seem to be anything wrong with eating meat long after the animal is dead, which is usually how it's done.

That said, you and I may make no practical difference to the lives of animals merely by shopping and dining, but we might have an effect on other people. We indicate to others that it is okay whenever we go along with it. We signal a demand for it when we buy it from a store or order it at a restaurant. We tacitly condone it whenever we tolerate it or eat it as freegans. Adrienne Martin argues that we "share in the responsibility of collective wrongs" when we participate, even if our individual actions make no difference. We are accomplices in something we know is wrong.[42] Or, as Andrew Chignell maintains, we have a collective obligation to dissociate ourselves from actions that violate our obligations not to financially support activities that harm others, in this case animals, workers, and the environment. We should always "stand with the good," even when doing so makes no causal difference.[43] We communicate to others where we stand on the ethics of eating meat through our purchases, consumption, and complicity with carnists. There really isn't much good about it. Can someone know the morally dubious origins of the meat and still eat it with an unconditionally good will?

Furthermore, there is the matter of one's integrity. Surely it is odd, if not contradictory, to maintain that it is wrong to eat meat but that there is nothing wrong with eating it. Even to claim that it is an acceptable moral mistake—something that is just a little wrong but not *that* wrong—is odd. Granted, we are fallible, and we can always do better, but can admit we are flawed without diminishing the wrongness of an action. However, if we truly believe something is unethical, then we should not do it simply as a matter of integrity. That is to say, our actions matter to each of us individually regardless of their consequences.[44] We don't always have to be saints or heroes, but we can surely aim higher than to routinely make moral mistakes. Or, to put it in Kantian terms, if we have obligations to animals, then we owe it to them to resist doing anything that makes their lives worse, practically or symbolically.

It is another story for the four billion people who live in fishing and livestock-dependent societies. It seems permissible for those with fewer options to use animals for food. If small-scale food-animal production causes no environmental harms and the animals are treated well and slaughtered without pain or fear, it is hard to find fault with meat eating under these circumstances. We can even imagine that farm animals might consent to some of the things we do to them, for example, chickens could agree to let us take their eggs and cows could let us milk them. There is nothing disrespectful to animals to take their products if nothing is done that would cause harm or distress.

Can we also imagine that an animal would consent to be painlessly slaughtered and fed to hungry humans? What if the animal was aging and had little left to live for anyway? Its life would not be cut short, if there even is such thing as animal dying before its time. We would simply be asking it to give up its life for others, or to put it more gently, to give up its interest in pursuing its ends to enable others to pursue theirs. Could a cow, pig, or chicken agree to give its life for others?

Mythology is filled with examples of animals who volunteer to be eaten. Jean Kazez wonders if these stories are "products of wishful thinking, tailor-made to make people feel better about the violent things they have to do to stay alive."[45] Worse, if animals really did have the capacity to put their needs aside for our welfare, "they should be seen as our fellows, not our fodder."[46] No one would ask humans to volunteer themselves to feed others. Although a hypothetical self-sacrifice may not violate an animal's dignity, it is too much to ask of it to comprehend such an action. There is only so much they can plausibly consent to.

In a traditional livestock-dependent or small-farm community, the practice is to eat only the aged animals that have outlived their usefulness. Young animals are needed for fertilizer, wool, and offspring. Older animals are only needed for their meat. Yet, even if the slaughter of these animals is as peaceful as possible, it is still violent, gruesome, and regrettable. Eating animals might be joyful but killing them never is. But if there really are no other viable alternatives, and the consequence of not eating them would be hunger or malnutrition, then it is (of course) okay to eat meat under these conditions.

The key to the moral permissibility is the animal's age. It must have already lived a full life and have appreciably less to live for than its younger counterparts. It must be on the decline, past its prime, and as close to death as possible while still being healthy and robust enough to feed people. I doubt there is a specific age or clear indication of when any living being has lived enough and could die without losing out on life. It is usually better to be living than dead unless ending a life is a better way to preserve one's dignity, for example, terminally ill patients who choose hospice rather than continuing medical interventions. For farm animals that are not given a say in the matter, the question is when their lives can reasonably be taken from them without the right to live a full life, or at least a full enough life.

Roger Scruton argues that there is no such thing as cutting a farm animal's life short in the way that we speak of an untimely death of a person. There is never anything tragic about the death of a pig or the waste of a life of a chicken. Therefore, if animals never really have anything to look forward to as they age, it is best to slaughter them on the farmer's schedule, when their meat is at its best for consumers. The lives of farm animals are for us, not for them.[47]

Scruton's argument has some plausibility. We never lament what kind of life a cow might have lived if it were allowed to live. Unlike a person, the cow would never develop into anything more remarkable than what it already is. We could say that animals reach their potential rather early in their lives and then plateau until they decline. But they still have the capacity to enjoy their lives and they are indeed capable of anticipating at least some future events, such as feedings, herding, and play. Scruton is partially right that farm animals should be allowed to develop for our sake, but he omits the fact that their lives matter for them. What is important is what *they* think about the value of their lives, not what we might think of it.

Typically, cattle can live to be fifteen to twenty years old but are slaughtered before three years. Pigs can live ten to twelve years but are slaughtered after six months. Goats can live for twelve to fourteen years and are killed after one or two. Chickens can live for seven years but are killed after seven weeks.[48] Ideally, each of these animals could live much longer before they begin to decline and have less to live for. The idea of a "full enough life" means that a food animal is entitled to most but not all of its life. It assumes that only humans have golden years to look forward to filled with grandchildren, retirement, and bucket lists. Presumably, there is nothing golden about aging for the animals.

Of course, it would be wrong to euthanize an aging human who is "done" and spends his or her time merely living out the days until the end. We respect the humanity of individuals to age as they wish, however dreary and dreadful they might appear to us. But we do not owe animals the same dignity. We can determine when they are done and then kill and eat them for food. The exact age would vary by species. I realize this is ageism (or animal *Logan's Run*), but I believe it is a feasible and respectful solution to the question about the moral permissibility of eating meat. Or, for those unmoved by ethical arguments, apparently older animals even taste better.[49]

For those of us who do not rely on livestock, it is also morally permissible to eat aging animals provided they were not mutilated and they were raised on farms where they can express their natural behaviors: happy meat from truly humane farms. The same applies to hunting and fishing: only aged animals, killed painlessly. As for other kinds of animal eating, it is permissible for anyone to eat humanely produced eggs and dairy, insects, bivalves, possibly crustaceans, road kill, laboratory meat, and minimally sentient animals, were they to be engineered. In addition, we can permissibly eat meat that is already purchased, free, leftover, or served by our hosts, even if it comes from unethical sources. The damage is already done after it is purchased, although, as we said earlier, there is nothing intrinsically good about eating meat and it does nothing to make the lives of animals better.

We will return to the ethics of meat eating in the next chapters to address political questions concerning the regulation of the food industry, the rights of domesticated animals, and existential questions about how we are affected by our meat-eating traditions. It really is more of a political issue.

WHAT'S WRONG WITH FOOD TECHNOLOGIES?

Some kinds of food and agricultural production methods are morally questionable, such as factory farming, bioengineered animals, and food irradiation. So are some foods themselves, particularly highly processed junk foods, functional foods, and anything with a lot of artificial ingredients. There is something about combining food and agriculture with science and technology that raises red flags. Public opinion surveys show that both Americans and Europeans are concerned that their food is becoming too high tech and industrialized.[50] People are generally skeptical about large-scale food production and believe that small family farms produce food that is safer, more nutritious, and better for the environment. Both American and European consumers are overwhelmingly willing to pay more for food from environmentally responsible farms.[51] The percentage of those willing to pay more in the United States has nearly doubled since 1990.[52]

One explanation for the increased awareness and concern about food production and environment is the prevalence of food scares. Everyone surveyed in a recent Kellogg Foundation survey was familiar with one or more stories about e-coli in ground beef, mad cow disease, contaminated produce, and other such things.[53] Food scares give the public a little glimpse at how agriculture and food production actually works—and sometimes fails. Although the effects are short-lived, scare stories teach people about food systems, regulatory oversight, health and environmental hazards, and other things we usually ignore.[54] They provide teachable, albeit fleeting, moments.

The reason food scares resonate might be because they tap into familiar narratives about the consequences of overindustrialization. The public has grown accustomed to these stories; the main actors and settings are almost interchangeable. They are set in a modernization narrative about an industrial process that has snowballed out of the control and we are helpless to do anything about it. It is like a runaway train or Frankenstein's monster: there is no stopping it, even though we know it is broken. For example, climate change and species extinction are seen as further proof of modernization gone awry. Each new food scare seems oddly familiar, as if we've heard the story before. Perhaps that is why the public only pays attention for so long.

According to the Kellogg Foundation study, the typical response to a food scare is resignation and helplessness. Although the modernization narrative explains the problem, it also explains away the problem. That is to say, people believe either industrialization has gone too far (farming relies too much on pesticides) or not far enough (safe pesticides have not been invented yet). Either way, the public accepts a story of inevitable modernization as the dominant framework for understanding how food systems work.[55] This is unfortunate because other stories are available to help us understand food production and what we might do about it.

The fact is, industrial technologies are far less autonomous than the modernization narrative makes them out to be. Technologies neither harm nor help us in themselves. Instead, they are designed by us to let us achieve our goals. They reflect our humanity, not lack of it. Granted, man-made things might have unforeseen or unintended consequences, but that does not mean the things we develop are entirely beyond our control. Technical systems are neither inevitable nor permanent, and they can always be designed differently. In the case of food, the goal should be to create production facilities that are safe to work in, produce safe foods, and cause no harm. In other words, whatever is bad about a technological system can be improved to embody our best, not worst, values.

There is, however, no agreement about what kinds of food and animal production are acceptable. It is not clear what better-designed technological systems would look like or what kind of food they would produce. Consider three classes of food technologies: genetically modified crops, bioengineered animals, and food additives. In each case there is disagreement about consequences and consumer (and animal) rights.

According to the National Academy of Sciences,[56] the American Association for the Advancement of Science,[57] and the World Health Organization,[58] the evidence suggests that genetically modified food and animals are safe to eat and do not harm the environment. Regulatory agencies in the United States[59] and European Union concur.[60] However, the public remains wary[61] and the Union of Concerned Scientists believes there is good reason for caution, particularly when there are more effective and economical ways to produce food.[62] There is also disagreement about labeling genetically modified foods. Scientific and regulatory agencies (not to mention the food industry) believe there is no good reason to label anything that is demonstrably safe to eat, while ethicists and advocacy groups believe consumers have a right to know where their food comes from. For example, Paul Thompson argues that consumers should always be able to opt out of eating anything they would rather not, however irrational their choices might be. Yet we cannot opt out unless food is labeled so we can know what exactly we are eating.[63]

There is also disagreement about food additives. Scientists and regulatory agencies affirm their safety,[64] while consumers[65] and advocacy organizations have their doubts.[66] The food industry, surprisingly, sides with the public: for the last few years they have been removing ingredients and colorings that consumers perceive to be unhealthy.[67] Then again, maybe it's not so surprising: "healthy" sells.

There are, of course, good reasons to oppose any food technology or production method that is unsafe to eat, pollutes the environment, harms animals, or in any way violates our rights. If, for example, herbicide-resistant genetically modified crops cross-pollinate and produce superweeds that cannot be removed, then we would have good reasons to oppose at least those crops. If we cause suffering while developing transgenic animals, or if artificial ingredients are unhealthy, then we should oppose those food technologies. These are the easy cases. The hard cases are when there are no clear harms and something is safe to eat, safe to grow, safe for animals, and produced and consumed without violating rights. Are there still moral reasons to disapprove of something that appears to be perfectly fine?

Yes, but not because of bad consequences, lack of consent, or disrespect. For those who believe food and agricultural should be natural and organic, or bound up with traditional cultural or religious practices, industrialized processing and biotechnology can be morally problematic, or at least undesirable things we should avoid. The framing of the issues is what matters. For those who already see food and agriculture as organic or sacred, or who frame actions in Romantic or agrarian narratives, then what we grow and eat can appear to be worsened and corrupted by technologies. For those who have more scientific and cosmopolitan inclinations, technologically mediated foods are less worrisome in themselves so long as they do not produce bad consequences or disrespect persons and animals.

This is not to suggest that beliefs in natural goodness or sacred traditions are hopelessly dated and provincial. They are not. If anything, the fact that so many believe that food should be natural, clean, and pure says something important about how people think about what they eat. However, the normative force that supports this kind of food Romanticism is hard to generalize because it is always related to things that are impossible to universalize, such as religions, customs, and strong feelings. Still, these can count as moral reasons to oppose some food technologies, even if the justification is not recognized by everyone—a soft, conditional, normativity. If you already believe food and agriculture should be a certain way (for this or that reason), then deviations may be seen as morally wrong.

One set of arguments against high tech foods appeals to an ideal wherein we live in harmony with our surroundings. Food, according to this ideal, should be natural and free from additives and excessive processing, agriculture should integrate farmers, communities, animals, and the environment, and eating traditions should support sustainable agriculture and lifestyles. On this reading, genetically modified foods, animal biotechnology, and foods with artificial ingredients are unnatural and disruptive to a harmonious life. They can be seen as impure, alienating, and disgusting.

- *Impure.* Foods that contain artificial ingredients are not found in nature. When we eat them, we introduce unnatural elements into our bodies. Unusual genes in crops and animals and chemical food additives are impurities that should be eliminated in the name of wholesome living. The more natural foods we eat and the more we live in accordance with nature, the healthier and more balanced our lives will be. Impurities are bad in themselves, not because of any consequences. It is simply better to be as natural and pure as possible.
- *Alienating.* People, food, and the environment are all connected in the act of eating, provided we eat the right foods in the right way. Bioengineering and foods with artificial ingredients are produced in high tech facilities that are the antithesis of traditional living. Worse, they disconnect us from the land and from each other. The closer we are to our food sources, the more in touch we are with a vital part of our health and traditions. The further we are from our food sources, the less knowledge we have about agricultural life, and the less aware we are of how our lives are connected to others. At the risk of oversimplifying: connection is good, disconnection is bad. It is better to be connected to than cut off from farming, neighbors, and nature.
- *Disgusting.* Genetically modified organisms and artificial food ingredients are intuitively unappealing. The uncomfortable feeling we get reading a long list of chemical ingredients on a food label is telling: there has to be something wrong with eating unnatural foods. The very idea is repugnant. The same with transgenic engineering—crossing animal and plant genes. Common sense tells us it is better to eat wholesome foods rather than bioengineered monstrosities.

Given the choice, most of us would choose food grown in the ground or raised on a ranch rather than anything synthesized in a laboratory. We might not be able to articulate the reasons why we prefer natural to artificial foods beyond saying "yuck!" but that does not mean our preferences are arbitrary or irrational. The expression summarizes our displeasure.

Another set of arguments is based on an ideal quality of life that we should aspire to. On this standard, we can do better than to manipulate genes and eat processed foods. Our lives are better without them: farming is better, animal lives are better, cooking and eating are better, and our overall quality of life is simply better with less technology. On this reading, food biotechnology and artificial additives are: undesirable, inappropriate, cheating, and sacrilege.

- *Undesirable.* Typically, we settle for high tech and processed foods; we rarely seek them out. Given the choice, we would opt for something whole and natural rather than processed and packaged. They are less desirable than their natural counterparts. We can offer dozens of good reasons to seek out all-natural foods, but very few reasons to seek out unnatural foods.
- *Inappropriate.* For those who honor long-standing customs and traditions, bioengineered crops and animals are out of place, out of sync, and inappropriate for all but a large-scale food system. The same is true for quality foods. Time-honored and traditional foods are more appropriate for special occasions than anything processed, packaged, or filled with food additives. High tech foods may be fitting for some settings but they are entirely inappropriate for anything ceremonial or traditional.
- *Cheating.* Techno-fixes are short cuts. Their functional properties can always be achieved by other means, albeit with more planning and effort. It might be more complicated, for example, to deal with weeds instead genetically modifying corn to be herbicide resistant, but there are always alternatives. The same can be said for animal biotechnology and food additives. The reasons farmers and food manufacturers turn to technologies is to optimize production and increase sales. The technologies solve problems for them, not for consumers. We usually have very little to gain from their conveniences, but we have a lot to gain from food and agriculture done in traditional ways. The product tastes better, it is better for the animals and the environment, and a litany of other reasons why time-honored traditions are better. This is the intuition behind

the Slow Food movement: quality food is good, clean, and fair. No biotechnology or artificial ingredients are needed.

- *Sacrilege*. Food, for some, can sanctify and elevate our lives above the mundane into the realm of the sacred. We have all had experiences where food becomes something greater than mere nourishment. Special meals and exquisite dishes can be transcendent experiences. The same can be said about traditional agriculture and animal husbandry. These are noble traditions that honor and respect the sanctity of nature. But there is nothing sacred about irradiated foods, bioengineered animals, or artificial ingredients. They not only make food and agriculture worse, they defile it. Technologically modified foods are tainted, corrupted, and stained.

It is debatable whether these kinds of appeals to nature and tradition are based on fact or nostalgia. It is not clear that traditional agricultural practices and foodways are as wonderful as they are made out to be. Traditions perpetuate as much violent ugliness as they do wholesome deliciousness. But for those who are looking for reasons why food technologies are intrinsically bad, one way to make the case is to contrast the virtues of the natural with the vices of the artificial. The moral force comes from the appeal to live a good life (maybe even the Kingdom of Ends) and to reject anything that makes it difficult to live harmoniously with nature and humanity. In other words, natural foods and traditional agriculture are not only better, but we should support them to improve our lives and to protect the dignity of humanity that is degraded by chemicals and machines. Romantic and agrarian narratives are enduring because they are animated by moral (and religious) force.

Then again, maybe the reason artificial and high tech foods seem to lower the quality of life has more to do with a context and setting than anything intrinsic to what the foods are or how they are processed. They don't *necessarily* diminish our experience; in fact, they can be parts of activities that engage with others and help make our lives more meaningful. For example, Diane Michelfelder fondly recounts eating fish sticks with her family outside on warm summer evenings:

> While drinking lemonade from the multicolored aluminum glasses so popular during the 1950s, we would eat Mrs. Paul's fish sticks topped with tartar sauce. With their dubious nutritional as well as aesthetic value, fish sticks are to fresh

fish as Cool Whip is to fresh cream. One doesn't know the seas in which the fish that make up fish sticks swim. Nearly anyone can prepare them in a matter of minutes. Still, despite these considerations, these meals were marked by family sociability and kindness, and were not hurried affairs.[68]

If eating processed foods together can have all of the virtues of the traditional family feast, then there is nothing intrinsically questionable about the foods. Instead, it's the social or unsocial setting that's the issue. The same goes for how the food was processed. It's conceivable that the lives of the fish stick fishermen could be as traditional as they were a hundred years ago, and the plant where the fish are processed could be family-run or worker-owned and managed. Unlikely, but not impossible.

The same can be said of food biotechnology. The *Retro Report* in the *New York Times* recounts the rise and fall of Calgene, the first company to bring a genetically engineered food to market, the Flavr Savr tomato. The story portrays an earnest group of geneticists who figured out how to make a tomato that stayed fresh longer by turning off the single gene that makes a tomato squishy. The tomato was generally embraced, in large part because the company had nothing to hide—and the product was designed to improve the experience of consumers, not the needs of producers. The question the story poses is, what is wrong with *this* company, *this* product, and *this* use of genetic engineering?[69]

For those who find arguments about the intrinsic goodness of food and agriculture questionable, there are no shortage of extrinsic arguments about industrialized food and agriculture. However, if the reasons are extrinsic, then it is possible that there could be beneficial and respectful high tech food and agriculture that are freely produced and knowingly consumed, and cause no harms to animals or the environment. If we take Monsanto and patent-protected seeds out of the picture, we can also imagine high tech foods using publicly owned or open-source genetic modification technologies, and grown on a kibbutz or collective, where profits are shared or at least wages are high. High tech foods made without alienation or exploitation. Or artificial ingredients designed to make foods safer, healthier, and tastier, maybe to prevent cancer or treat malaria. The challenge to technology critics is if there are only extrinsic problems with foods, then what could be wrong with something that is neither bad to eat nor bad for the environment; if it is grown and eaten with knowledge and consent; and if it is not privately owned and patented?

The answer to the question "what's wrong with food technologies?" is either that they are intrinsically bad or that they may or may not produce bad consequences and violate rights—which leaves open the possibility that there could be nothing wrong with them at all.

Chapter Five

FOOD POLITICAL PHILOSOPHY

The most pressing political food issues are what to do about massive, remediable, undeserved suffering from hunger and malnutrition, and how to feed people using means that are just, fair, and culturally appropriate. Each year hundreds of millions suffer from a lack of food and not enough is done about it. When the food justice literature joins the fray, it is usually to help make the case that people have the right to safe and healthy food and that governments have an obligation to provide the means to it. Arguably, governments have obligations to noncitizens, refugees, and to other nations, which means that they have to secure food access for everyone regardless of nationality. Another set of the food justice literature argues that governments should deal with the underlying social and economic issues that erode food safety and security. They should create opportunities for people to feed themselves, protect national food sovereignty, and support alternative food systems. These wide-ranging justice issues are held together by the idea that our current food and agricultural system fails to feed everyone and is damaging both to peoples and environments. Sometimes the food justice literature remembers that animals matter too.[1]

The liberal political response to food injustices is simply to apply democratic principles of rights, freedom, and equality, and to seek fair political mechanisms to address whatever is problematic. Food justice can be handled by the usual political theories and governing mechanisms. The only challenge food poses is the perennial issue of cultural pluralism: finding consensus in light of deep social divisions and conflicting convictions. But that is not unique to food. There are a lot of things people disagree about in pluralistic, multicultural societies. Any liberal government has to figure out how to balance the rights of individuals, the general welfare of everyone, and longstanding cultural traditions.

Some philosophers believe that food justice is so unique that it can neither be understood in terms of our usual political concepts nor regulated by our current political institutions. Michael Walzer, for example, argues that the liberal political tradition underestimates the extent to which people fundamentally disagree in pluralistic societies, and he warns that if we ignore the different ways people understand social goods, such as food, then any attempted political action is doomed to fail. Furthermore, if we ignore how food politics is not the same as, for example, the politics of immigration, health care, or gender, we ignore the complexities of social life. He argues that we need plural theories of justice to account for these differences and to ensure that everyone's rights, interests, and (in this case) tastes are respected. We need a more relational, less absolute theory of justice that is sensitive to the different responsibilities we owe to others depending on the specifics of our relationships.

Walzer retains traditional liberal ideals of freedom and equality but challenges political theory (and governments) to acknowledge the social meanings and real-world contexts in which our ideals matter.[2] This chapter examines how Walzer's political theory can help us address food justice.

In addition to theoretical questions, food political philosophy can help clarify what we should do to regulate the food system: an eight trillion dollar industry that employs approximately 30 percent of the world's workforce.[3] Governments are forced to contend with things that stretch the limits of their authority, such as transnational corporations and climate change. It is not clear how national governments can oversee the food system, or what they can do to balance the rights of producers and consumers with the legitimate claims of cultural traditions. To complicate matters, the food system is increasingly inseparable from the entire global economy; therefore, questions about governing the food system are about governing the economy itself. No small task.

And then there are the animals—the billions and billions that are raised, caught, and killed for food each year. How do they figure into political systems? Animals clearly deserve moral consideration (otherwise there would be nothing wrong with playing pin the tail on a real donkey), and they clearly are political subjects, given the number of laws devoted to them. The question remains (even for meat lovers), what obligations do governments have to animals raised, caught, and killed for food? Do we have the right to eat them? Arguably, liberal political theory does not even apply to animals and communitarian concerns for cultures do not take animal lives very seriously. Will Kymlicka and Sue Donaldson's version of multicultural citizenship theory is better equipped to deal with questions concerning what we owe to the animals we eat. They try to strike a (better) theoretical and practical balance between humans, animals, and cultural traditions.[4]

This chapter examines what justice in food should consist of, how the food system should be regulated, and what kind of protections food animals deserve.

WHAT IS FOOD JUSTICE?

Food justice is usually understood as a political response to a range of social and economic injustices in the food system. Food justice shares the same goals as ordinary justice theory, to recognize everyone's basic rights and freedoms, but it includes concerns for such things as diet, farming, and ecology. It examines how inequalities of race, class, and gender permeate our food system, and how social and economic justice should tend to both communities and the environment. As theory, food justice is about finding the right concepts to explain and evaluate food issues; as a practice, it is a social movement that engages with communities, farmers, and stakeholders with the aim of transforming our food system.

Walzer's version of egalitarian liberalism, or communitarianism, is an overlooked theoretical source both for food justice theory and practice. He believes that a good political philosophy can do more than just analyze and criticize; it should actually be helpful. Rather than prescribe principles of justice in advance of any concrete application, political philosophy should start from the bottom and work its way up: from practice to theory.

> One way to begin the philosophical enterprise—perhaps the original way—is to walk out of the cave, leave the city, climb the mountain, fashion for oneself . . . an objective and universal standpoint. Then one describes the terrain of everyday life from far away, so that it loses its particular contours and takes on a general shape. But I mean to stand in the cave, in the city, on the ground. Another way of doing philosophy is to interpret to one's fellow citizens the world of meanings that we share.[5]

His intuition is that real-world political issues require several principles of justice, not just one overarching principle, such as equality or fairness. Justice is ultimately about distributing goods: about who can rightly have what. Yet Walzer believes our ideas of justice should be related to the meanings cultures attach to those goods and reflect the actual ways people experience them. Goods mean different things, are valued differently, and play different roles in people's lives. For example, power, fame, clothing, and work are not the same thing for everyone and, therefore, no single principle of justice should be applied to them. The principle of equality may make sense for voting and free speech but not for grading, where the principle of merit makes more sense. Committees can rightfully award prizes, but the market determines success in business. Yet, it might be entirely different in another society.

Walzer thinks this kind of diversified distribution system is fair, and argues that we should think about justice in terms of "complex equality": different social goods should be distributed for different reasons, by different procedures, and by different agents. The way goods are distributed should vary by culture and context because our understanding of goods is "thick" and bound up with meanings. In other words, there are many senses of justice because justice deals with many different things that are understood differently by different people.[6]

Walzer uses food as an example of something that could plausibly be seen as a cross-cultural good but in fact has different meanings in different places. We characterized this conception of food as meaning in chapter 1. Walzer argues that a food like bread can be seen as "the staff of life, the body of Christ, the symbol of the Sabbath, the means of hospitality, and so on."[7] We can imagine a scenario where the religious uses of bread might conflict with its nutritional uses and a culture might favor the religious. Bread might be reserved for religious observation even though people might be hungry and simply need it for nourishment. Or it might be a subsidized staple in one society but an ordinary consumer good in another. There is no such thing as generic "bread" that is universally recognized by everyone as the same thing, and there is no common practice of its distribution. The same goes for any food. It is always someone's food, not generic human chow that means the same thing for everyone.

Another way that the meaning of food affects food justice is in emergency disaster relief. Typically, emergency aid disregards culturally specific meanings and treats food as fuel and nutrition. It immediately goes to the neediest and bypasses the usual channels of distribution, like grocery stores. Obviously, in disaster scenarios, it makes sense to conceive of food as a basic good necessary for survival and to distribute it equally to everyone who needs it. Yet, the fact that food is conceptualized and distributed differently during emergencies attests to Walzer's claim that the meanings that cultures attach to food and the way that it should be distributed go together.[8]

Injustice, according to Walzer, is when a social good in one sphere of life dominates the distribution of a different good in another sphere of life, for example, when people have political power because they are rich, or good jobs because they are attractive and thin. Dominance across spheres is more unjust than monopolies within spheres. Walzer calls the imposition of power outside of its own sphere "tyranny."[9] Justice amounts to patrolling the borders between goods and blocking conversion between goods whose principles of just distribution are distinct. "The regime of complex equality is the opposite of tyranny."[10] Food justice, then, is about protecting its own standards of distribution from nonfood influences. That means there might be different food laws for different people, or protections for food activities from the influences of money and power, or food activities promoted or discouraged by governments. It is hard to say in advance without specifying the meanings assigned to something. There is no one-size-fits-all food justice.

Another challenge Walzer poses to liberal political theory is the idea of "involuntary associations." These are the familial and cultural relationships we never choose but which deeply affect how we think, act, and feel about things. We never enter into these relationships freely, the obligations our memberships generate were never consented to, and the attitudes and ideas we acquired as a result of them were never chosen. Nor do we choose the languages and cultures we are born into and that we pass onto our children without asking them. Walzer's point is not that some associations are good and some bad because of the choices they afford. His point is that it is impossible to imagine our lives without them, and, therefore, any political theory and practice has to contend with the unchosen associations we all have. It would be foolish to deny them and impossible to eliminate them. He explains that "dealing with the constraints of family, ethnicity, class, race, and gender is, in large measure, what democratic politics is about."[11]

I would add that involuntary associations also influence our understanding of food ethics, taste, and disgust. Our basic attitudes about what and how we should eat, what tastes good and what is off-limits, are formed by unchosen relationships that are difficult if not impossible to free ourselves from. We are all born into a world of foods, tastes, and practices that shape our identities and values. Walzer argues that we need to look at our social structures in order to have a better understanding of our experience and to seek out overlooked sources of injustice and inequality. He says we move toward equality "when we open paths within involuntary associations."[12] In the case of food, we should examine the background conditions of our lives to see if they foster equality, not antiquated social meanings and tyranny, for example, women generally prepare food for families, the rich eat better than the poor, or farmworkers have no health care. In other words, the place to look for food injustice is within traditions, groups, and cultures, which makes food justice less a search for correct principles than an activity aimed at identifying inequalities and changing cultural practices.

There are three consequences to framing food justice issues in terms of Walzer's version of communitarianism.

(1) There are many food justices. It is not the same in the world's wealthiest nations as it is in the world's poorest; even within a country there might be different food rights for different groups. There may be several conceptions of justices depending on the context of food production and consumption. A food political theory should, therefore, be attentive to the ways that food systems interact differently with food cultures and lifestyles. That means that different paths to equality should be opened in different contexts. In the United States, that might mean making it easier for people to choose healthier foods than

they traditionally eat (maybe subsidize spinach or mandate meatless Mondays); in a poor nation, it might mean providing education and technical assistance for women farmers; in another context, it might mean protecting a food culture from globalization. Food justice means something different in different parts of the world and for different peoples.

(2) Food should be protected from the capitalism. We need our civic and political institutions to monitor and regulate the economy so that it doesn't interfere with food meanings and practices, including different cultural conceptions of nourishment and taste. Food-related social goods include having sufficient food, healthy food, and good food jobs for humans and environments. When capitalism helps achieve these ends, it should be supported. When it does not, it is tyrannical, as Walzer dramatically puts it.

(3) Ordinary things people care about are political. Things like diet, farming, and food preparation are fundamentally political issues embedded within our involuntary associations and traditions. To change them requires changes in our habits and practices. Walzer implores us to look for inequalities in the most mundane parts of our everyday lives and to think about political actions in terms of things that people feel strongly about, like how food tastes, being healthy, and having good jobs. People are passionate about their involuntary associations, so any food philosophy and politics should be driven by not only rational deliberation but also "passionate intensity" for things people are willing to protest and lobby for.[13] Politics should reach people on issues they care deeply about, and it should deal with everyday problems in ways that make the most sense for our everyday lives. Food should be just, of course, but it also has to be meaningful and delicious for people to really care about it.

HOW SHOULD FOOD SYSTEMS BE REGULATED?

All nations regulate food in some way or another, even those that claim to have free markets and business-friendly governments. Every country has laws, rules, and systems of inspection and management that regulate production and commerce. In industrialized nations like the United States, there is a maze of regulatory agencies responsible for the implementation and enforcement of a dizzying number of food laws. For example, the Food Safety and Inspection Service of the U.S. Department of Food and Agriculture is responsible for making sure that meat and poultry products are safe, labeled, and packaged properly. The U.S. Food and Drug Administration is responsible for the safety of every other kind of food other than meat and poultry. The Centers for Disease Control and Prevention investigate foodborne illnesses and monitor the effectiveness of efforts designed to prevent outbreaks. And that's just food safety.

Governments also make laws about water quality, pesticides, advertising, animal welfare, food assistance programs, imports and exports, nutritional guidelines, and maintenance on facilities. It would be tedious to list every state and federal program dedicated to food regulation, even more so to compare U.S. laws to those in other countries. The simple fact is that governments regulate food and agriculture according to some principles of justice (whatever they might be) while nongovernmental actors, producers, and consumers also play a role in the food system and bear some responsibility for it.

One way to understand food justice is to consider some of the injustices caused by the food system. By following the path of food from farm (or factory) to plate, we find a number of relatively noncontroversial injustices that *someone* should be responsible for, either a government with coercive powers, commercial self-regulation, or consumer ethics. There is a long list of interrelated issues involving vast networks of plants, animals, people, and machines and soil, water, chemicals, and markets. And more. Its complexity is mind-boggling—and it's not all bad.

Between 1900 and 2000, the world population increased from 1.5 billion to 7 billion, yet food production managed to keep pace. By some estimates, we could feed another 1.6 billion people if food were distributed more evenly (and wasted less).[14] The successes are due to innovations in production and distribution, including better fertilizers and transportation, and improved storage and refrigeration. At the start of the century, food production was small-scale and diversified: family farms in rural communities produced a variety of crops, animals lived and worked on farms, and the labor was done by humans, often women and children, and tenant farmers and sharecroppers. These conditions persist today, but by the end of the twentieth century they were largely replaced by a globalized food system. Production is mechanized, farms are larger, there are more chemicals inputs and pharmaceuticals, and markets share is concentrated into the hands of fewer and fewer companies.

However, the current food system also creates injustices. The main problem for a political theory of food is how should a global food system be regulated and governed—and who is responsible, to what extent, and at what cost?

Consider the litany of the food system injustices.

Industrial food crop production injustices: soil compaction and erosion pollution and waste; water pollution, overuse, and depletion; loss of agrobiodiversity; air pollution; oil and phosphorus (fertilizer) depletion; pesticide effects on humans, animals, and nontarget insects; insect resistance to pesticides; plant resistance to herbicides; nutrient pollution (from fertilizers, minerals, animal waste, and human sewage) in water and ecosystems; poverty, unemployment, crime, loss of rural community; farm worker poverty, exploitation, even suicide; exposure to health and safety hazards, intimidation, sexual harassment; and child and slave labor.

Industrial food-animal production injustices: physical and psychological harms to animals; antibiotic overuse and resistance; animal waste pollution; worker health and safety hazards; exploitation of workers; negative impacts to communities from environmental contaminants and nuisance flies; and greenhouse gas emissions that contribute to climate change.

Industrial seafood injustices: overfishing and fish depletion; ecological damage from bycatch, bottom trawling, and dredging; environmental and health problems from aquaculture waste and antibiotics; contaminated seafood; fish pain and stress; and trafficking and slavery.

Industrial food processing injustices: worker safety and exploitation in animal slaughter and meat processing; animal welfare issues; food contamination, foodborne illness, and food safety; fast food, junk food, and foods with little nutritional value; waste from discarded packaging materials; environmental hazards from synthetic materials.

Industrial food distribution injustices: large scale food distributors with concentrated economic power, eroded competition, and privileged large-scale buyers; limits to consumer choices; cultural homogenization; fossil fuel use and greenhouse gas emissions from transportation, refrigeration, and storage; food deserts and limited access to healthy foods; lack of food sovereignty and representation; food insecurity, malnutrition, and hunger; corporate agriculture subsidies, food dumping, and deregulation; underfunded food assistance programs; dubious labeling and marketing, especially to children; and food waste.

Industrial food consumption injustices: diet-related diseases, chronic illness, and obesity; unhealthy diets high in saturated fats, added sugar, and animal products; energy use and waste in food preparation; social inequalities and poor diet; large restaurant portions and unhealthy school food; and bad food environments.

The food system lies within a network of geographic, biological, technological, and social systems. In the United States, it is woven seamlessly into our everyday lifestyles. Agriculture and processing are mostly hidden, food is available year-round, we shop in supermarkets, and other hallmarks of our food environments. It is hard to isolate what belongs to the food system and what is simply the texture of our daily lives. Yet, surveys in the United States and Europe show an increasing wariness to industrialized food and a preference for foods that are more healthy, wholesome, and natural.[15] There is a general sense that something is wrong with our food, and that it could be better.

However, critics of globalized food often miss just how deeply entrenched it is with the most important national and international institutions. Making better consumer choices or voting with your fork are not enough. The food system is so inseparably related to our political and economic lives that real alternatives or even lasting reforms or are unlikely if not impossible (not to sound too pessimistic). The reason, simply put, is capitalism. The food system, based on the private ownership of property and market system of production and distribution, sells more than $1.8 trillion in goods and services each year in the United States alone. It accounts for over 13 percent of the U.S. gross domestic product,[16] one-fifth of U.S. private sector jobs,[17] and 10 percent of personal income spending.[18] Global estimates are harder to pin down, but all estimates point to the same fact that food and agriculture form a significant portion of the world economy, around 10 percent of the total market, $8 trillion in food sales, and 30 percent of the workforce.[19]

And it's not all bad. The money flowing through the food economy is not only the source of goods, employment, and profit, but it also incentivizes genuine innovation and creativity. Not just for the sake of new snack foods and crass commercialism, but for good things, like products that make our food safer and more nutritious with reduced environmental harms.

For example, innovations such as "active packaging" extend shelf life and improve food safety through new materials that are biodegradable, pathogen resistant, and edible. New developments in plant-based foods promise to provide meat and dairy replacements that consumers might be more willing to embrace than soy-based products. And new developments in sustainable agriculture, renewable energy, and environmental biotechnology promise a lighter environmental footprint. These market- and technology-driven innovations are spurred by investment capital, and, although they are not inconceivable under a different political economy, they are present under the current one and generally recognized as steps in the right direction.[20]

However, in recent years, as the food economy has become more globalized, the roles of producers, consumers, and even governments have been surpassed by financial markets and transnational corporations, creating new challenges (and threats) to political governance. As more and more money flows into the agri-food sector of the economy, financial intermediaries exert greater influence over the food system. Banks, commodity trading companies, and investment funds increasingly treat food and agriculture as any other speculative financial product completely detached from its use value. This is known as the "financialization of food": trillions of dollars in transactions that affect everything from the cost of food, the prevalence of malnourishment, and the ecological state of nations. The main engines of agro-industrialism and agricultural trade have shifted from national governments to transnational corporations and financial institutions. State power is being replaced by economic power.

The influence of finance on agriculture is not new and not necessarily a bad thing. If done right, it helps farmers get their products to the market and helps buyers get affordable goods. Farming is notoriously unpredictable: some years are plentiful, and some years are unavoidably disastrous. To mitigate this annual uncertainty, centuries ago farmers and buyers devised a mechanism called a "forward contract" that specifies a predetermined price and delivery date for a good before the actual harvest.[21] That way both parties can guard against unpredictability and be assured of a fair price and decent profit regardless of what the market value of the good is at the time of delivery. Some years it might be higher (and better for the producer), some years it might be lower (and better for the consumer). Forward contracts are perfectly reasonable financial arrangements that still exist today.

In the eighteenth century, a new kind of contract called "futures contracts," or simply "futures," emerged to guard against the risk that either the producer would fail to deliver the goods or the consumer would fail to pay.[22] Futures are like forward contracts but they are not bilateral agreements between two parties; instead, they are standardized agreements about the commodity's quality, quantity, and delivery date so that the prices are the same for everyone in the market. They represent portions of a commodity, not an entire delivery like a forward contract. In fact, futures may be bought and sold many times (or liquidated) before delivery, so that no one knows which exact portion or with whom they have traded. All that matters is the value of the "derivative," or the underlying asset that is traded without necessarily even directly transferring that product.

Speculators buy agricultural derivatives essentially as bets that the future value will be greater than the contracted value. Hedgers buy agricultural derivatives to try to protect themselves from price swings. Futures markets are designed to solve the concerns of farmers to secure buyers and to lock in prices, as well as the concerns of financial investors to trade in a relatively stable market. They help bring in private capital that would otherwise be reluctant to invest in farming, which is risky compared to manufacturing or durable goods.

Global trade in agricultural-based derivatives increased significantly with the liberalization of financial markets in the 1980s and 1990s and shows no signs of slowing. The government-backed institutions that used to support agriculture through loans, credit, and subsidies after World War II are giving way to private financial institutions. The 1994 World Trade Organization Agreement on Agriculture helped to institutionalize neoliberal principles by requiring that nations lower subsidies, harmonize food standards, and eliminate "non-tariff barriers to trade": any domestic laws or policies that make importing and exporting more costly or difficult.

In 2000, the U.S. Commodity Futures Modernization Act (CFMA) further relaxed regulations on financial speculators allowing them to increase the number of futures contracts they could hold and removing mandated reporting of activities by traders. This allowed for increased trading as well as the creation of new financial products linked to agricultural commodities, such as "commodity index funds" (CIF) and "commodity exchange-traded funds." Investment in CIFs increased from $10 billion in 2000 to $260 billion in 2016.[23] Financial investment in agricultural derivatives increased nearly seven times from 2005 to 2016 (from $65 billion to $448 billion).[24]

The major financial actors in large-scale agricultural investments include private equity funds, hedge funds, investment banks, mutual funds, pension funds, commodity trading firms, asset management firms, and insurance companies.[25] Food and agriculture are entrenched in the financial system as a form of capital investment, often with real consequences for those whose lives depend on farming and food production.

An example is the troubling triad of agricultural commodity speculation, biofuel investment, and foreign land acquisition, know ominously as "land grabbing." Trade in land-based derivatives, such as land funds and land index funds, allows investors to deal with farmland as if it were any financial product, not an actual place where people work and live. International investors own the land and can use it however they please, no matter what the social and environmental consequences might be for the locals.[26]

And therein lies the problem with the financialization of food: it turns food into something else entirely and treats it like any other financial product in an increasingly deregulated global economy. It takes the commodification of food a step further and treats it like a stock, a bond, or any other profit-earning device. The financial sector has turned to the food and agricultural sectors for investment and capital accumulation, creating new investment funds based on agricultural commodities. To be clear, there is nothing intrinsically wrong with profiting from food, investing in it, or even speculating on it. Nor is there anything intrinsically wrong with turning food into an object, even something as abstract as a commodity derivative. The problem is that the current food economy, driven by massive, unregulated, centralized financial markets, has resulted in:

- high food prices and market volatility,[27]
- increased power of financial institutions,[28]
- land grabbing,[29]
- hunger, malnutrition, and obesity,[30]
- rural poverty and displacement of farmers,[31] and
- ecological damages.[32]

Of course, if the financialization of food were to magically disappear, there would still be food injustices, albeit for different reasons. There would still be food insecurity, trade imbalances, and environmental costs because many of the problems caused by the industrialization of the food system precede financialization, and many issues remained the same even as state intervention in agriculture and financial institutions has diminished. Arguably, political food issues are endemic to industrialization not Wall Street.[33]

But some things have indeed changed with neoliberal reforms. Not only has it worsened food insecurity and fostered land grabbing, it has also consolidated wealth and power as a result of concentrated market exchanges and clearinghouses—in spite of the rhetoric of democratization and freedom from government control. As governments refrain from guiding food and agricultural policies in the name of deregulation, big financial institutions fill the gap. At this point, the plot thins: the winners and losers are entirely predictable. Big farms, big corporations, and big investors benefit from deregulation, while small farms, rural communities, and developing nations are left out and impoverished. The big overwhelms the small, and the rich benefit while the poor suffer.

Although imagining away food financialization is an interesting thought experiment, it won't actually happen anytime soon, if ever. Capitalism is here to stay and if we are to heed Walzer and engage with and help communities confront "the struggles and wishes of the age" as Marx says,[34] then we have no choice but to deal with food financialization as one of the main obstacles to food justice. There is no way around it. Furthermore, financialized food is no longer food: it is not even a commodity but a derivative based on a commodity—far removed from anything grown and eaten. The question is, what should we do about the financialization of food—and can anything even be done about it if it is so thoroughly enmeshed in the global economy?

There are three main political responses: reforms, resistance, and tweaks. Food justice reforms aim to lessen or eliminate harmful effects of injustices while accepting that the food system involves large-scale actors (governments, corporations, financial institutions), large-scale enterprises (consolidated, integrated production), and large-scale inputs (capital, technology, resources). Reforms will eliminate neither the massive scale nor the economic conditions of the food system.

However, these efforts at reform are far from trivial. For example, one of the long-stated goals of the United Nations and the World Health Organization is the elimination of hunger and malnutrition. They have always recognized the importance of food security and access to the means of producing sufficient, nutritious, and culturally appropriate foods. Numerous governmental and nongovernmental organizations are also committed to worker rights, women's rights, consumer health and safety, marketing and labeling, animal welfare, cultural preservation, and ecological impacts—essentially, every major food injustice is addressed by powerful actors, often with the coercive powers of the law, albeit within the constraints of a market-oriented, export-based, global system.

Reformers propose a number of ways to stabilize markets and ensure protections for both producers and consumers, such as renewed regulation of financial markets, government-backed guaranteed prices for farmers and protection from risk, help for small farmers to gain access to markets, a return of national food boards (such as the Canadian Wheat Board and Latin American Coffee Board), reinstating the 1932 Glass–Steagall Act (which separated commercial from investment banking), enforceable rules to control financialization and international trade, and regulation of agri-food transnational corporations (TNC).[35]

A second political response is resistance. Alternative food systems have been around in the United States since the 1960s when the health-food movement was a part of a larger counterculture.[36] The health-food movement rejected industrialized agriculture in favor of small farms, organic foods, shorter supply chains, farmer's markets, and community supported agriculture (CSA)—many of the same features of the Slow Food and Local Food movements. The latter are a loose association of farmers and consumers who believe it is better to sell and buy locally grown food directly in order to circumvent the existing distribution networks. They are less organized than the Slow Food movement, which not only champions "good, clean, and fair" traditional food systems but also engages in education, organization, and lobbying against globalized foods.[37]

A food sovereignty movement has been growing since the 1990s, and, like Slow Food, is committed to creating an alternative food system. It is less concerned with aesthetic quality and taste than challenging the corporate control of the food supply. Food sovereignty has been described as "the right of peoples to healthy and culturally appropriate food produced through ecologically sound and sustainable methods, and their right to define their own food and agriculture systems."[38] The largest grassroots organization, La Via Campesina, advocates for food as a basic human right, agrarian reform and agroecology, protecting natural resources, reorganizing food trade, ending hunger, democratic controls, and dignity for migrants and workers. They are fighting against transnationals and agribusiness, capitalism and free trade, and patriarchy.[39] Quixotic, to be sure, but at least they know what they are up against.

Food-system resisters believe the best option for farmers is to create their own food networks to ensure a market and fair prices by cutting out the mediating role of financial institutions and TNCs. To achieve these ends, they focus on alternative markets, sometimes on state-managed markets and national governments, and sometimes on local community organizations. For example, fair-trade products try to bypass the global food market to deal directly with food distributors. Fair-trade products rely on producer unions that give small farmers the ability to negotiate prices themselves, often using (old fashioned) forward contracts. Other versions of food sovereignty would have government policies protect national sovereignty from international trade in order to ensure food security and promote domestic food production.[40]

However, some in the food sovereignty movement are skeptical of state authority and instead advocate for community-level organization and food networks.[41] An extreme form of resistance is to truly go local and avoid even the commercial retailers that sell fair-trade products. For example, urban agriculture, rooftop farming, and even dumpster diving and freeganism can be considered alternative food systems. (It is not always clear what the role of either governments or markets should be in achieving food sovereignty.)

A third political response proposed by the main actors in the world food economy is to tweak the financialized food system. Tweak advocates recognize that the globalization of the world food economy causes price hikes and market volatility, record levels of hunger, and ecological harms, among other problems. In 2001, the Doha Declarations of the World Trade Organization recognized the special place of agriculture by noting that "non-trade concerns" such as food security and social stability must be taken into account in establishing trade rules and in mediating disputes between nations.[42] In response, advocates of trade liberalization recommend tweaking the system to encourage more investment to increase food productivity (such as improved information sharing and transparency in futures markets), more agricultural biotechnology, and more integration within food markets with better technologies.[43]

The World Bank, World Trade Organization, and public-private partnerships, such as the Alliance for a Green Revolution in Africa, promote responsible agricultural investment, or what is sometimes called "sustainable intensification." The idea is to increase private investment, relax trade regulations, and to increase production in environmentally sound ways. This approach is endorsed by major philanthropic organizations, such as the Rockefeller and Bill and Melinda Gates foundations, the G20 nations, and partnerships between environmental organizations Rainforest Alliance and World Wildlife Foundation and TNCs such as Coca-Cola and Walmart.[44]

Jennifer Clapp explains the difference between food justice reformers and tweakers (on one side) and food sovereignty resisters (on the other) in terms of conflicting narratives about trade and food security.[45] The "trade as opportunity" narrative draws on the eighteenth- and nineteenth-century economic theories of Adam Smith and David Ricardo, and maintains that everyone benefits from commercial trade. Lower trade restrictions help "food self-reliance" as a way to promote food security and general economic prosperity—not to mention world peace and cosmopolitanism. Their classical theories of "comparative advantage" maintain that specialization based on advantages in geography, labor, and technology encourages competition, efficiency, and economic growth.[46]

The "trade as threat" narrative worries that free trade undermines "food self-sufficiency," the rights of states and communities to choose their own food systems and to protect both food and national security. The assumption is that a nation that cannot feed itself is vulnerable to foreign interests. The trade as threat narrative does not oppose all trade, only the kind that prioritizes financial institutions and TNCs over the "multifunctionality of agriculture," such as fair-trade products. According to this counter-narrative, food should be treated as an exceptional case within trade policies because it is more consequential than other social goods. Existing trade regimes pose risks to food security and can devastate communities and ecosystems, not to mention the increased health risks as ultra-processed foods pervade global food chains.[47]

The competing narratives of trade are about more than economics; they go to the heart of the concerns of both progressives and conservatives that the current global order is doing more harm than good. We have seen more and more nations embrace their own versions of nativism and provincialism in response to economic globalization. Many nations are turning inward, becoming protectionist, and disengaging from international institutions and alliances. Ironically, the liberal language of food sovereignty, consumer protection, and environmentalism harmonizes with the conservative rhetoric of nationalism, xenophobia, and authoritarianism keen to preserve a version of a traditional of social order that is hostile to foreigners and suspicious of cosmopolitan political institutions.

The question posed at the start of this section was, how should a global food system be regulated and governed—and who is responsible, to what extent, and at what cost? What can be done about injustices in the food system caused by the financialization of food? Which kinds of reforms and resistance can, following Walzer, combat financial tyranny, open paths for freedom in light of our involuntary associations, and communicate and engage with communities? Or, following Rawls, which ones would help share the benefits and burdens of social life and ensure than none are disadvantaged by undeserved social circumstances? I really do not know what can be done about the financialization of food except to recognize its effects so we know what we are up against, to defend the institutions that might be able to change it—and to engage in food politics.

WHAT ARE THE POLITICS OF FOOD ANIMALS?

The injustices caused by industrialized food-animal production are well-known by now. It is bad for the land, air, and water, bad for public health, and rural life, and really, really bad for animals, who we can be certain do not want to be killed to feed humans. On the other hand, people need to eat, food animals provide a lot of nourishment, and small-scale animal agriculture is not that bad. Eating meat is a thoroughly political issue bound up with the global economy, equally driven by financialization and TNCs as it is by tastes and traditions.

The amount of meat and animal products produced and consumed has radically increased over the last half-century. People now eat twice as much chicken, pork, and beef as they did fifty years ago. From 1961 to 2011, the world population doubled but meat production quadrupled and egg production increased by even more.[48] If predictions from the Food and

Agricultural Organization of the United Nations hold, by 2050 the population will increase threefold while meat consumption will increase sevenfold. Unless things change, they predict environmental disaster around the corner.[49]

Furthermore, the consumption of meat is unevenly distributed across the globe: people in wealthy countries eat far more than people in poor countries. The average American eats eight times more meat than someone in Africa, with the biggest increases in consumption coming in fast-growing economies in China and Brazil.[50] This change in diet is typically seen as an inevitable consequence of development and is euphemistically called the "livestock revolution" and "nutritional transition." Tony Weis calls it the "meatification" of diets: the push to have everyone eat as much meat as the world's wealthiest consumers.[51]

One of the main engines of meatification is a modernization (or utopian) narrative of economic development. According to this generally accepted story, industrialization and economic development, in conjunction with science and technologies, lead to social and political progress. The wealthier and more advanced a nation is, the more open and democratic it is. Or put more crudely, consumer societies are free societies.[52] According to Weis, one of the assumptions along the path to modernization is that the wealthier a society becomes, the more meat it will want to consume. "The climb up the 'animal protein ladder' is part and parcel with the climb up the 'development ladder.'"[53] A meat-based diet is viewed as a visible sign of prosperity compared to a plant-based diet, and animal proteins are viewed as superior in every way to plant proteins.

Yet the increased consumption of meat is far from natural and inevitable, but rather it is the result of political choices often tied to national development aspirations. In the nineteenth century, Britain fostered the idea that eating meat was a source of class status, nationalist pride, and imperialist power.[54] In the mid-twentieth century, the U.S. Department of Agriculture recommended four daily servings of both milk and meat.[55] And, at the start of the twenty-first century, the Chinese health minister issued dietary guidelines that recommend forty to seventy-five grams of meat per person each day.[56] East Asia is not known for its beef production but demand for western-style meals is growing rapidly, particularly among younger people and urbanites. Increased meat consumption is driven by rising incomes, changing cultures, and international trade. In the 1980s, beef in China was so rare it was called "millionaire's meat." Now it's commonplace.[57]

Another engine of meat consumption is what Weis calls the "industrial grain-oilseed-livestock complex." In the 1950s and 1960s, state-supported agriculture and industrialized farming technologies produced a surplus of grain. In the 1970s and 1980s, trade protectionism and government subsidies spurred more production that led to the dumping of cheap food on the international market. In the 1990s and 2000s, trade liberalization and food financialization led to even more surplus production. But because it is difficult to "absorb" the excess grains and oilseeds, governments buy it to protect farmers and use it for biofuels or animal feed—which in turn spurs industrial animal agriculture that fuels the demand for more grains, feed, and meat.[58]

Predictably, the benefits and burdens of cheap food surpluses are not shared equally within or among nations. Surpluses reflect and exacerbate global inequalities. It reflects them in the uneven geography of both meat consumption and poverty. There is nearly an inverse relationship between per capita meat consumption and hunger. Wealthy industrialized countries eat the most meat; poor countries, mostly in Africa and the southern hemisphere, eat the least and experience the highest rates of hunger and food insecurity. Yet food surpluses also exacerbate inequalities by increasing dependence on grain imports in poor countries, by land grabbing, deforestation, and resources depletion, as well as by water scarcity and climate change, which have a greater effect on countries that have neither the financial nor technological means to adapt.[59]

Advanced, industrialized countries can contend with the meat economy through reforms, resistance, or tweaks. However, the situation is very different for approximately 1.3 billion people who survive on less than two dollars a day and for whom animal agriculture is not optional. Three-quarters of the poorest of the poor depend on farm animals as an important source of income.[60] For example, livestock contributes 30–40 percent of the agricultural gross domestic product for a significant portion of sub-Saharan Africa and South Asia.[61]

Women farmers are particularly vulnerable. They have less access to improved inputs, training, and markets, so their yields are typically less than men's, which puts families (and entire communities) at risk when there is not enough to eat or extra to sell.[62] Farm animals are crucial for agricultural productivity in poor and rural communities, but especially for women and children. Livestock provide food, extra income to send children to school, and help to reduce gender gaps and inequalities, all of which makes communities healthier and stronger. If livestock help to improve the lives of one billion people affected by hunger and poverty, then it would be unconscionable to advocate for worldwide animal liberation. Too many people would literally die without food animals.

The choices of those in livestock-dependent societies are so severely limited that it is not clear they have the option not to eat meat. Justice, according to Rawls (following Hume) is required only under conditions of "moderate scarcity." If we all had everything we needed, so the argument goes, there would be no need for justice. Everything would already be just. It is only when there are not enough basic goods for everyone that we need justice to ensure a fair distribution. Furthermore, if we are outside of the circumstances of justice in a condition of "total scarcity," like on a lifeboat, then all kinds of things that are normally unjust are now okay, such as stealing food or survival cannibalism. For the one billion who are not in circumstances of justice, they can understandably disregard animal lives for the sake of their survival. The same should apply for the approximately three billion living on three dollars per day—not the world's poorest but nevertheless living in severe poverty.[63]

The fact that half of the world lives in poverty does not negate the rights of animals to pursue their lives. It only means that there are exceptions to the rule in how we may treat them. However, for those of us who live in circumstances of justice—over half of the world—there are fewer compelling reasons to take the life of an able-bodied animal merely to satisfy either hunger or taste, or to enjoy traditions. Or, to frame the issue in economic and political terms, we do not have the right to raise and kill animals for food so long as there are other viable options to earn a living and to feed people. In fact, we have the obligation to respect all life but above all sentient creatures that have lives that matters to them. Like us, animals have subjective experiences and, therefore, basic interests that cannot be sacrificed for the greater good of others. That means no animal killing, harming, or confining —even if it benefits humans. Unlike animal welfarists, who argue for utilitarianism for animals and deontology for people, the more consistent, easier to defend, position is universal rights for all humans and sentient animals.[64]

In addition to respecting the universal negative rights of animals, we also have positive obligations to care for them. We always have negative obligations not to do certain things, such as enslaving, torturing, and killing animals for fun (although eating aging animals seems okay), as well as not to keep them in zoos and circuses or use them for entertainment and medical experimentation. But we also have positive relational obligations to care for, accommodate, and rescue them depending on what the nature of the relationship is. (Walzer agrees that we have both universal rights to equality and particular responsibilities that are related to cultures.)[65]

Will Kymlicka and Sue Donaldson propose an extension of animal rights with citizenship theory to account for both our negative and positive obligations. The intuition is that universal rights are not dependent on relationships within a particular political community, yet the rights of citizens are. For example, citizens, tourists, temporary residents, and refugees all have the same right to life but they do not all enjoy the same rights to political participation. No one can be enslaved, but only people who live there get to vote in local elections. In other words, we have both universal negative rights (about what not to do) and positive relational obligations (about what we owe to others) depending on our citizenship. The context and setting do not matter for negative rights, but they are crucial for our positive obligations to each other.[66]

It is the same with animals. Specifically, we have an obligation to leave wild animals alone, to accommodate urban animal denizens, and to protect our domesticated animals. All animals have the right to life, but they are owed different treatment according to our different relationships with them. Wild animals live in their own communities whose sovereignty and territory we should respect. Urban "liminal" animals are like temporary visitors that live among us and whose interests set side-constraints on how we may pursue the collective good. And domesticated animals are vulnerable dependents whose interests should count in determining our collective good. All animals are sentient creatures who deserve respect, but only some of them deserve the benefits of citizenship.[67]

Kymlicka and Donaldson point out that there are three aspects of citizenship:

(1) Citizenship can mean nationality, as in having residence in a particular place that can be considered to be home. It entails, minimally, residence within a national territory.
(2) Citizenship can mean popular sovereignty, in that the state speaks in the name of the people. A legitimate state claims to belong to the people, express their interests, and to represent them.
(3) Citizenship can mean involvement in civic goings on, civic virtue, and participation in civic life.

Clearly no animal can engage in public debate but neither can some humans. Animal citizenship is contingent on the first two senses, of residency and sovereignty, not democratic agency.

Domesticated animals meet two of the three senses of citizenship. Pets and farm animals are nationals who live squarely within our political communities and are among the sovereign people in whose name the state governs. They would be citizens in the third sense but they cannot participate in civic life due to a lack of language and cognitive capacities—like children, those with severe cognitive disabilities, and immigrants who are not yet conversant. Animals are vulnerable, dependent, and need our help like other vulnerable and dependent members of society.[68]

Yet domesticated animals may indeed have some form of political agency even if they are incapable of public reasoning. Cattle, pigs, and even chickens can decide and choose for themselves based on their subjective sense of the good. They can cooperate with each other and with humans, sometimes seeking us out, not only for food but also for help and assistance. And they can also communicate their preferences to us. Farm animals depend on us to live, to be sure, but so do some humans. Kymlicka and Donaldson draw on disability theories of citizenship for models of "dependent agency" to account for the various ways in which our political agency relies on supportive and trusting relations with others.

All of us need the help of others to articulate our subjective good; all of us need the help of supportive social structures to participate in schemes of social cooperation. We are all interdependent, relying on others to enable and sustain our (variable and contextual) capacities for agency.[69]

It is a mistake to think of agency as a precondition for inclusion in a political community, as if having certain capacities is a criterion for citizenship. All of us need help at some point in our lives, yet if our vulnerabilities and dependencies have no bearing on our citizenship, then why should we view domesticated animals differently? They should be entitled to the same rights and protections as any of us who need help and advocacy in order to participate in social life.

It is not clear how we can have the right to eat the animals that we have domesticated and rendered dependent. If we are responsible for the care and protection of our charges, then we cannot claim to treat an animal with respect by taking its life. The best arguments for animal welfare and happy meat have a hard time explaining how killing an animal for food somehow does not harm it. Simply put, there is no *right* to eat meat. There are only obligations to respect animals and to care for the ones who depend on us.

Fish are a little different. Twelve percent of the world's population live in fish-dependent societies that rely on fishing and aquaculture for food and livelihood.[70] They are free to eat fish, preferably happy fish who have lived full lives. That squares with standard management practices for protecting fishing stocks. Aquaculture (properly managed) is preferable to wild caught in order to avoid a litany of environmental harms, and to respect the rights of wild animals to be left alone. That means that those of us who have choices should choose to eat (happy and aged) farm-raised fish over wild-caught fish.

Fish enjoy none of the legal protections that livestock receive, perhaps because sea creatures are generally harder to read and awaken less sympathy in us (although that may say more about our insensitivity than their lack of trying).[71] Given the fact of fish suffering, there is no reason not to extend animal welfare laws to them. Granted, fishing is notoriously difficult to regulate, and it is not clear how humane standards could be enforced either internationally or on the high seas, but the political case is clear: fish deserve justice (although I am sure that slogan won't move many people).

Consumers recognize the need to cut back on animal products even as the total amount of meat consumed increases worldwide. Surveys show that Americans are trying to eat less meat, primarily for the cost and health risks, but over half mention environmental and animal welfare as reasons for cutting back.[72] Similarly, attitudes about meat eating among Europeans is souring, particularly among people age eighteen to twenty-four.[73] After recently promoting meat consumption, the Chinese government is now trying to get people to eat less meat to improve public health and reduce greenhouse gas emissions.[74] Around the world, policy makers are starting to recognize the need to shift consumer diets away from animal proteins and toward plant-based and high tech alternatives. Lab-grown meat companies in the United States, Israel, and the Netherlands have attracted major investors including nations (China), food giants (Cargill and Tyson Foods), and billionaires (Bill Gates and Richard Branson).[75]

There are a number of ways to reduce the demand for meat. Governments and nongovernmental organizations (NGOs) can educate the public about health risks, animal welfare, and environmental harms, they can issue new dietary guidelines, and they can improve public perception of alternative proteins. Food producers, retailers, and restaurants can advertise and market nonmeat options, they can increase vegetarian and vegan options, and they can help shift the social environment in which meat consumption is the norm, perhaps even influencing tastes so that consumers will happily choose alternatives without needing to be nudged. And consumers can advocate, lobby, and engage with public institutions to cut down on the amount of meat served—Meatless Mondays, for example.

Another option is to gross people out and disgust them into cutting back on animal products. A 2013 video by the animal advocacy NGO Mercy for Animals does just that. In "Mad Sausage," a talking piece of meat warns a would-be diner about the horrendous, disease-ridden conditions where he (the sausage) came from. He explains that he was raised in prison, deprived of fresh air, and exposed to sickness. He sneezes on the diner's face and says, "I hope I'm not contagious." When the diner ignores his dire warnings and takes a bite, we see a montage of miserable caged animals, squealing pigs, slaughter, meat processing, and images of cells, microorganisms, and what we assume are pathogens. The diner's eyes grow wide and he spits the sausage out of his mouth. He's revolted and so are we.[76]

Is there anything wrong with this kind of raw plea not to eat meat? Is there any place for political uses of disgust to motivate people to act, or should we keep public debate as rational as possible? Nussbaum, as we said early, is skeptical about the role of emotions in public life because they are too often used to justify discrimination. Kelly is even more emphatic: appeals to emotion have no place whatsoever in political liberalism. Walzer urges political passions for the things we care about but says nothing about strong emotions for the things we detest. Dr. King and Nelson Mandela didn't rely on disgust to motivate people and promote change; neither did abolitionists, suffragettes, or anti-colonialists.

Nevertheless, in the United States, both conservative and progressive uses of disgust are already part of the political landscape, albeit for different purposes: conservatives use it for fear, progressives for health and safety. Conservatives dabble in disgust to help draw strict moral boundaries around things to prevent what are seen as impurities that can spread and infect others. For example, "immoral" people (such as gay Boy Scout leaders) should be kept away from "moral" people so as not to risk contagion. The metaphors of dirt and disease can explain why conservatives advocate for things like segregation, incarceration, and stigmatization of otherness. Donald Trump repeatedly evokes the concepts of disgust and purity when he promises to build a wall along the border to protect us from immigrants who "infest" the country. Conservative talk show host Tucker Carlson warned that immigrants make "our own country poorer and dirtier and more divided."[77] Georg Lakoff calls the conservative worldview a "strict father morality" that stresses order, discipline, authority, boundaries, homogeneity, purity, and self-reliance.[78]

Lakoff describes the progressive worldview in terms "nurturance"—or "mommy morality"—which stresses empathy, care, protection, social ties, fairness, and happiness. We find nurturance in the politics of protection: health care, worker safety, environmental protection, consumer protection, and gun control.[79] Progressives rarely appeal to disgust, except for occasional public health campaigns against things like pollution, smoking, and soft drinks. For example, in 2001, the Brazilian government mandated that graphic photos be put on each cigarette pack sold in the country and saw the number of smokers drop significantly. According to the director of Brazil's National Cancer Institute, "The images are meant to cause repugnance in using a product that is associated with the injuries that are being shown."[80] Strong visceral reactions to graphic images resonate with both progressive and conservative values, in this case protection and purity.

Is there is anything intuitively wrong with emotional appeals in public health campaigns? The concept of protection has always been central to liberal political theory: modern contract theories are about protecting property rights and protecting each other from vigilante justice, Mill argues that justice should protect our liberties, Kant argues for a league of nations to protect against external aggression, and Nussbaum argues that a society should protect basic human capacities.

If there is nothing wrong with public policies that protect the things we value deeply, then there may be a legitimate political role for appeals to disgust. The feelings of empathy and responsibility for others are very much aligned with cosmopolitan values, anyway. It is perfectly reasonable to be worried about bad food, pollution, and animal welfare, and it is perfectly reasonable to bring our passions into the political arena—so long as we use our words and don't just show pictures and say "ew!"

There's a reason why large-scale farmers and state farm bureaus in the United States support ag-gag laws that criminalize the acts of filming or photographing farms and livestock facilities without the consent of the property owners. These laws are designed to silence whistleblowers who expose worker safety and animal welfare violations. Supporters of ag-gag laws are well aware of the powerful emotional effect of videos to evoke empathy for animals. These laws exist only to hide animal agriculture from public scrutiny because the industry is well aware that meat can easily be made distasteful when we are aware of its origins. The sights and sounds of distressed animals, blood, and innards are not only unpleasant but may also be an indication of wrongdoing; our strong feelings may indicate that there is something wrong with the way they are raised and killed. If factory farms and slaughterhouses really believed they enjoyed public support, they wouldn't act like they have something to hide. They know that the only thing that can shake our love of meat is the even stronger feeling of disgust.

Research into consumer behavior has shown how effective disgust-oriented messages are in influencing attitudes toward meat, even more effective than health-oriented messages.[81] For example, sales went down in the United Kingdom after horsemeat was found in ground beef.[82] The same happened in the United States when media reported that hamburger contained "pink slime."[83] Some research shows that the response to these food scandals was based more on disgust and animal welfare than health.[84]

Appeals to disgust seem to work—and not necessarily because they appeal to the worst in us but because they speak to our reasonable desire for self-protection. Disgust appeals also resonate with conservatives, who are more likely to respond to threats of danger than progressives. But the results are the same: one group avoids meat for self-protection, the other avoids it out of fear.[85] They might even be able to find common ground in what Rawls calls an "overlapping consensus" of worldviews.[86]

Given the grip that meat has over us, and given the dire predictions about eating meat and the fate of the planet, what is really wrong with emotional appeals to get people to cut back? Nothing else seems to work. Good reasons and rational persuasion are defenseless against our tastes. Even vegetarians and vegans backslide. How bad would it be to shock people off meat if the worst predictions are right and we're truly facing environmental calamity? Walzer recommends that we engage in politics about things people care about and meet them where they're at. Why not fear and disgust about bad food?

Or, for those who oppose of any form of disgust politics what so ever, another option is to emphasize the positive in nonmeat alternatives. Highlight what's wholesome and good about plants. Entice people with a delicious a carrot instead of a disgusting stick.

Chapter Six

FOOD EXISTENTIALISM

Food touches on a number of existential themes that concern what it's like to be human, or what used to be called "the human condition." Existentialist philosophers examine the basic states of being that characterize what we are and how we fundamentally relate to the world.[1] They recognize that our experiences are not a generic state of affairs that anyone could have but always the particular experiences of someone in a particular situation. The existentialists assume an individual's perspective of what it is like to be involved in the world and that our experiences matter uniquely to each of us. But where philosophers had traditionally found rationality and purpose in life, the existentialists find irrationality and paradox. They believe that life is ultimately meaningless and it's up to us to give ourselves direction and purpose.

Food is, obviously, an essential part of our lives, but not in a trivial way, like Feuerbach's platitude that you are what you eat. (Kass rightfully notes that it's the other way around: what you eat becomes part of you.[2]) Food fundamentally shapes our lives and figures into our agency, enabling some actions and closing off others. We are driven by hunger and thirst, limited by satiety, and have tastes for things we know we shouldn't eat. Our very freedom requires we have enough (but not too much) to eat. Yet how free are we when so much of food experience is determined by our bodies and by circumstances beyond our control? And if we are not free, then how can we be held responsible for our food choices? The existentialist response might be that we are neither absolutely free nor determined, but inescapably bound by our *factical* food lives: the situations that we have no choice but to contend with—and often try to escape from.

Food also affects into our identities and relationships with others. We are all shaped by the food evolution, geography, history, and culture that form the situations we are born into and that delimit our choices. Arguably, cooking made us who we are today: from the development of our brains to technologies to cooperative activities. Then agriculture led to a new era driven in large part by food, including domesticated animals, governments, trade routes, religions, and other hallmarks of social life. Food continues to play a role in who we are and how we live together, as seen in the food customs and tastes we are socialized into, or more significantly, for those who have dietary restrictions, are subsistence farmers, or suffer malnutrition. Food plays a huge role in the identities of people everywhere.

Sometimes societies use food to exclude people from full membership, or they assimilate and mainstream a minority group's traditional dishes, or they mischaracterize people on the basis of food, such as Hawaiian people who, apparently, put pineapple on everything. Food can be used to heighten both our similarities and our differences; it can help us feel united with or alienated from others. And there is always the question, even for those who are comfortably assimilated, as to what extent people should go along with what everyone else does—as Kierkegaard says, between authenticity to oneself and conformity to the crowd. We inherit the diets and cuisines of others and can accept them, resolutely affirm them, or reject them. Our choices may be limited, but we can always take a stand on our lives.

Another food existentialist theme is absurdity: the groundlessness of our existence and the ultimately arbitrariness of our choices. Nietzsche noted that a mechanistic world is a meaningless world and, ever since we made God irrelevant, there is nothing beyond ordinary life that makes it significant. But if life is basically pointless and there is nothing out there to help us make sense of it all, then what are we really doing with our lives? If we really are just chewing animals like the rest, living from meal to meal, how can we live with any sense of purpose? We live and we eat; it is both obvious and incomprehensible, maybe impervious to reason. Yet, for some reason, food and eating seem particularly important even when we have enough. Affirming the importance of food in our lives is either a lovely little truth or a really sad fact. When you think about it, if we have enough to eat, what does it really matter *what* we eat?

DOES FOOD DELIMIT OUR FREEDOM?

One of the contributions the existentialists make to food philosophy is the importance they place on the body in everyday experience. Several of them argue that our experience is more affective and emotional than cognitive and rational. Our bodies matter as much as our minds, or as Maurice Merleau-Ponty puts it, we are a "lived-body" that engages in the world. Our consciousness is "less a matter of 'I think this' than 'I can do that.'"[3] Our experience of the world is always given "through the intermediary of the body."[4] The "knowing-body"[5] gives us access to the world and "teaches me what space is."[6] In fact, "there would be no space at all were it not for the body."[7] Jean-Paul Sartre also claims that experience is a mix of mind and body. Instead of Descartes's "I am, I exist," he says, "I exist my body."[8] We are "flesh": partly subjective, partly objective, and partly social. Yet the body is also "inapprehensible"[9] and "ineffable,"[10] which means our experience is always ambiguous and indeterminate, making certainty about things all but impossible.

Paul Ricoeur, the often-overlooked contemporary of Merleau-Ponty and Sartre, says that the notion of the lived-body obscures how much we can actually know about our experience. The fact that we are always related to our bodies doesn't mean that certainty is impossible and experience is always ambiguous; it just means that the voluntary (mind) and involuntary (body) are interrelated. Like Merleau-Ponty, Ricoeur claims that we understand ourselves based on our ability to say, "I can," not "I think," and this ability presupposes what is involuntary: the will bound to the body and the body that is known by the will. In *Freedom and Nature*, Ricoeur describes the act of willing as both the "realization of freedom and the reception of necessity."[11] We are both free and determined, capable of voluntary actions within the limits of involuntary bodily functions.

He describes willing in terms of three parts, each related to the body: (1) "I decide," (2) "I move my body," and (3) "I consent." Each part has a correlate: (a) the decision or project, (b) the action or motion, and (c) the acquiescence or consent. And each correlate is related to different aspects of the involuntary: (i) decisions to motives, needs, and values, (ii) actions to skills, emotions, and habits, and (iii) consent to character, unconscious, and life. Ricoeur finds a dualism at the heart of experience instead of a lived-body that unifies the will. "The circular relation" of voluntary and involuntary implies a notion of the body that is a "body-for-my-willing, and my willing as project-based-(in part)-on my body. The body is *for* the will and the will is *by reason* of the body."[12] That means that the act of willing can be distinguished from the body, and the body is not inscrutable. If Ricoeur makes the will embodied, he also makes our bodily experience knowable. In other words, he largely agrees with Merleau-Ponty and Sartre, but he frames the relationship between mind and body differently. Instead of lived-experience, he proposes a dialectical relation between the voluntary and involuntary—a fragile, fractured unity of mind and body.

Now, food is nowhere to be found in *Freedom and Nature*, other than a few passing remarks about needs. But considering the extent to which food is woven into our daily activities, we should be able to find it in each of the correlates to voluntary actions. Starting with a decision, there are food-motives, food-needs, and food-values, and each has an involuntary dimension that explains why we act. Our motives, needs, and values are not always known to us but, unlike something completely involuntary (like the circulatory system), we can at least try to know what's behind our decisions.

Food-motives are like impulses that incline the will toward its project. In turn, every motive is a motive for a decision. I decide *in order to* as well as *because of.* The main motivation to eat is hunger, or perhaps taste, but there are countless other motives that vary by the meal type, the type of food, the activity, and so on. Think of all of the things we do related to food, from farming to butchering to shopping and more. It would be futile to try to enumerate every food-motive for every food action. Ricoeur's points are that our motives are often unknown, and they are often related to something involuntary.

An example would be food-needs, which are more bodily and harder to identify than motives. Food-needs don't cause us to act as much as they lend themselves to motivation to acquire something lacking. Hunger and thirst are obviously needs, but so are other things we lack and want, such as enough food, desirable foods, reliable foods, and new foods.[13] Similarly, food-values also incline the will to pursue something perceived to be good for me to have or to do. They include the usual consumer preferences that influence food choices: price, convenience, taste, health, appearance, familiarity, novelty, mood, diet, and ethics.[14]

Our food-needs and values provide reasons for acting but are more closely related to the involuntary than other food-motivations. Our food-needs and values originate both in our bodies as well as elsewhere in food environments. That means they are susceptible to external influences and internal forces that are only partially within our control. The moral implications are not trivial. For example, how can we take responsibility for our diets if our choices are not entirely our own? How can we ask people to stop guzzling soda or cut back on meat when those needs and values are neither completely voluntary nor entirely known? If our bodies and surroundings limit our choices and restrict our freedoms, we need a subtler account of personal responsibility that acknowledges our vulnerability to manipulation.

Advertisers and marketers know exactly how to do it. They provide us with motivations, they create needs, and they skew values to get us to buy what they're selling. It is not always terrible, and sometimes our needs and values square with their messaging—but sometimes not. Herbert Marcuse argues that capitalism creates false needs that manipulate us into seeking out momentary pleasures (like shopping and entertainment) that do little for us except to perpetuate a life of conformity and alienation.[15] The more we act on false needs, the worse off we become. Ricoeur adds the possibility of false and repressive motives and values to the ways we can be inclined to act for the sake of someone else's profits, not our own best interests.

For example, if our lives are dull after long days of joyless work, it may seem reasonable to purchase a little distraction to brighten our dreary lives, but that may do little to satisfy our needs for something genuinely new and meaningful. Values can also be manipulated, for example, when marketers try to persuade us to prioritize convenience and price over more lasting and important values, such as health and ethics. Food-needs and values are routinely targeted by food companies to motivate us to act against our self-interests and responsibilities to others. We would be wise to be aware of how and why we're motivated to buy and eat. I get duped all the time by green marketing: anything packaged in earth-tones and labeled "sustainable" or "organic." My green values are used to get me to spend money, which, though not always bad for me, is always good for the seller.

The same type of analysis can also be applied to the involuntary correlates of movement and action: food-skills, food-emotions, and food-habits, the vehicles of the will that allow us to move our bodies and to act. Each was learned and gradually become ingrained and involuntary. If Ricoeur is right and our food-skills are acquired, then we should, in principle, be able to change them. Even skills like drinking from a cup or using a spoon, which seem like second nature, are not so different from more obviously learned skills, like making bread or operating a tractor.

The same with habits. Some theorists (including Merleau-Ponty and some readers of Heidegger) argue that our experience is less cognitive than philosophers would have us believe and more practical and habitual.[16] But if Ricoeur is right, then a habit doesn't eliminate all conscious experience, only *self-conscious* knowing and willing. If our habits are more chosen and deliberate than they initially appear, then they too can be changed. Food-skills and food-habits only move us to act; they don't cause us to do anything. If food-motives are more involuntary than we might think, food-skills and habits are more voluntary.

According to Ricoeur, our food emotions—even our passions and revulsions—are also learned and acquired. The idea that the emotion of disgust is more like a habit than a reflex might seem counter-intuitive, but as any parent knows, infants and toddlers have to learn to feel it, otherwise they are totally fine with everything from mucus to spit to feces. They will touch everything, eat kibble, and stick their dirty fingers right in their mouths. Eventually, they learn from our facial reactions to feel the same way we do about the things we deem to be disgusting. But if the emotion of disgust is learned, then perhaps it can be unlearned. In fact, it happens all the time when people overcome their initial revulsion to new foods, like when a Westerner tries insects for the first time and finds them surprisingly good. Or when Sam I Am finally convinces that reluctant guy to try green eggs and ham.

Maybe the reason emotional appeals are seen as irrational and manipulative is because of a misunderstanding of what they are: they are perceived to be objective things that get triggered deep in the brain when, in fact, they are ingrained responses to past situations and contextual cues.[17] They are more like motives than causes. They are like a vehicle for the will, not an involuntary force behind it. Maybe if emotions were seen as involuntary correlates of action that are amenable to reason rather than irrational impulses, then moral appeals to them might be more acceptable. Then, perhaps, the politics of food disgust might not be as unseemly as its critics claim[18]—no better or worse than any other appeal to change your mind about something. Emotional responses are a part of moral reasoning, not the antithesis of it. Even Kant appreciates their role in helping us fulfill our obligations.

Finally, to conclude Ricoeur's cycle of food willing, is our food-character, food-unconscious, and food-life that we have no choice but to consent to. For example, someone's food-character might be temperamentally brave and adventurous, another is anxious and fearful. One person loves to try new foods, another is wary of anything new. That's just how it goes. The same for the food-unconscious that affects how and what we eat, and how we think and feel about food. Advertisers and marketers are well aware of how the unconscious "lizard brain" influences our basic drives and fears.[19] Social influencers tap into our deep desire for recognition, belonging, and love. Interestingly, Ricoeur treats the unconscious as an enduring feature of the will that is always a part of our decisions and actions. We can recognize signs of it, but there is little we can do to change it, which is not what Freud says.

The least accessible aspect of the will is one's food-life, the closest we can come to being conscious of embodiment itself. The experience of being alive, having a will, and being free is a mystery: something we participate in and can know but only up to a point. As Gabriel Marcel, Ricoeur's teacher in the 1930s, explains, "A mystery is something in which I am myself involved, and it can therefore only be thought of as a sphere where the distinction between what is in me and what is before me loses its meaning and initial validity."[20] Isn't it the same with our basic experiences of food: hunger, appetite, and tasting? When pressed, can we really say what they are, except maybe mysteries? They are what Marcel would call "insoluble but not senseless."[21]

There are three advantages of Ricoeur's dialectical model of the voluntary and involuntary for food existentialism.

(1) The model of the voluntary and involuntary is more articulated than an undifferentiated conception of the lived-body, which helps us understand ourselves

better and see more clearly how we are affected by outside influences. I've been focusing on consumerism but there are other reasons our motives, needs, and values might be targeted, for example, by public service announcements or not-for-profits that nudge us to think differently about food. Or perhaps our cultural obsession with "good eating" has less to do with our value of health than with being thin and feeling bad about our appearance. Maybe the values of health and wellness need to be reframed (less as science and more as social-psychology) in order to encourage a better relationship between food and our bodies.

(2) Voluntary decisions and actions are always affected by involuntary things that are beyond our control, which means that our food-freedoms are always limited by our food-nature. Ricoeur maintains that our bodies are always a part of every decision and action, and that our autonomy is unavoidably limited. That not only means we need a subtler understanding of our food responsibilities but also a broader understanding of corporate liability. For example, maybe the concept of addiction is too narrow to analyze products that are designed to be irresistible, such as sugar and snack foods, and we should debate other kinds of psycho-social manipulation at the border of our experience.

(3) The involuntary aspects of our decisions and actions can be identified, experienced, and possibly changed. If we don't like our food-skills, emotions, and habits, we can do something about them, or maybe develop new ones. Ricoeur helps to push conscious experience as far as it can go into our bodies until we reach dimensions that are beyond possible experience—but until then we can know quite a lot about how the involuntary affects the voluntary. Body politics after Ricoeur is more nuanced and detailed.

There are other ways that food mediates our experience that do not quite map onto his phenomenology of the will. I have in mind things that are both physiological and psychological, such as mood, energy, and indigestion. Food can affect our self-esteem in the quality of our skin and hair, teeth and breath, and our size and weight. Food can color our experience and affect how others perceive us. It can influence how we think and act, it can make us drowsy or alert, and, if aphrodisiacs were real, it could enhance our sex lives. In short, food acts on us, in us, and through us, sometimes causing physiological changes, other times influencing us at the border of the will.

Jane Bennett sees food as more than "inert matter" but a "lively force with agentic capacity." We not only act on it; it also acts on us.

> Human intentionality is surely an important element of the public that is emerging around the idea of diet, obesity, and food security, but it is not the only actor or necessarily the key operator in it. Food, as a self-altering, dissipative materiality, is also a player. It enters into what we become. It is one of the many agencies operative in the moods, cognitive dispositions, and moral sensibilities that we bring to bear as we engage the questions of what to eat, how to get it, and when to stop.[22]

While it might be a reach (if not incoherent) to say that food has agency, it is undoubtedly a major player that limits our freedom and independence. Everything we eat subtly exerts an influence on us and forces *us* to accommodate *it* in order to do whatever it is we want to do with it. For example, seeds can only grow in so many ways, fish have to be captured in water where they live, and livestock have to be cared for or else they die. Perishables have to be refrigerated or consumed before they spoil, meat needs to be cooked with a safe source of heat, liquids need vessels, and dry goods need containers. We can only tolerate so much salt, sugar, and spice; we can only eat and drink so much before we are stuffed. Food pushes back on us—maybe not with agency but with efficacy. Maybe the truth about our bodies and food lies somewhere in between Feuerbach and Sartre: neither transforms entirely into the other. People make and eat edible things; that, in turn, delimits our freedom and, therefore, what kind of persons we can be.

DOES FOOD MAKE US WHO WE ARE?

Food plays a key role in who we are as individuals and as members of groups. It played a role in shaping human evolution, in the geographies of where we live, in the histories that precede us, and in the cultures we inherit.

Evolution. Part of who we are can be explained by how our diets evolved. Long before agriculture came on the scene, early humans hunted, gathered, and scavenged. Eating meat was important because it is energy dense, nutritious, and hard to get. It was probably a big deal to scare away lions and take their prey, or to spear a medium-size animal. It involved a lot of coordination beforehand and a lot of congratulations afterward—both good social skills. But it is more likely that cooking, not hunting, was the main reason the early humans developed their cognitive and social capacities. By ingesting calories rapidly and efficiently over a relatively short time, our ancestors developed tremendous numbers of neurons in the cerebral cortex. In turn, their bigger brains needed more energy than raw foods could provide.[23] We should probably thank cooking for language, technology, and most of our evolutionary advantages.[24]

There is also the argument that foraging led to other kinds of cooperation, such as sharing of food and work responsibilities, making and maintaining cooking technologies, and preparing edible plants. In other words, many of our basic cooperative activities and moral knowledge developed alongside of food practices.[25] A lot of what we do with food has prehistoric origins, such as dining together, serving food, eating while seated, using spoons, and other common activities.

Geography. The places we live also influence how we make and eat food. We grow it on a farm, catch it in an ocean, eat it in a country—all within a cultural practice. From an existentialist perspective, these geographical conjunctions of food and place influence the social norms and practices that shape who we are. Not entirely as if we live in Plato's *Republic*, where people completely identify with their roles, but in a subtler way in which a food geography sets limits on what one can do and become. For example, the geographic differences between living in rural poverty, urban prosperity, or a Pacific Island contribute to an identity, as do the effects of globalization, the availability ingredients, and regional tastes. Food taboos seem to be geographic: no dog eating in some parts of the world and no horses and pigs in others.[26] Given that the world is organized around the nation state, a good number of people are affected by their national foods and national cuisines (to the extent there really are such things).[27] Although the role of nations in establishing cuisines, and of globalization in eroding them, is debatable, both play at least some role in what and how we eat.[28]

Eating—or disliking—national cuisines can also affirm one's identity. Many nations and regions have foods that are singularly important to their history, including dishes that are hard for outsiders to enjoy unless they have had enough exposure to them. These usually fermented or pungent foods are prized because they indicate membership in a group, such as Vegemite in Australia or natto in Japan. They take on added significance when immigrants miss them, or when shared with outsiders who wrinkle their noses in disgust.

History. Food can also play a major role in shaping historical events, arguably, as *the* principle driver of world history.[29] It molds social and economic life, transforms environments, and shapes both politics and tastes. It has been at the center of social upheavals, migrations, and wars. Sugar, for example, was not only the heart of the transatlantic slave trade, it also changed the face of West Africa, Europe, and the Americas for the next three hundred years. The same is true of other foods that shaped nations and peoples: potatoes and Ireland, cod and Scandinavia, tea and India, and bananas and Central America. Corn and soy gave rise to the highly processed Western diet; agriculture gave rise to civilization itself. The third part of the food-history dialectic are the myriad of machinery and devices that make it all possible. Food, history, and technologies influence, if not determine, one another.

Incidentally, food not only moves history but can also move a plot forward, for example, the apples for Eve and Snow White, the bear family's porridge, and Proust's madeleines. In each case, food is more than a prop; it is an important element that explains events and serves dramatic purposes. It can also provide background information and round out a character. The petulant person is shown to be a picky eater, or the reserved character gains complexity when shown devouring a meal. Food can shed light on a character in the same way it affects our identities.

Culture. Finally, there is food and culture, the well-known pairing that identifies peoples and cuisines: we develop self-identities in relation to how our societies produce and consume food.[30] Members identify with their cultures as they identify with their foods, usually what they grew up eating and what tastes like home. Sometimes we identify others by the foods they eat, or more likely stereotype and misidentify them by what *we think* they eat. Or another way food affects cultures can be seen in immigrant communities who try to retain their identities by importing ingredients, opening restaurants as cultural havens, or by modifying old recipes with regional ingredients, like when Acadians created the Cajun trinity from the French mirepoix. Sometimes an imported food gains such widespread acceptance that it becomes assimilated into the culture, like pizza in the United States and Spam throughout the Pacific.

Other times, cultures resist changes in their foodways, for example, France's longstanding resentment (and embrace) of the "Americanization" of food,[31] or the ban on new "ethnic" restaurants from opening in Verona, Italy.[32] Other Italian cities have tried to preserve their culinary traditions from immigrant foods, albeit kabob shops not French restaurants or chic sushi bars.[33] The fact that food is used to preserve cultural identity is telling. It means that changes in food traditions can threaten a society's self-conception. Food is a stand-in for the politics of a cultural heritage.

Sometimes countries use food laws to resist integrating immigrants, for example, the laws in Poland, Belgium, France, and the Netherlands that ban kosher and halal animal slaughter, where animals are not stunned but completely conscious when their throats are cut. Right-wing politicians have embraced the restrictions under the guise of animal rights, or *laïcité* in France (the complete secularization of the state). Not all advocates of retaining traditions (for example, Slow Food), or of animal welfare (for example, the European Food Safety Authority), have ulterior, bigoted motives. But Europe has always had its share of right-wing nationalists intent on making life difficult for religious minorities. Germany, for example, instituted its ban on religious slaughter in the 1930s under Nazi rule.[34] Given the long history of anti-Semitism and anti-Muslim sentiment in these types of laws, animal welfarists might want to think twice before collaborating with those who are inspired by hate.[35]

Food issues are particularly charged when a group's social standing is vulnerable or threatened; less so when the group is more comfortable in its relations to a dominant culture or accepting of foreign influences. Established immigrant communities are usually more secure in their social standing and, therefore, more amenable to cultural borrowings—and a confident dominant culture more tolerant of foreign cuisines. Sometimes groups resent when their foods are mainstreamed by the dominant culture, like when a chef becomes famous for cooking another culture's food. Food appropriation is fairly routine and doesn't strike the same nerves as appropriating clothing (which might make some people feel like their traditions are treated like Halloween costumes), but I can understand if a Chinese person does not like the way his or her culture is represented in a

"Chinese chicken salad," with canned mandarin oranges on iceberg lettuce and other things that have nothing to do with China.

Michael Twitty argues that (innocent) cultural diffusion is different from (disrespectful) cultural appropriation. Cultural diffusion is "a natural process when people of multiple different cultures live close together in some environment and can't help but rub off on one another. No fault, no shame." Cultural appropriation is "about exploitation, abuse, theft. You know it when you see it, it's like obscenity—so don't get the two confused."[36] Twitty argues that the cuisine of a people is "a source of cultural power that they have an inherent right to. It's their thing that they use to mitigate the forces of oppression. And when you take that thing away, then you're really robbing them of something very significant."[37] Lisa Heldke adds that the attitude one takes towards the cuisines of others makes all the difference: we can exoticize cuisines as mere novelties, or we can treat their delicious foods as an occasion to think about other peoples. When we experience different cuisines, we get a little window in the lives of others and a glimpse of what they hold dear. Surely, we can do better than to gawk and chew—or expect others to satisfy our desires for "ethnic" cuisines.[38]

Food-identity passions can run so high because food is so thoroughly woven into our lives that it can be hard to imagine how things could be different. It is baked into our evolution, geography, history, and culture. Our relation to food is like Heidegger's notion of being-in-the world: as something we are intimately bound up, and involved, with. Heidegger likens being-in-the-world to dwelling in a house. The relationship between my dwelling and me cannot be understood in terms of subjectivity and objectivity, but it is more like an animal in its habitat or a fish in water. Being-in-the-world means that we are always connected and concerned with our surroundings even before we are aware of them.[39]

Heidegger calls our basic understanding of the world and our place in it the "worldhood," like the "world of home" or the "world of school." Usually, it remains in background, like a theoretical holism that we can never make fully explicit.[40] The *worldhood of food* comprises all of the ways we habitually encounter things without really paying attention to, or reflecting on, them in any detail. All of the little things we do that make up the worldhood of food are significant: they meaningfully relate us to the world and to other people. For Heidegger, the basic way we encounter things is like tool-use, or as equipment to contend with (as opposed to objects we observe). Everything we deal with as equipment implicitly relates us to other things, other people, and social practices.

Similarly, we deal with food as practical and meaningful, with predefined purposes and ways to relate to it. For example, *what* one cooks, *with what* one cooks, *why* and *how*, *when* and *where*, and *with whom* are all related and governed by conventional social practices. We deal with it the way others have before us; we do what *they* do, however things are conventionally done. The unwritten rules of proper conduct and our expectations of others are often hard to see because we are born into them and have no reason to question them. Heidegger's point isn't to endorse the status quo but simply to characterize how we relate to ordinary things. We primarily deal with food practically and habitually; we only secondarily perceive it as an object with qualities and properties. The food conceptualizations and narratives we discussed earlier would be, on this model, secondary and derivative analyses that presuppose a more ordinary, unreflective way we usually deal with food.

In addition to tool-use, another way to understand the worldhood of food is in terms of social roles and practices. We take on roles and conduct ourselves as anyone would in the same position, following established sets of behaviors and dispositions. We do what a typical fisherman, cook, or dieter would do in similar situations. We assume the same activities, beliefs, and relations to other social roles as anyone would. That means we take on identities in relation to the identities of others. Furthermore, our roles are normative: they determine the right way to act and the right way to do things. Roles "stabilize behavior" and set expectations for others about the way things should be done.[41] Social roles and social norms vary by culture and evolve over time. Sometimes they are codified into laws and customs, other times they're in the background as subtle social pressures.

Furthermore, roles and norms are internalized and taken for granted. They figure into our decisions and actions without our even noticing it. Social roles and norms can feel natural, and conforming to them like listening to one's own conscience. They have a remarkable grip over us with an internal motivating force that has little to do with either external coercion or personal desire. In fact, the hold that social roles and norms have over us is so strong that they are incorporated into our very identities, which might explain why people respond so defensively when accused of violating a role or norm: it feels like a personal attack. As Hilde Lindemann puts it, "identities are normatively prescriptive—they tell you what you are supposed to do and how others may, must, and mustn't treat you."[42]

Food is always in the background, subtly worked into our lifestyles in rather ordinary ways. Yet for some people, food plays an extraordinary role in their lives. Obviously, it's important for those whose roles are bound up with producing or preparing it (farmers, inspectors, anyone in food service, and so on). Some other ways food can be paramount in one's identity include the following:

Malnutrition: For the millions who eat too little or cannot access nutritious foods, diet is a pressing issue with lasting effects. Undernutrition leads to wasting, stunting, and irreversible cognitive and physical development; it leads to health problems, educational challenges, and limited social mobility. It also leads to obesity from a limited diet of inexpensive, nutrient-poor foods. From an existentialist perspective, malnutrition largely makes up a personal identity as the dominant feature of a life.

Food preoccupation. Food is an ongoing issue for those who are living in a food shortage, who have an eating disorder, or who have a medical condition. For those who constantly think about it and organize their entire days around it, if meal preparation is an all-day affair, or if one experiences body dysmorphia (beyond ordinary body dissatisfaction), then food plays an outsized role in one's life.

Mealtime concern. Food can be the cause of real concern and anxiety at mealtime for a diabetic, vegan, or dieter, or for an observant Muslim or Jew, a denture-wearer, or person with food allergies or reflux. If eating is always fraught, the reason for social alienation, or a reminder that you are different from those around you, then food plays a bigger role in an identity than for those who eat worry-free.

Meat eating. Eating meat is universally associated with feasting and celebrating, wealth and strength, social status and power over animals, and national aspirations—climbing up the animal protein and development ladders.[43] The reason people stay hooked on meat might be because of the powerful symbolism behind it. If we give it up, we give up the aspects of our identities that meat stands for.[44] It might be magical thinking, but people seem to feel more wealthy and powerful when they eat animals.[45]

And more masculine. The connection between being a man and eating animal flesh has a strong enough cultural currency in Western societies to disincline men from becoming vegetarian, or even ordering vegetarian dishes at restaurants. More women than men restrict their consumption of meat, and for men to give it up for something like tofu, "they would have to give up a food they saw as strong and powerful like themselves for a food they saw as weak and wimpy."[46] Granted, there are a lot of stagnant gender concepts at play here, but the point is that eating meat reflects and reinforces gender roles.

Bodily purity. The connection between purity and identity is about what we would never touch and how we see ourselves.[47] Our norms (and taboos) work in two directions: to protect us from sickening things and to motivate us to eat wholesome things. For some, vegetarianism is about preserving moral and spiritual purity by avoiding unclean animals, blood, and death.[48] I imagine the desire for purity keeps people away from food additives and genetically modified foods in favor of natural and "clean foods." The decision to keep one's body pure—maybe to cleanse—reflects a desire to be a certain kind of person by eating, or refraining from eating, certain foods.

Abominable foods. Dietary prohibitions set groups of people apart and unite them against others. It might not seem like much, but Americans are united against dog eaters, horse eaters, and the rat and bat eaters. Others unite against our pig and cow eating, or in our condemnation of *their* protein choices. According Anthony Podberscek, in South Korea, where dog eating is considered by some to be a part of their traditions, "calls from the West to ban the practice are viewed as an attack on the South Korean national identity."[49] For whatever reason, eating certain types of animals elicit solidarity within groups, or scorn and contempt for others. Not eating disgusting foods is part of our identity, while the disgusting foods other people eat contributes to how we see them.

Weight stigma. When we make people the objects of disgust, it is easy to think less of them and maybe even treat them as if they don't have equal moral worth. We see this kind of dehumanization in judgments about overweight people, one of the last socially acceptable forms of discrimination. Even well-intentioned public service announcements meant to promote healthy eating have portrayed the overweight as gluttonous overeaters who consume disgusting amounts of food.[50] Daniel Kelly and Nicolae Morar argue that the use of disgust "is likely to bleed beyond its intended boundaries, encompassing not just the sin but also the sinner, bringing its dehumanizing stigma with it."[51] That's exactly what happens in weight stigma: it leads to lower wages and less professional advancement, worse health care and educational opportunities, and lower social acceptance and marriage rates. Women are affected more by weight stigma than men.[52] (That's why it's important only to direct disgust toward animals, not people.)

Gender inequality. Some food activities constitute gender relations and identities.[53] Across cultures, women have different eating habits, nutritional needs, and food preparation roles.[54] In general, women participate more in the private than public spheres of food production. Furthermore, gendered restrictions in poor nations deny women authority, education, and access to technology and financial resources, which keeps them out of the marketplace, in poverty, and more vulnerable to hunger and malnutrition. Women's empowerment and food security go hand in hand.[55] And there is always a connection between a woman's diet and a body-shape norm. For men, it's more about muscles and exercise than food.[56]

Dietary misrecognition. Sometimes our identities are related to roles that we are not aware we occupy, or that are even thought of as roles, such as membership in a racial, class, or ethnic group. Often nonvoluntary or "covert" identities[57] are symptomatic of social oppression, for example, when people are misidentified or have their identities shaped by dominant groups. Class and race often function in this way when members are thought to have identical tastes ("Those people sure love X!") or food practices they may not actually have. It's commonly called stereotyping and not taken very seriously, but misidentifying, misrecognizing, and treating people as if they are invisible can inflict harms by failing to see them as deserving equal moral consideration.[58] One of the intuitions of the food sovereignty movement is that the integrity of peoples depends on their ability to determine their own foodways, and when cultural practices are mischaracterized, members can suffer the harms of misrecognition.

For example, Africa is typically portrayed as a place of poverty and starvation: primitive, corrupt, and war-torn.[59] The Western media and foreign aid agencies play up narratives of Africa's helpless victims that can only be saved by the West. One critic calls it the "foreign-aid industrial complex" that feeds off of the problems facing the continent.[60] Even well-meaning people accept it: respondents to surveys on foreign poverty perceived less agency and less capacity for self-improving actions in Africans than poor people in other continents.[61] The victim narrative is stereotypical and simplistic; it fails to see how African problems are connected to industrialized nations and foreign corporations, and it fails to respect the agency and resilience of Africans to overcome the obstacles they face. In other words, to see malnourished people simply as hungry mouths that should be fed as fast as possible misidentifies the problem and misrecognizes the people.

Another example of food misrecognition is the not-uncommon experience of first- or second-generation immigrant children shamed by their classmates for bringing foreign and unknown foods to school. These "lunchbox moments" occur when a child is made to feel othered by his or her peers. In a video for NBC Asian America, a South Asian interviewee recalls a time he brought rice and curry to school and someone asked, "Why are you eating dog food?"[62] Another NBC interviewee says, "I remember kids laughing at my food and telling me that I had diarrhea for lunch. In some ways it made me feel a little bit like an outsider because I didn't have a peanut butter and jelly sandwich."[63] Hannah Kim explains how her lunch box moment affected not only her relationship with food, but also her relationship with her culture: "I remember one time where I cried and yelled at my mom for not giving me lunch like the other kids at my school. My mom sat with me and the next day gave me money that we didn't really have to go buy a hot lunch from my school cafeteria. I realize now that I wasn't only ashamed of my lunches but I was also slightly ashamed of my heritage."[64] Some Asian Americans carry their embarrassing childhood moments of food shaming into adulthood. As user DNA_ligase put it in response to a Reddit thread: "I'm a grown adult, but my sister and I still pack 'non-smelly' lunches for our first day of work at a new place to test things out."[65]

Although food plays a role in all of our lives, for many it plays an even bigger role—especially for those who are malnourished, overweight, food-preoccupied, on special diets, defensive around vegans, concerned with purity, repelled by what others eat, or mischaracterized as starving or a weird food eater.

Assuming everyone has at least some kind of food identity, the existential question is what to do about it: go along with it, take ownership of it, or question and change it. Even though few things have as strong a grip on us as food, there is no reason why we cannot reflect on it, take a different attitude on it, and do something about it instead of blindly following our cultures and habits. We can always hold our stories lightly and imagine other food possibilities, can't we?

WHY DOES IT MATTER WHAT WE EAT?

From a biological perspective, humans are no different from any other animal in that we all have to eat other living things in order to survive. From an existential perspective, the difference is that humans have, as Sartre puts it, both *facticity* and *transcendence*: we exist in the world as any other thing yet we also consciously evaluate and take a stand on our lives. In fact, our lives are defined by the kinds of stances we take on ourselves and what we make of our situations.[66] For example, food takes on different meanings depending on how we understand it and what we do with it. The same thing can either be a pleasure or a chore depending on how you take it. It's up to each of us to make our food experiences meaningful—assuming Nietzsche is right and there is nothing intrinsically meaningful about anything.

The reason the existentialists urge us to find our own meanings is because the ones we inherit from others are not always so great. The existentialists were concerned about how blandly dull and homogenizing social life tends to be. For example, Kierkegaard warned against the complacent indifference of "the crowd": the ordinary, taken-for-granted ways people do things is a shallow and empty "untruth." Nietzsche warned of blind obedience to "the herd": living as docile, faceless, obedient animals. Sartre criticized the dull, alienated life of the bourgeoisie, who live in bad faith and refuse to take ownership of their freedom. And Heidegger is critical of our "average everydayness," where we take on the roles that "anyone" could occupy, absorbed into the "groundlessness and nullity" of our inauthentic daily lives.[67]

The existentialists also believe we can overcome the worst tendencies of social life and find better ways to live together. Usually, the sign that there is something wrong is more affective than cognitive—a feeling that something is deeply off about life. For Kierkegaard, despair (possibly fear and trembling) alerts us to the empty reality of our lives and how we can both live ethically and aspire to the religiosity of the "knight of infinite faith" (who transcends social norms). For Nietzsche, the madman and the idea of an eternal recurrence can awaken our capacities for creativity and exhort us to live by the "master morality" of the ancient Greeks and Romans. For Sartre, nausea and anguish are signs that we are ultimately responsible for our lives, and an important step toward freedom and social cooperation. And for Heidegger, anxiety wakes us up from being absorbed in the world so we can decide how to cope with daily life.

Our day-to-day food lives are made up of ordinary activities, roles, and dishes, the restaurants, stores, and bars we visit, and the food environments we live in. As we said earlier, the worldhood of food (the background conditions, attitudes, and practices) infuses our identities and prescribes appropriate behavior. It determines "what one does," "what one eats," and "how it should be prepared" and other conventional actions and attitudes. The problem from an existentialist perspective is when societies ask more of us than a harmless acceptance of social norms but instead demand mindless conformity to an oppressive social order. There is usually nothing wrong with doing things the way anyone would. You can make and eat a sandwich the same way everyone else does without worrying that you'll lose your individuality. But sometimes social life is "normalizing," in Michel Foucault's ominous sense of standardizing and regulating down to the minutiae of our lives.[68] Social conformity is not reserved for totalitarian states or science fiction dystopias but exists in our ordinary lives where we habitually go along with however things are done without every really stopping to think about what we're doing.

Take the typical American diet. Americans eat more food now than they did in 1970—a total of 23 percent more calories a day. They eat more chicken and cheese, and less beef and ice cream. They drink a lot less milk but eat a lot more yogurt. And they eat significantly more grains and cooking oils than they did fifty years ago.[69] About 75 percent of Americans say they are very focused on their health and nutrition, yet Americans lead the world in diabetes, hypertension, and cancer.[70] About the same percentage eat less fruit and vegetables than the USDA Dietary Guidelines recommend.[71]

Regular meat eating is also part of the typical diet. It's cheap, familiar, and available. In addition to mindless habituation, people eat it because of emotional attachments to tastes, unconscious urges, and cognitive dissonance between food animals and pets.[72] It is easier to eat meat than avoid it. Only 4 percent of the adult U.S. population is vegetarian, according to a

Harris Poll.[73] Most eat a Westernized diet: high saturated fats, high sugar, and low fiber.

The typical diet relies on a lot of prepared foods. Since 2016, retail sales at restaurants have been higher than grocery stores, which means people spend more money eating out than eating at home.[74] People are cooking less than they used to. The total time devoted to meal prep is about thirty minutes per day (thirty-seven minutes if you include serving and clean up).[75] Only 10 percent surveyed said they enjoy cooking; the other 90 percent were either ambivalent or said they hated it.[76] Millennials (born between 1981 and 2001) cook less and spend more on prepared foods than any other generation.[77]

Another way we typically encounter food is mindless eating: consuming without paying attention to what and how much is eaten. As we saw in chapter 2, our habitual eating is influenced by environmental factors: friends and family, the size of plates and portion size, and background noise. Eating while watching television, working, or distracted prompts us to eat more. Attention and memory play important roles, as well. If you don't pay attention while you eat, you can't remember much about it, and without memory of having eaten, you are more likely to eat again sooner than had you eaten more mindfully. Memory, distraction, awareness, and attention all influence food intake.[78] So do boredom, anxiety, and fatigue, stress, coping, and strong emotions, the presence of food, special occasions, free food, when other people are eating, when the clock says so, and when we are pressured to—all typical things that usually go unnoticed.

Another feature of food in the United States is the ubiquity of branded products, stores, and restaurants. Stores are designed to create "branded environments," where people can feel imbued with a company's messaging. McDonald's franchises set the standard years ago; now Apple Stores have taken over as the standard bearer. There is ample research on the effects of brand names on consumer preferences and perceptions.

Advertisers and marketers try to create emotional attachments between consumers and brands so that we identify with them and feel like we are a part of something greater. As a marketing executive for Chipotle puts it: "Our ultimate marketing mission is to make Chipotle not just a food brand but a purpose-driven lifestyle brand . . . that people want to know about, want to be a part of and want to wear as a badge."[79] Other major companies are using terms like "societal brand" to describe their strategy to use emotions and values to become part of our lives and, hopefully, sell us more stuff. When people feel that buying a brand says something important about them, according to the Chipotle executive, the brand "transcends being a utility and becomes a more special, integral part of a consumer's life."[80]

What's wrong with having a typical diet and mindlessly enjoying branded products? The diet is not particularly healthy, we eat poorly when we don't pay attention, and living a branded life is better for companies than it is for consumers, who may or may not benefit from the products. The conventional social world of food is part of a trillion-dollar industry that is much better at production and distribution than offering high quality and good-tasting foods. There are better ways to shop and eat than to go along with it.

That said, there is nothing immoral about conventional food consumerism. As Heidegger says, we deal with the world in fairly typical ways, doing whatever seems normal to do. He calls it "average everydayness" for a reason: it is perfectly average, no better or worse. It is good enough for us to get by as we usually do, coping with things as they arise, and for going about our daily concerns. We are basically conformist, norm-following creatures. Average everydayness simply refers to what is normal: how to wear shoes, how to pronounce words, and what to eat for lunch. It is part of a nexus of normality that connects what one eats, how one eats, and when and where one eats, related to with-what and thanks-to-what one eats.

For Heidegger, the problem with average everydayness is that it makes itself out to be more than it actually is. When we say "this is normal," "this is what people do," or "that's what they say," we act as if we are offering reasons when, in fact, they are nothing more than banal truisms. Everydayness is simply made up of the ordinary ways of understanding the world that we falsely take to have some kind of special standing. It may not be as bad as the crowd is for Kierkegaard or the herd is for Nietzsche, but it is a kind of habitual conformity in a negative sense.

Heidegger calls it "falling." *Dasein* (our existence) "turns away from itself"[81] and "falls-away" into the everyday world of "being-busy which is absorbed in the thing one is handling."[82] In other words, we fall into distraction in order to avoid facing the pointlessness of everydayness: there is nothing there but what *they* do, or what *one* does. We plunge into the world, completely identify with things and with tasks, and become so caught up that we cannot stand back and ask ourselves what we are doing. Heidegger calls a life that is "completely fascinated by the world" *inauthenticity*.[83] We are distracted by, yet gripped by, ordinary life. In fact, whenever we start to feel lost or uprooted (usually by anxiety), we quickly cover it up by being distracted by mindless concerns, like surfing online or checking social media. Or eating.

Hubert Dreyfus distinguishes between two senses of social conformity: *falling-in* with the one (falling away from itself) and *falling-for* the one (turning away from itself). The first is our typical, mindless but harmless *conformity*. The second is an indifferent, levelling, dull *conformism*—which is as bad as the crowd and the herd.[84] Conformism "plunges out of itself and into itself, into the groundlessness and nullity of inauthentic everydayness."[85] When Dasein chooses "the *one* for its hero,"[86] we conform so much to the way things are that we gain a "pseudoidentity."[87] Marcuse calls it a "one-dimensional person" who willingly conforms to a "one-dimensional society" that erodes our capacity for individuality, creativity, and critical thinking.[88]

The Heideggerian alternative to inauthentic conformism is to be resolute and own up to your life and your choices. An authentic life takes responsibility for itself and doesn't simply accept the dominant social practices. Instead, we can engage in social life with a clear understanding that it is merely social life, nothing more, nothing less. We can realize that ultimately our lives are our own and no one else can give us meaning or purpose. So rather than flee from the world or become absorbed into it, we can counteract the drift by resolutely affirming ourselves in the face of it: choose to choose. Participate in social life but with eyes wide open, knowing full well what we are doing. When we cope with anxiety instead of distracting ourselves from it, we can see that the world we live in is merely a social product and nothing we cannot deal with.

We all have to contend with our customs and traditions, and we can either go along with whatever is customary or step out of it. Coping strategies have their place, given the unlikelihood that we are going to improve all of the social structures involved in the food system. In the meantime, it might be a good idea for those who find it shallow and soulless to figure out a way to live with it, maybe by changing your attitude from despair to acceptance. Or ironic detachment. That might make it easier the next time you feel numbed in a supermarket or annoyed that the only place to eat is a boxy franchise restaurant—inexplicably anxious or depressed by it all.

Or, to apply the concept of inauthenticity outside of a western, bourgeois context (where lunch at the shopping mall food court might actually be a treat), people everywhere find themselves having to contend with big crowds, long lines, and other situations where we are just part of a mass of humanity. Everyone has had the experience of being in a throng or a group going along with whatever everyone else does. It is not just a First World problem of conformism to the latest trends, but how you feel about what is considered normal: should you affirm, reject, despair, conform, and so on. These are perennial issues of the relationship between individuals and communities recast in terms of the moods, dispositions, and lifestyles. In one society, what *they* do might be to eat processed and branded food, in another society, they demand meat in every meal, in another, women do all of the food preparation. In each case, we can always take a stand on our social conventions and decide whether or not to go along with them. Or, when people aren't allowed to, it is a sign of an overly repressive society.

But is that really the best we can do: to accept our powerlessness, take a deep breath, and take it for what it is? For those living in particularly repressive societies, an attitude adjustment might be the only option if there really are no other food choices available. But those living in advanced industrialized societies have more choices and can actually take steps to improve their lives. Furthermore, our average everydayness is not only inexplicably conditioned by the past but also organized by entirely explicable political decisions, economic policies, and technological consequences. In other words, our typical food experiences are the result of more than cultural traditions but also the deliberate decisions by a food industry that tries to get us to buy whatever they're selling, and by social-political structures that sometimes demand conformism. It takes a lot of work to create a food environment. Maybe the reason people are conforming creatures is not because we are *fallen* but because we are *pushed!*

A number of existentialist (and sort-of existentialist) philosophers have argued that modern mass societies are products of an increasingly technological, bureaucratic, and capitalist social order. Many of them attempted to reconcile existentialism with Marxism[89] and anti-totalitarianism.[90] The general idea is that free, authentic existence is either enabled or prevented by social-political conditions, and the key to overcoming alienation and dehumanization requires more than an attitude adjustment but some kind of meaningful social change. Marxist-existentialist alternatives have included socialism, liberalism, humanism, and counterculture. It is hard to generalize about this movement in twentieth-century intellectual history, not only because the philosophers are so diverse (albeit white German or French men), but also because they formed their ideas in response to post-WWII issues that have long since passed and are not all relevant today.

But two Marxists ideas that the existentialists embraced remain pertinent to food philosophy. The first is *alienation*, the idea that people in advanced industrialized societies are detached from food production, that food labor is generally unfulfilling, and that food consumption appears fragmented and disconnected from food systems. The second is *reification*, the idea that food is commodified, depersonalized, and processed, that the production system seems dauntingly vast and incomprehensible, and that food commercialism is such a permanent feature it is hard to imagine alternatives. Food is too often experienced as foreign, inexplicable, and other, with mysterious origins and unpronounceable ingredients.[91]

There are two advantages to this Marxist-existentialist interpretation of food. One, it demystifies our everyday food experience and sets it in a social-political context. It tells us where to look for explanations and what we might do to change things in the face of food conformity. Instead of looking to the structures of human nature to get to the bottom of our practices and preferences, we should look outward for answers. When we do, we find a number of familiar actors: food producers, governments, financial institutions, and other major players in the food system. They may not explain everything about why we feel the way we do about food, but it's a good place to start—if for no other reason than it suggests something we can do about it other than just changing our attitudes. In addition to Heideggerian resoluteness, we can also follow the lead of Marcuse and work toward a new, liberated society: the "Great Refusal" that says "no" to repression and "yes" to liberation. No to food conformity, yes to food counterculture; no to false needs, yes to true needs; no to technologies of consumerism, yes to technologies of creativity.

Marxist-existentialism can also make sense of the dissatisfaction (even disgust) many people feel about their food that leads them to romantic and religious alternatives, longing for unity to overcome social alienation. This desire for connection is a very real phenomenon that should be taken seriously. It not only underlies religious convictions but also many of the narratives discussed in chapter 2 that seek to counter the disconnect from food people feel because of modernization and technology. It drives people to seek a connection to nature, spiritual unity with a community, and sometimes bodily purity. As I argued before, these romantic responses cannot be prescriptive beyond those who already share the same religious-spiritual convictions. But for those that do, at least the Marxist-existentialist framework can give a political bite to a holistic embrace of unity. The Great Refusal is entirely compatible with religious feelings: "say no to food capitalism, yes to this-or-that reasonable comprehensive doctrine (if you're looking to Rawls for sloganeering).

Another response to food consumerism is the existentialist conception of "positive affirmation": embracing and committing oneself to life in spite of its ultimate meaninglessness. It is hard to talk about without falling into clichés or sounding hokey, but the idea is that maybe at bottom we are only human, nothing more and nothing less, and when we realize that there's no there-there, we don't have to experience anguish, anxiety, or nausea but maybe a *vouloir-vivre*, an attachment to life, and a positive affirmation of our existence. Our negative moods are "detectors," as Ricoeur says, of a more fundamental and positive aspect of existence: the "goodness of being."[92] We can affirm our lives in spite of our insignificance in the scheme of things; we can live from a basic attitude of affirmation about the basic goodness of life. And what better way to affirm the goodness of life than with food?

NOTES

1. FOOD METAPHYSICS

1. Lisa Heldke, "An Alternative Ontology of Food: Beyond Metaphysics," *Radical Philosophy Review* 15, no. 1 (2012): 82.
2. Raymond D. Boisvert, "Convivialism: A Philosophical Manifesto," *Pluralist* 5, no. 2 (2010): 58.
3. Leon Kass, *The Hungry Soul: Eating and the Perfecting of Our Nature* (Chicago: University of Chicago Press, 1994).
4. John Searle, *The Construction of Social Reality* (New York: Free Press, 1995).
5. W. V. O. Quine, "Ontological Relativity," in *Ontological Relativity and Other Essays* (New York: Columbia University Press, 1969), pp. 26–68.
6. Donald Davidson, "On the Very Idea of a Conceptual Scheme," in *Inquiries into Truth and Interpretation*, 2nd ed. (Oxford: Clarendon Press, 2001), pp. 183–198.
7. It is debatable if Kuhn and Feyerabend endorse epistemic relativism; however, both indeed argue that scientific development is not an approximation to truth. See Thomas Kuhn, *The Essential Tension* (Chicago: University of Chicago Press, 1977); Paul Feyeraband, *Against Method: Outline of an Anarchist Theory of Knowledge* (New York: Verso Press, 1975).
8. Hans-Georg Gadamer, *Truth and Method*, trans. Joel Weinsheimer, 2nd ed. (New York: Continuum, 1989).
9. Gadamer, pp. 278–317.
10. Gadamer, pp. 355–382.
11. A scholarly, pedantic work, study, or thought.
12. Frank Sibley, "Tastes, Smells, and Aesthetics," in *Approach to Aesthetics: Collected Papers on Philosophical Aesthetics*, ed. John Benson, Betty Redfern, and Jeremy Roxbee Cox (Oxford: Clarendon Press, 2001), pp. 235–237.

13. Decomposers break down the dead tissue of other species, similar to scavengers and creatures like earthworms and sea cucumbers, but they do not digest their prey. Instead, they convert it into nutrients and absorb it externally. The most common decomposers are fungi, bacteria, and archaea (single-celled organisms that belong to their own domain). See C. Michael Hogan, "Archaea," in *The Encyclopedia of the Earth*, last modified August 23, 2011, https://editors.eol.org/eoearth/wiki/Archaea#Archaea.
14. See, for example, Wendell Berry, *Bringing It to the Table: On Farming and Food* (Berkeley, CA: Counterpoint, 2009).
15. United States Department of Agriculture, www.nutrition.gov; United Kingdom Food Standards Agency, www.food.gov.uk; European Union European Commission, www.efsa.europa.eu/en/topics/topic/nutrition.
16. "Food as Fuel Before, During and After Workouts," American Heart Association, updated January 2015, https://www.heart.org/en/healthy-living/healthy-eating/eat-smart/nutrition-basics/food-as-fuel-before-during-and-after-workouts.
17. Marnae Ergil and Kevin Ergil, *Pocket Atlas of Chinese Medicine* (Valencia, CA: TPS, 2009), pp. 54–97.
18. K. T. Achaya, *Indian Food: A Historical Companion* (Delhi: Oxford University Press, 1998), pp. 77–81.
19. J. Worth Estes, "Food as Medicine," in *Cambridge World History of Food*, ed. Kenneth Kiple and Kriemhild Coneè Ornelas (Cambridge: Cambridge University Press, 2000), pp. 1534–1553.
20. In chapter 5, we will examine Michael Walzer's argument that different goods have different meanings and should be distributed for different reasons by different agents.
21. Charlotte Hess and Elinor Ostrum, eds., *Understanding Knowledge as a Commons: From Theory to Practice* (Cambridge, MA: MIT Press, 2007).
22. David Bollier and Silke Helfrich, eds., *The Wealth of the Commons: A World Beyond Market and State* (Amherst: Levellers Press, 2013).
23. Jose Luis Vivero-Pol et al., eds., *Routledge Handbook of Food as a Commons* (New York: Routledge, 2018).
24. Carolyn Korsmeyer, *Making Sense of Taste: Food and Philosophy* (Ithaca, NY: Cornell University Press, 1999), pp. 118–128.
25. Korsmeyer, p. 132.
26. Marta Zaraska, *Meathooked: The History and Science of our 2.5-Million-Year Obsession with Meat* (New York: Basic, 2016).
27. Monika K. Hellwig, "Eucharist," in *Encyclopedia of Religion*, ed. Lindsay Jones, 2nd ed. (New York: Macmillan Reference, 2004).
28. For the connection between recipes and scripts, see Dave Monroe, "Can Food Be Art? The Problem of Consumption," in *Food and Philosophy: Eat, Think, and Be Merry*, ed. Fritz Allhoff and Dave Monroe (New York: Blackwell, 2007), pp. 133–144.
29. For a good discussion of the role of recipes in the identity of food, see Andrea Borghini "What Is a Recipe?," *Journal of Agricultural and Environmental Ethics* 28, no. 4 (2015): 719–38.
30. "Frequently Asked Questions about Medical Foods, Second Edition," Food and Drug Administration, May 2016, https://www.fda.gov/downloads/Food/Guidance Regulation/GuidanceDocumentsRegulatoryInformation/UCM500094.pdf.

31. "Dietary Supplements," U.S. Food and Drug Administration, accessed January 2017, https://www.fda.gov/ForConsumers/ConsumerUpdates/ucm153239.htm.
32. "Adverse Event Reports Allegedly Related to 5-Hour Energy, Monster and Rockstar," U.S. Food and Drug Administration, November 2012, http://www.fda.gov/OfficeofFoods/CFSAN/CFSANFOIAElectronicReadingRoom/UCM328270.pdf.
33. "Guidance for Industry: Distinguishing Liquid Dietary Supplements from Beverages," U.S. Food and Drug Administration, January 2017, https://www.fda.gov/downloads/Food/GuidanceRegulation/GuidanceDocumentsRegulatoryInformation/DietarySupplements/UCM381220.pdf.
34. "Medicines in Our Home: Caffeine and Your Body," U.S. Food and Drug Administration, Fall 2007, http://www.fda.gov/downloads/Drugs/ResourcesForYou/Consumers/BuyingUsingMedicineSafely/UnderstandingOver-the-CounterMedicines/UCM205286.pdf.
35. Kevin Alexander, "Why 'Authentic' Food is Bullshit," *Thrillist*, July 15, 2017, https://www.thrillist.com/eat/nation/why-authentic-food-is-bullshit.
36. Todd Kliman, "Debunking the Myth of Authenticity," *Lucky Peach*, no. 1 (July 2011): 82–92.
37. Megan McArdle, "'Authentic' Food Is Not What You Think It Is," *Bloomberg*, February 24, 2017, https://www.bloomberg.com/view/articles/2017-02-24/-authentic-food-is-not-what-you-think-it-is.
38. John DeVore, "Life in Chains: Finding Home at Taco Bell," *Eater*, November 5, 2014, https://www.eater.com/2014/11/5/7155501/life-in-chains-kfc-taco-bell.
39. Krishnendu Ray, *The Ethnic Restauranteur* (New York: Bloomsbury Academic, 2016).
40. Stephen Castle and Doreen Carvajal, "Counterfeit Food More Widespread than Suspected," *New York Times*, June 26, 2013, http://www.nytimes.com/2013/06/27/business/food-fraud-more-widespread-than-suspected.html.
41. "Put Your Ethics Where Your Mouth Is," *New York Times Magazine*, April 20, 2012, www.nytimes.com/interactive/2012/04/20/magazine/ethics-eating-meat.html.
42. Yehuda Shurpin, "Is the Lab-Created Burger Kosher?: The Halachic Status of Lab-Created Meat," Chabad.org, accessed June 2017, www.chabad.org/library/article_cdo/aid/2293219/jewish/Is-the-Lab-Created-Burger-Kosher.
43. Thomas Billinghurst, "Is 'Shmeat' the Answer? In Vitro Meat Could be the Future of Food," *Gulf News*, May 2, 2013, https://gulfnews.com/going-out/restaurants/is-shmeat-the-answer-in-vitro-meat-could-be-the-future-of-food-1.1176127.
44. Joanna Sugden and Aditi Malhotra, "In India, Lab-Grown Meat Still Taboo," *Wall Street Journal*, August 6, 2013, https://blogs.wsj.com/indiarealtime/2013/08/06/lab-grown-beef-still-taboo.
45. "Food Dressings and Flavorings," Code of Federal Regulations, 21 CFR 169.
46. "Warning Letter: Hampton Creek Foods," U.S. Food and Drug Administration, August 12, 2015, www.fda.gov/ICECI/EnforcementActions/WarningLetters/2015/ucm458824.htm.
47. Sera Young, *Craving Earth: Understanding Pica—The Urge to Eat Clay, Starch, Ice, and Chalk* (New York: Columbia University Press, 2011).
48. American Psychiatric Association, *Diagnostic and Statistical Manual of Mental Disorders*, 5th ed. (New York: American Psychiatric Publishing, 2013), pp. 556–558.

49. Paul Rozin, "Disgust," in *Handbook of Emotions*, ed. Michael Lewis and Jeannette M. Haviland (New York: Guilford, 1993), pp. 757–776.

2. FOOD EPISTEMOLOGY

1. John Rawls, *Political Liberalism* (New York: Columbia University Press, 1993).
2. I use "story" and "narrative" interchangeably to mean an account of connected events.
3. Alasdair MacIntyre, *After Virtue: A Study in Moral Theory* (Notre Dame, IN: University of Notre Dame Press, 1981); Paul Ricoeur, *Time and Narrative 1*, trans. Kathleen Blamey and David Pellauer (Chicago: University of Chicago Press, 1984); Arthur Danto, *Narration and Knowledge* (New York: Columbia University Press, 1985); Peter Swirski, *Of Literature and Knowledge* (New York: Routledge, 2007).
4. Lawrence A. Blum, *Friendship, Altruism and Morality* (London: Routledge and Kegan Paul, 1980); Martha C. Nussbaum, *Love's Knowledge: Essays on Philosophy and Literature* (New York: Oxford University Press, 1992); Margaret Urban Walker, *Moral Understandings: A Feminist Study in Ethics*, 2nd ed. (New York: Routledge, 2007).
5. Arthur Frank, *The Wounded Storyteller: Body, Illness, and Ethics* (Chicago: University of Chicago Press, 1995); Hilde Nelson, ed., *Stories and Their Limits: Narrative Approaches to Bioethics* (New York: Routledge, 1997); Rita Charon and Martha Montello, *Stories Matter: The Role of Narratives in Medical Ethics* (New York: Routledge, 2002).
6. Paul Ricoeur, *Oneself as Another*, trans. David Pellauer (Chicago: University of Chicago Press, 1992), p. 143.
7. Gary D. Fireman, Ted E. McVay, and Owen J. Flanagan, eds., *Narrative and Consciousness: Literature, Psychology, and the Brain* (New York: Oxford University Press, 2003); Daniel B. Hutto, *Folk Psychological Narratives: The Sociocultural Basis for Understanding Reasons* (Cambridge, MA: MIT Press, 2008).
8. Muhammad Amer, Tugrul U. Daim, and Antonie Jetter, "A Review of Scenario Planning," *Futures* 46 (2013): 23–40.
9. Lisa Kern Griffin, "Narrative, Truth, and Trial," *Georgetown Law Journal* 101 (2013): 281–335.
10. Martha C. Nussbaum, *Cultivating Humanity: A Classical Defense of Reform of Liberal Education* (Cambridge, MA: Harvard University Press, 1998).
11. Walker, *Moral Understandings*, pp. 72–77.
12. Meg Shields, "The Future of Food: Five Ominous Trends in Science Fiction Cuisine," *Film School Rejects*, March 14, 2017, https://filmschoolrejects.com/science-fiction-food-trends-6ecccad9b291.
13. James R. Chiles, *Inviting Disaster: Lessons from the Edge of Technology* (New York: Harper Business, 2002); Steven M. Drucker, *Altered Genes, Twisted Truth: How the Venture to Genetically Engineer Our Food Has Subverted Science, Corrupted Government, and Systematically Deceived the Public* (White River Junction, VT: Clear River Press, 2015). The Union of Concerned Scientists worries less about exaggerated risks of genetically engineered crops than the crops' exaggerated benefits, see

"Monsanto's Claims for Their Genetically Engineered Crops Seem Too Good to be True—But What Are the Alternatives?" *Union of Concerned Scientists*, February 2012, https://www.ucsusa.org/publications/ask/2012/modern-farming.html.

14. "Perceptions of the U.S. Food System: What and How Americans Think about Their Food," *W. K. Kellogg Foundation*, 2012, accessed January 2017, http://www.topospartnership.com/wp-content/uploads/2012/05/Food-Systems.pdf.
15. Paul Ehrlich, *The Population Bomb* (New York: Ballantine, 1971).
16. Warren Belasco, *Meals to Come: A History of the Future of Food* (Berkeley, CA: University of California Press, 2006).
17. Michael Pollan, *In Defense of Food: An Eater's Manifesto* (New York: Penguin, 2009).
18. Leonard Dinnerstein, *Antisemitism in America* (New York: Oxford University Press, 1995), pp. 35–57.
19. Simon Fairlie dabbles in agrarian anti-Semitism when he wonders if the "Jewish lobby" played a role when the USDA defined the hamburger as entirely beef and no pork in "one of the biggest ecological cock-ups in modern history." See Simon Fairlie, *Beef: A Benign Extravagance* (White River Junction, VT: Chelsea Green, 2010), p. 6.
20. Eric T. Freyfogle, ed., *The New Agrarianism: Land, Culture, and the Community of Life* (Washington, DC: Island Press, 2001); Norman Wirzba, ed., *The Essential Agrarian Reader: The Future of Culture, Community, and the Land* (New York: Counterpoint, 2004).
21. Wenonah Hauter, *Foodopoly: The Battle over the Future of Food and Farming in America* (New York: New Press, 2012); David Kirby, *Animal Factory: The Looming Threat of Industrial Pig, Dairy, and Poultry Farms to Humans and the Environment* (New York: St. Martin's Press, 2010); Maria-Monique Robin, *The World According to Monsanto* (New York: New Press, 2012).
22. John Bellamy Foster, *Marx's Ecology: Materialism and Nature* (New York: Monthly Review Press, 2000); Fred Magdoff, John Foster, and Frederick H. Buttel, eds., *Hungry for Profit: The Agribusiness Threat to Farmers, Food, and the Environment* (New York: Monthly Review Press, 2000).
23. Marion Nestle, *Food Politics* (Berkeley, CA: University of California Press, 2003).
24. See, for example, Sidney Mintz, *Sweetness and Power: The Place of Sugar in Modern History* (New York: Penguin, 1986) and Dan Koeppel, *Banana: The Fate of Fruit that Changed the World* (New York: Plume, 2008).
25. Upton Sinclair, *The Jungle* (New York: Doubleday, 1906); Michael Pollan, *Omnivore's Dilemma: A Natural History of Four Meals* (New York: Penguin Press, 2006); Eric Schlosser, *Fast Food Nation: The Dark Side of the All-American Meal* (New York: Houghton Mifflin, 2001).
26. Robert Kenner, dir., *Food Inc.* (United States: Magnolia Pictures, 2008).
27. The research paints a more complex picture of what actually motivates ethical consumerism, including the burdens and guilt it places on us. See, for example, Clarrisa J. Morgan, Candace C. Croney, and Nicole J. Olynk Widmar, "Exploring Relationships Between Ethical Consumption, Lifestyle Choices, and Social Responsibility," *Advances in Applied Sociology* 6, no. 5 (May 2016): 199–216.
28. Calin O'Connor and James Owen Weatherall, *The Misinformation Age: How False Beliefs Spread* (New Haven, CT: Yale University Press, 2018).

29. Carolyn Korsmeyer, *Making Sense of Taste: Food and Philosophy* (Ithaca, NY: Cornell University Press, 1999), pp. 189–194.
30. Leon Kass, *The Hungry Soul: Eating and the Perfecting of Our Nature* (Chicago: University of Chicago Press, 1994), pp. 95–128. In Cormac McCarthy's *The Road* (New York: Vintage, 2006), the bad postapocalyptic survivors eat other people; the good survivors do not.
31. Hans-Georg Gadamer, *Truth and Method*, trans. Joel Weinsheimer, 2nd ed. (New York: Continuum, 1989), pp. 298–304.
32. For Christianity and food see Gary W. Fick, *Food, Farming, and Faith* (Albany, NY: SUNY Press, 2008); Ellen F. Davis, *Scripture, Culture, and Agriculture: An Agrarian Reading of the Bible* (Albany, NY: SUNY Press, 2004). For Judaism and food see Mary L. Zamore, ed., *The Sacred Table: Creating a Jewish Food Ethic* (New York: CCAR Press, 2011). For Islam and food see Ibrahim Abdul-Matin, *Green Deen: What Islam Teaches about Protecting the Planet* (San Francisco: Berrett-Koehler, 2010). For Hinduism and food see Whitney Sanford, *Growing Stories from India: Religion and the Fate of Agriculture* (Lexington, KY: University of Kentucky Press, 2011). For Buddhism and food see Mary Evelyn Tucker and Duncan Ryuken Williams, *Buddhism and Ecology: The Interconnection of Dharma and Deeds* (Cambridge, MA: Harvard University Press, 1998).
33. See, for example, Carole M. Counihan and Stephen L. Kaplan, eds., *Food and Gender: Identity and Power* (New York: Routledge, 1998).
34. Lierre Keith, *The Vegetarian Myth: Food, Justice, and Sustainability* (Oakland, CA: PM Press, 2009). Kass, in *The Hungry Soul*, tells an even more elaborate story that connects our physiology, omnivory, and table manners. We are said to be designed by nature to eat everything, and to eat in an upright seated position, using utensils, in harmony with others and with God—ideally keeping Kosher.
35. Peggy Lowe, "Working 'The Chain,' Slaughterhouse Workers Face Lifelong Injuries," *National Public Radio*, August 11, 2016, https://www.npr.org/sections/thesalt/2016/08/11/489468205/working-the-chain-slaughterhouse-workers-face-lifelong-injuries.
36. I will use the terms "taste" and "tasting" to refer to the perception of flavors with the understanding that most of tasting relies on the sense of smell.
37. Food and Agricultural Organization of the United Nations, *The State of Food Insecurity in the World 2015* (Rome: FAO, 2015), http://www.fao.org/3/a-i4646e.pdf.
38. Alexandra W. Logue, *The Psychology of Eating and Drinking*, 4th ed. (New York: Routledge, 2014), pp. 22–29.
39. Logue, *The Psychology of Eating and Drinking*, pp. 22–29.
40. The American Psychiatric Association's *Diagnostic and Statistical Manual of Mental Disorders*, 5th ed. (Arlington, VA: American Psychiatric Publishing, 2013), details three kinds of pathological eating: anorexia nervosa, bulimia nervosa, and binge eating. Each manifests a different relationship with food. A person with anorexia typically portions food carefully and only eats exceedingly small amounts of only certain kinds of food. A person with bulimia will consume an excessive amount over a short period of time, feel out of control and distressed, then purge to compensate. A person who binge eats compulsively overeats and typically feels extreme guilt, remorse, or self-loathing.
41. Logue, *The Psychology of Eating and Drinking*, pp. 14–22.

42. Devina Wadhera and Elizabeth D. Capaldi-Phillips, "A Review of Visual Cues Associated with Food Acceptance and Consumption," *Eating Behaviors* 15, no. 1 (January 2014): 132–143.
43. Jane Ogden et al., "Distraction, the Desire to Eat and Food Intake. Toward an Expanded Model of Mindless Eating," *Appetite* 62, no. 1 (2013): 119–126.
44. Remco C. Havermans et al., "Food Liking, Food Wanting and Sensory-Specific Satiety," *Appetite* 52, no. 1 (2009): 222–225.
45. Nicole Larson and Mary Story, "A Review of Environmental Influences on Food Choices," *Annals of Behavioral Medicine* 38, no. 1 (2009): 56–73.
46. Larson and Story, "Environmental Influences on Food Choices," 56–73.
47. Jennifer Orlet Fisher et al., "Parental Influences on Young Girls' Fruit and Vegetable, Micronutrient, and Fat Intakes," *Journal of the American Dietetics Association* 102, no. 1 (2002): 58–64.
48. Gebra Cuyun Grimm, Lisa Harnack, and Mary Story, "Factors Associated with Soft Drink Consumption in School-Aged Children," *Journal of the American Dietetics Association* 104, no. 8 (2004): 1244–1249.
49. Glorian Sorensen et al., "The Influence of Social Context on Changes in Fruit and Vegetable Consumption: Results of the Healthy Directions Studies," *American Journal of Public Health* 97, no. 7 (2007): 1216–1227.
50. Logue, *The Psychology of Eating and Drinking*, pp. 45–61.
51. Knvul Sheikh, "How Gut Bacteria Tell Their Hosts What to Eat," *Scientific American*, April 25, 2017, https://www.scientificamerican.com/article/how-gut-bacteria-tell-their-hosts-what-to-eat.
52. Massimiliano Zampini et al., "The Multisensory Perception of Flavor: Assessing the Influence of Color Cues on Flavor Discrimination Responses," *Food Quality and Perception* 18, no. 7 (2007): 975–984.
53. Betina Piqueras-Fiszman, Agnes Giboreau, and Charles Spence, "Assessing the Influence of the Color of the Plate on the Perception of a Complex Food in a Restaurant Setting," *Flavour* 2, no. 24 (2013).
54. Amy Fleming, "Restaurant Menu Psychology: Tricks to Make Us Order More," *Guardian*, May 8, 2013, https://www.theguardian.com/lifeandstyle/wordofmouth/2013/may/08/restaurant-menu-psychology-tricks-order-more.
55. Sarah Kershaw, "Using Menu Psychology to Entice Diners," *New York Times*, December 22, 2009, https://www.nytimes.com/2009/12/23/dining/23menus.html.
56. Maria Konnikova, "What We Really Taste When We Drink Wine," *New Yorker*, July 11, 2014, https://www.newyorker.com/science/maria-konnikova/what-we-really-taste-when-we-drink-wine.
57. Michael Shaffer, "Taste, Gastronomic Expertise, and Objectivity," in *Food and Philosophy: Eat, Think, and Be Merry*, ed. Fritz Allhoff and Dave Monroe (New York: Blackwell, 2007), pp. 73–87.
58. Shaffer, p. 77.
59. Jamie Goode, "Wine and the Brain," in *Questions of Taste: The Philosophy of Wine*, ed. Barry Smith (New York: Oxford University Press, 2007), p. 80.
60. Gordon M. Shepherd, *Neurogastronony: How the Brain Creates Flavor and Why It Matters* (New York: Columbia University Press, 2010), p. 3.
61. Barry Smith, "The Objectivity of Tastes and Tastings," in *Questions of Taste*, pp. 41–78.

62. Smith, "The Objectivity of Tastes and Tastings," p. 64
63. Smith, "The Objectivity of Tastes and Tastings," pp. 68–78.
64. Kendall Walton, "Categories of Art," *Philosophical Review* 73, no. 3 (July 1970): 338.
65. Cain Todd, *The Philosophy of Wine: A Case of Truth, Beauty, and Intoxication* (Montreal: McGill-Queen's University Press, 2011), p. 104.
66. Todd, *The Philosophy of Wine*, pp. 130.
67. "Flavor Descriptors," Fona International, accessed February 2017, https://www.fona.com/discover-fona/FlavorDescriptors_Discover.
68. "Flavour Descriptors," Novotaste, August 30, 2017, http://www.novotaste.com/content/flavour-descriptors.

3. FOOD AESTHETICS

1. This chapter will not examine whether or not food should be considered art but instead focus on aesthetic experience, judgment, and enjoyment. The point of food is to taste and eat it, however lovely it might be to look at. For the three main arguments about whether food should be considered art, see Dave Monroe, "Can Food Be Art? The Problem of Consumption," in *Food and Philosophy: Eat, Think, and Be Merry*, ed. Fritz Allhoff and Dave Monroe (New York: Blackwell, 2007); Elizabeth Telfer, *Food for Thought: Philosophy and Food* (New York: Routledge, 1996), chapter 3; and Carolyn Korsmeyer, *Making Sense of Taste: Food and Philosophy* (Ithaca, NY: Cornell University Press, 1999), chapter 4. Monroe argues that neither the acts of consumption nor the lack of permanence should exclude food from being considered to be art; Telfer considers food to be a minor art because it cannot express as much as traditional artforms; and Korsmeyer argues that food is more expressive than Telfer gives it credit for, but it stands on its own merits regardless of its likeness to art. I don't have much to add to the issue other than to register my general agreement with all three of them. Eating and permanence are irrelevant for something to be considered art, food expresses less than art, and there are some things that art does that food cannot, and vice versa. I would side-step the question and maintain that food has aesthetic value in its own right and does not need to be considered as art to be taken seriously—which, ironically, lowers its status and suggests that it is lowly unless elevated into a more refined category. It's like calling Bob Dylan lyrics poetry: can't lyrics stand on their own?
2. Georg Lukács, *History and Class Consciousness: Studies in Marxist Dialectics*, trans. Rodney Livingston (Cambridge, MA: MIT Press, 1972).
3. Pierre Bourdieu, *Distinction: A Social Critique of the Judgment of Taste*, trans. Richard Nice (Cambridge, MA: Harvard University Press, 1984).
4. Korsmeyer has an excellent discussion of the challenges of applying Enlightenment conceptions of taste to gustatory aesthetics. See Korsmeyer, *Making Sense of Taste*, pp. 103–145.
5. David Hume, "Of the Standard of Taste," in *Essays: Moral, Political, and Literary* (Boston: Little, Brown, & Company, 2004), p. 268.
6. Hume, p. 268.
7. Hume, pp. 280–284.
8. Hume, pp. 272–280.

9. Jerrold Levinson, "Hume's Standard of Taste: The Real Problem," *Journal of Aesthetics and Art Criticism* 60, no. 3 (Summer 2002): 227–238.
10. Levinson, pp. 227–238.
11. Noël Carroll, "Hume's Standard of Taste," *Journal of Aesthetics and Art Criticism* 43, no. 2 (Winter 1984): 181–194. The same point is made by Barry Smith, "The Objectivity of Tastes and Tastings," in *Questions of Taste: The Philosophy of Wine*, ed. Barry Smith (New York: Oxford University Press, 2007), pp. 68–72, and Cain Todd, *The Philosophy of Wine: A Case of Truth, Beauty, and Intoxication* (Montreal: McGill-Queen's University Press, 2011), pp. 115–122.
12. Immanuel Kant, *Critique of Judgment*, trans. Werner Pluhar (Indianapolis, IN: Hackett, 1987).
13. Kant, p. 55:

> Hence, if he says that canary wine is agreeable he is quite content if someone else corrects his terms and reminds him to say instead: It is agreeable to *me*. This holds moreover not only for the taste of the tongue, palate, and throat, but also for what may be agreeable to anyone's eyes and ears. To one person the color violet is gentle and lovely, to another lifeless and faded. One person loves the sound of wind instruments, another that of string instruments. It would be foolish if we disputed about such differences with the intention of censuring another's judgment as incorrect if it differs from ours, as if the two were opposed logically. Hence about the agreeable the following principle holds: *Everyone has his own taste* (of sense).

14. Kant, pp. 55–56:

> It would be ridiculous if someone who prided himself on his taste tried to justify [it] by saying: This object (the building we are looking at, the garment that man is wearing, the concert we are listening to, the poem put up to be judged) is beautiful *for me*. For he must not call it *beautiful* if [he means] only [that] *he* likes it. Many things may be charming and agreeable to him; no one cares about that. But if he proclaims something to be beautiful, then he requires the same liking from others; he then judges not just for himself but for everyone, and speaks of beauty as if it were a property of things. . . . He reproaches them if they judge differently, and denies that they have taste, which he nevertheless demands of them, as something they ought to have.

15. Korsmeyer, *Making Sense of Taste*, pp. 54–58; Raymond D. Boisvert and Lisa Heldke, *Philosophers at Table: On Food and Being Human* (London: Reaktion, 2016), pp. 76–82; Nicola Perullo, *Taste as Experience: The Philosophy and Aesthetics of Food* (New York: Columbia University Press, 2016), pp. 17–18, 46–47; Kevin W. Sweeney, "Hunger is the Best Sauce: The Aesthetics of Food," in *The Philosophy of Food*, ed. David M. Kaplan (Berkeley, CA: University of California Press, 2012), pp. 52–68.
16. Gordon S. Wood, *The Radicalism of the American Revolution* (New York: Vintage, 1991), pp. 243–270. According to Wood, the primary virtues of republicanism were disinterestedness and honor. All good citizens, and particularly political leaders, were expected to be able to rise above their private interests and to sacrifice personal desires for the sake of the common good. If disinterestedness used to mean

an ideal of civic humanism then, perhaps, we should read Kant more charitably as a typical Enlightenment thinker who challenged the assumptions and practices of monarchy, and who simply contrasted such concepts as hierarchy, kinship, and patronage with reason, freedom, and disinterest.

17. George Dickie makes a similar argument about disinterestedness and the impossibility of disentangling our interests and values from our aesthetic experiences. See George Dickie, *The Century of Taste: The Philosophical Odyssey of Taste in the Eighteenth Century* (New York: Oxford University Press, 1996), pp. 123–141.
18. Frank Sibley, "Aesthetic Concepts," in *Approach to Aesthetics: Collected Papers on Philosophical Aesthetics*, ed. John Benson, Betty Redfern, and Jeremy Roxbee Cox (Oxford: Oxford University Press), pp. 1–23.
19. "Food writing is a uniquely physical category of criticism, and Gold applied himself to the business of eating with an ambitious formalism, often trying every single restaurant on a particular stretch, or chasing down every iteration of a particular dish, putting tens of thousands of miles a year on his faithful pickup truck." Helen Rosner, "That Guy Who Won That Thing: What Jonathan Gold Meant for Food Writing," *New Yorker*, July 24, 2018, https://www.newyorker.com/culture/annals-of-gastronomy/that-guy-who-won-that-thing-what-jonathan-gold-meant-for-food-writing.
20. "There are so many food writers that never vary their gaze six inches from what's on the plate. They'll describe one dish, then another dish and then another dish, and then they'll look around the room for a second and try to tell you what the people are wearing and then look at another dish. When you look at food without referencing who's cooking it and what the ingredients are and how they might've been produced, you might as well be describing a stamp collection." Jonathan Gold, quoted in Rosner, "That Guy Who Won That Thing."
21. Jonathan Gold, "Pie's the Limit," *Los Angeles Times*, October 7, 1993, http://articles.latimes.com/1993-10-07/food/fo-42909_1_pie-n-burger-burger.
22. Jonathan Gold, "Crullers That Bloom in Spring," *LA Weekly*, March 21, 2007, https://www.laweekly.com/restaurants/crullers-that-bloom-in-spring-2147969.
23. Telfer, *Food for Thought*, p. 26.
24. Telfer, pp. 26–27.
25. Plato, *Republic*, trans. G. M. A. Grube (Indianapolis, IN: Hackett, 1992), p. 260.
26. Telfer, *Food for Thought*, pp. 27–28.
27. Telfer, pp. 28–29.
28. John Stuart Mill, *Utilitarianism*, 2nd ed. (Indianapolis, IN: Hackett, 2002).
29. Peter Singer, *Animal Liberation* (New York: Random House, 1990), p. 171.
30. James Rachels, "The Basic Argument for Vegetarianism," in *Food for Thought: The Debate over Eating Meat*, ed. Steve Sapontzis (New York: Prometheus, 2004), p. 71.
31. Gary L. Francione, "The Problem of Happy Meat and the Importance of Vegan Education," in *The Philosophy of Food*, ed. David M. Kaplan, p. 176.
32. Mylan Engel, "Do Animals Have Rights and Does it Matter if They Don't?" in *The Moral Rights of Animals*, ed. Mylan Engel and Gary Lynn Comstock (Lanham, MD: Lexington, 2016), p. 59.
33. Tristram McPherson, "Why I Am a Vegan," in *Philosophy Comes to Dinner: Arguments about the Ethics of Eating*, ed. Andrew Chignell, Terence Cuneo, and Matthew C. Halteman (New York: Routledge. 2015), p. 82.

34. Gary L. Francione and Anna Charlton, *Eat Like You Care: An Examination of the Morality of Eating Animals* (New York: Exampla Press, 2013), p. 59.
35. Mill would agree with Telfer. The difference between higher and lower pleasures is that lower pleasures merely feel good whereas higher pleasures give us more to think about and experience. The source of higher pleasures involves the imagination and intellect, which allow us to go beyond our sensations to conceive of something better and more worthwhile. A good life is not only about pleasant sensations but the pleasures of improving oneself and others. Aesthetics pleasures—including eating and drinking—are higher (not lower) pleasures for Mill. For a good analysis of Mill's conception of pleasure, see Susan L. Feagin, "Mill and Edwards on the Higher Pleasures," *Philosophy*, Vol. 58, No. 224 (1983), pp. 244–252.
36. Lizzie Widdicombe, "The End of Food: Has a Tech Entrepreneur Come Up with a Product to Replace Our Meals?" *New Yorker*, May 5, 2014. https://www.newyorker.com/magazine/2014/05/12/the-end-of-food.
37. Alysia Santo and Lisa Iaboni, "What's in a Prison Meal?" *Marshall Project*, July 7, 2015, https://www.themarshallproject.org/2015/07/07/what-s-in-a-prison-meal.
38. Paul Rozin and April E. Fallon, "A Perspective on Disgust," in *Psychological Review* 94, no. 1 (1987): 23.
39. Rozin and Fallon, p. 24.
40. Jonathan Haidt, Clark McCauley, and Paul Rozin, "Individual Differences in Sensitivity to Disgust: A Scale Sampling Seven Domains of Disgust Elicitor," *Personality and Individual Differences* 16, no. 5 (1994): 701–713.
41. William Ian Miller, *The Anatomy of Disgust* (Cambridge, MA: Harvard University Press, 1997).
42. Martha C. Nussbaum, *Hiding from Humanity: Disgust, Shame, and the Law* (Princeton, NJ: Princeton University Press, 2004), p. 96.
43. Carolyn Korsmeyer, *Savoring Disgust: The Foul and the Fair in Aesthetics* (New York: Oxford University Press, 2011), p. 59.
44. Korsmeyer, p. 62.
45. Korsmeyer, p. 63.
46. Rozin and Fallon, "A Perspective on Disgust," p. 24.
47. Aurel Kolnai, *On Disgust*, ed. Barry Smith and Carolyn Korsmeyer (Chicago: Open Court, 2004).
48. Edmund Burke, *A Philosophical Enquiry into the Origin of Our Ideas of the Sublime and Beautiful*, ed. James T. Boulton (South Bend, IN: University of Notre Dame Press, 1968).
49. Korsmeyer, *Savoring Disgust*, p. 78.
50. Boyka Bratanova et al., "Savouring Morality. Moral Satisfaction Renders Food of Ethical Origin Subjectively Tastier," *Appetite* 91 (August 2015): 137–49.
51. Carolyn Korsmeyer, "Ethical Gourmandism," in *The Philosophy of Food*, ed. David M. Kaplan, p. 97.
52. Lisa Heldke nicely complicates the ethics of foie gras by noting how caring and cooperative the relationships between farmers and geese can sometimes be. See Heldke, "An Alternative Ontology of Food: Beyond Metaphysics," *Radical Philosophy Review* 15, no. 1 (2012): 74–77.
53. Leon R. Kass, "The Wisdom of Repugnance," *New Republic* 216, no. 22 (1997): 17–26.
54. Nussbaum, *Hiding from Humanity*, pp. 125–171.

55. Daniel Kelly, *Yuck!: The Nature and Moral Significance of Disgust* (Cambridge, MA: MIT Press, 2011).
56. Simone Schnall et al., "Disgust as Embodied Moral Judgment," *Personality and Social Psychology Bulletin* 34, no. 8 (2008): 1096–1109.
57. Simone Schnall, Jennifer Benton, and Sophie Harvey, "With a Clean Conscience," *Psychological Science* 19, no. 12 (2008): 1219–1222.
58. Yoel Inbar, David A. Pizarro, and Paul Bloom, "Conservatives are More Easily Disgusted than Liberals," *Cognition and Emotion* 23, no. 4 (2009): 714–725.
59. Justin F. Landy and Geoffrey P. Goodwin, "Does Incidental Disgust Amplify Moral Judgment? A Meta-Analytic View of Experimental Evidence," *Perspectives on Psychological Science* 10, no. 4 (2015): 1018–1036.
60. Joshua May, "Does Disgust Influence Moral Judgment?" *Australasian Journal of Philosophy* 92, no. 1 (2014): 125–141.
61. Robert William Fisher, "Disgust as Heuristic," *Ethical Theory and Moral Practice* 19, no. 3 (2016): 679–693.
62. Joshua May, "Why Do Politicians Appeal to Our Disgust?" *Birmingham News*, May 5, 2016, https://www.al.com/opinion/index.ssf/2016/05/why_do_politicians_appeal_to_o.html.

4. FOOD ETHICS

1. Immanuel Kant, *The Groundwork for the Metaphysics of Morals*, trans. James W. Ellington, 3rd ed. (Indianapolis, IN: Hackett, 1993).
2. Immanuel Kant, *The Metaphysics of Morals*, trans. Mary Gregor (New York: Cambridge University Press, 1991).
3. Kant calls them duties of virtue ("ends that are also duties"). They are freely chosen pursuits that we all should do in order respect our dignity and humanity. We all have an obligation to set ends and goals that are part of a meaningful and good life for ourselves and for others. We should all do something with our lives and not waste them by doing nothing.
4. Kant, *The Metaphysics of Morals*, pp. 200–201.
5. Kant, p. 222–223.
6. Kant, pp. 223–224.
7. Luke Harding, "Victim of Cannibalism Agreed to Be Eaten," *Guardian*, December 4, 2003, https://www.theguardian.com/world/2003/dec/04/germany.lukeharding.
8. For a good discussion of the ethics of cannibalism, see J. Jeremy Wisnewski, "Cannibalism," in *Encyclopedia of Food and Agricultural Ethics*, ed. Paul B. Thompson and David M. Kaplan (New York: Springer, 2014), pp. 279–286.
9. Beckett Mufson, "This Guy Served His Friends Tacos Made from His Amputated Leg," *Vice.com*, June 12, 2018, https://www.vice.com/en_us/article/gykmn7/legal-ethical-cannibalism-human-meat-tacos-reddit-wtf.
10. Samantha Schmidt, "Anorexic Woman Weighing 69 Pounds Has the Right to Starve, Court Rules," *Washington Post*, November 22, 2016, https://www.washingtonpost.com/news/morning-mix/wp/2016/11/22/anorexic-woman-weighing-69-pounds-has-a-right-to-starve-court-rules.

11. Ronald Sandler disagrees with Peter Singer that to fail to give to charity to alleviate hunger is like failing to save a drowning child in a shallow pond a few feet away from you. Instead, Sandler argues that individuals only have an obligation to give their fair share. Ronald L. Sandler, *Food Ethics: The Basics* (New York: Routledge, 2014), pp. 66–73.
12. Immanuel Kant, "To Perpetual Peace: A Philosophical Sketch," in *Perpetual Peace and Other Essays*, trans. Ted Humphrey (Indianapolis, IN: Hackett, 1983), p. 217.
13. Elizabeth Telfer, *Food for Thought: Philosophy and Food* (New York: Routledge, 1996), pp. 82–102.
14. One exception is Peter Carruthers, who does indeed defend factory farming. Peter Carruthers, *The Animals Issue: Moral Theory in Practice* (New York: Cambridge University Press, 2002).
15. "CAFOs Uncovered: The Untold Costs of Confined Animal Feeding Operations," Union of Concerned Scientists, April 2008, https://www.ucsusa.org/food_and_agriculture/our-failing-food-system/industrial-agriculture/cafos-uncovered.html.
16. Peter Singer and Jim Mason, *The Ethics of What We Eat* (Emmaus, PA: Rodale, 2007), pp. 111–134.
17. Jeffrey Moussaieff Masson, *The Pig Who Sang to the Moon: The Emotional World of Farm Animals* (New York: Ballantine, 2003).
18. Christine M. Korsgaard, "Interacting with Animals: A Kantian Account," in *The Oxford Handbook of Animal Ethics*, ed. Tom L. Beauchamp and R. G. Frey (New York: Oxford University Press, 2011), pp. 91–118.
19. Food and Agricultural Organization of the United Nations, *Livestock's Long Shadow: Environmental Issues and Options*, (Rome: FAO, 2006), p. xxi, http://www.fao.org/3/a-a0701e.pdf.
20. The Food and Agricultural Organization of the United Nations estimates that agricultural production is responsible for 18 percent in the United States; the U.S. Environmental Protection Agency puts it at 24 percent but notes that 20 percent of the carbon dioxide produced is offset by carbon sequestration; and the U.S. Department of Agriculture estimates that 9 percent of greenhouse gas emission are due to agriculture and forestry. Food and Agricultural Organization of the United Nations, pp. 79–113.
21. Food and Agricultural Organization of the United Nations, pp. 125–150.
22. Harrison Wein, "Risk in Red Meats?" National Institutes of Health, March 26, 2012, https//www.nih.gov/news-events/nih-research-matters/risk-red-meat.
23. Nicholas Bakalar, "Red Meat Increases Risk of Dying from 8 Diseases," *New York Times*, May 15, 2017, https://www.nytimes.com/2017/05/15/well/eat/red-meat-increases-risk-of-dying-from-8-diseases.html.
24. Mariëtte Berndsen and Joop van der Pligt, "Ambivalence Towards Meat," *Appetite* 42, no. 1 (February 2004): 71–78.
25. Temple Grandin's website provides information on animal welfare standards as well as videos of typical stockyards, livestock production facilities, and slaughterhouses. See www.grandin.com.
26. Temple Grandin, *Human Livestock Handling: Understanding Livestock Behavior and Building Facilities for Healthier Animals* (North Adams, MA: Storey, 2008).

27. Judith D. Schwartz, *Cows Save the Planet and Other Improbable Ways of Restoring Soil to Heal the Earth* (White River Junction, VT: Chelsea Green, 2013). See also, Nicolette Hahn Niman, *Defending Beef: The Case for Sustainable Meat Production* (White River Junction, VT: Chelsea Green, 2014) and Kristin Ohlson, *The Soil Will Save Us: How Scientists, Farmers, and Foodies Are Healing the Soil to Save the Planet* (Emmaus, PA: Rodale, 2014).
28. U.S. Department of Health and Human Services and U.S. Department of Agriculture, *2015–2020 Dietary Guidelines for Americans*, 8th ed., December 2015, https://health.gov/dietaryguidelines/2015/guidelines.
29. Food and Agricultural Organization of the United Nations, *World Livestock 2011: Livestock in Food Security* (Rome: FAO, 2011), http://www.fao.org/3/i2373e/i2373e.pdf.
30. Food and Agricultural Organization of the United Nations, *Livestock's Long Shadow*, p. xx.
31. Food and Agricultural Organization of the United Nations, "Major Cuts in Greenhouse Gas Emissions from Livestock within Reach," Food and Agricultural Organization of the United Nations, September 26, 2013, http://www.fao.org/news/story/en/item/197608/icode.
32. Simon Fairlie, *Meat: A Benign Extravagance* (White River Junction, VT: Chelsea Green, 2010), pp. 12–43.
33. U.S. Department of Health and Human Services and U.S. Department of Agriculture, *2015–2020 Dietary Guidelines for Americans.*
34. W. J. Craig and A. R. Mangels, "Position of the American Dietetic Association: Vegetarian Diets," *Journal of the American Dietetic Association* 109, no. 7 (2009): 1266–1282.
35. Carol Torgan, "Vegetarian Diets Linked to Lower Mortality," National Institutes of Health, June 10, 2013, https://www.nih.gov/news-events/nih-research-matters/vegetarian-diets-linked-lower-mortality.
36. Food and Agricultural Organization of the United Nations, *World Livestock 2011.*
37. Anup Shah, "Poverty Facts and Statistics," Global Issues, updated January 7, 2013, http://www.globalissues.org/article/26/poverty-facts-and-stats.
38. For a balanced assessment of the use animals for food, see David Fraser, "Animal Ethics and Food Production in the Twenty-First Century," in *The Philosophy of Food*, ed. David M. Kaplan (Berkeley, CA: University of California Press, 2012), pp. 190–213.
39. Singer, *The Ethics of What We Eat*, pp. 241–284; James Rachels, "Vegetarianism," in *The Oxford Handbook of Animal Ethics*, ed. Tom L. Beauchamp and R. G. Frey (New York: Oxford University Press, 2011), pp. 877–905.
40. For a good discussion of the limits of ethical consumerism, see Andrew Chignell, "Can We Really Vote with Our Forks?: Opportunism and the Threshold Chicken," in *Philosophy Comes to Dinner: Arguments about the Ethics of Eating*, ed. Andrew Chignell, Terence Cuneo, and Matthew C. Halteman (New York: Routledge, 2015), pp. 182–202.
41. Elizabeth Harman, "Eating Meat as a Morally Permissible Moral Mistake," in *Philosophy Comes to Dinner*, pp. 215–231.
42. Adrienne M. Martin, "Factory Farming and Consumer Complicity," in *Philosophy Comes to Dinner*, pp. 203–214.

43. Chignell, "Can We Really Vote with Our Forks?" pp. 197–199.
44. Bernard Williams, "A Critique of Utilitarianism," in *Utilitarianism: For and Against*, ed. Bernard Williams and J. J. C. Smart (New York: Cambridge University Press, 1973), pp. 108–118.
45. Jean Kazez, *Animal Kind: What We Owe to Animals* (New York: Wiley-Blackwell, 2010), pp. 15–16.
46. Kazez, p. 18.
47. Roger Scruton, "The Conscientious Carnivore," in *Food for Thought: The Debate over Eating Meat*, ed. Steve Sapontzis (New York: Prometheus, 2004) pp. 81–91.
48. "Age of Animals Slaughtered," Aussie Farms Repository, accessed September 2017, http://www.aussieabattoirs.com/facts/age-slaughtered.
49. Eve Fox, "The Case for Eating Older Animals," *Modern Farmer*, January 20, 2015, https://modernfarmer.com/2015/01/case-eating-older-animals.
50. W. K. Kellogg Foundation, "Perceptions of the U.S. Food System: What and How Americans Think about Their Food," 2012, accessed January 2017, http://www.topospartnership.com/wp-content/uploads/2012/05/Food-Systems.pdf; European Commission, "Europeans, Agriculture, and the Common Agricultural Policy," *Eurobarometer* 80.2, March 2014, http://ec.europa.eu/commfrontoffice/publicopinion/archives/ebs/ebs_410_en.pdf.
51. W. K. Kellogg Foundation, p. 29; European Commission Directorate-General for Agriculture and Rural Development, *Report on the Results of the Public Consultation on the Review of the EU Policy on Organic Agriculture*, September 19, 2013, pp. 17–19, https://ec.europa.eu/agriculture/sites/agriculture/files/consultations/organic/final-report-full-text_en.pdf.
52. W. K. Kellogg Foundation, p. 30.
53. W. K. Kellogg Foundation, p. 49.
54. W. K. Kellogg Foundation, pp. 49–52.
55. W. K. Kellogg Foundation, pp. 49–52.
56. National Academies of Sciences, Engineering, and Medicine, *Genetically Engineered Crops: Experiences and Prospects*, (Washington, DC: National Academies Press, 2016), https://doi.org/10.17226/23395.
57. "Statement by the AAAS Board of Directors on Labeling of Genetically Modified Foods," American Associate for the Advancement of Science, October 20, 2012, https://www.aaas.org/sites/default/files/AAAS_GM_statement.pdf.
58. "Food Safety: Frequently Asked Questions on Genetically Modified Food," World Health Organization, May 2014, http://www.who.int/foodsafety/areas_work/food-technology/faq-genetically-modified-food/en.
59. "Consumer Info About Food from Genetically Engineered Plants," U.S. Food and Drug Administration, current as of January 4, 2018, https://www.fda.gov/food/food-new-plant-varieties/consumer-info-about-food-genetically-engineered-plants.
60. European Commission, *A Decade of EU-Funded GMO Research (2001–2010)*, 2010, https://ec.europa.eu/research/biosociety/pdf/a_decade_of_eu-funded_gmo_research.pdf.
61. Cary Funk and Brian Kennedy, "Public Opinion About Genetically Modified Foods and Trust in Scientists Connected with These Foods," Pew Research Center,

December 1, 2016, http://www.pewinternet.org/2016/12/01/public-opinion-about-genetically-modified-foods-and-trust-in-scientists-connected-with-these-foods.

62. Margaret Mellon, "Biotechnology—A Failed Promise," Union of Concerned Scientists, August 25, 2011, https://blog.ucsusa.org/margaret-mellon/biotechnology-a-failed-promise.
63. Paul B. Thompson, "Shall We Dine? Confronting the Strange and Horrifying Story of GMOs in Our Food," in *Food and Philosophy: Eat, Think, and Be Merry*, ed. Fritz Allhoff and Dave Monroe (New York: Blackwell, 2007), pp. 208–220.
64. "Substances Added to Food (formerly EAFUS)," U.S. Food and Drug Administration, current as of June 26, 2018, https://www.fda.gov/food/food-additives-petitions/substances-added-food-formerly-eafus.
65. Nielsen Company, "We Are What We Eat: Healthy Eating Trends from Around the World," January 2015,https://www.nielsen.com/content/dam/nielsenglobal/eu/nielseninsights/pdfs/Nielsen%20Global%20Health%20and%20Wellness%20Report%20-%20January%202015.pdf.
66. "Chemical Cuisine," Center for Science in the Public Interest, accessed September 2017, http://www.cspinet.org/reports/chemcuisine.html.
67. Kate Bratskeir, "11 Food Companies Removing Artificial Colors and Flavors by 2018," *Huffington Post*, July 28, 2015, https://www.huffingtonpost.com/entry/11-companies-that-plan-to-remove-artificial-flavors-before-2019_us_55b6a777e4b0074ba5a5d327.
68. Diane P. Michelfelder, "Technological Ethics in a Different Voice," in *Technology and the Good Life?*, ed. Eric Higgs, Andrew Light, and David Strong (Chicago: University of Chicago Press, 2000), pp. 231–232.
69. Michael Winerip, "You Call That a Tomato?" *New York Times*, June 24, 2013, https://www.nytimes.com/2013/06/24/booming/you-call-that-a-tomato.html.

5. FOOD POLITICAL PHILOSOPHY

1. For a representative survey of food justice issues, see Roger Gottlieb and Anupama Joshi, *Food Justice* (Cambridge, MA: MIT Press, 2013) and Alison Hope Alkon and Julian Agyeman, eds., *Cultivating Food Justice: Race, Class, and Sustainability* (Cambridge, MA: MIT Press, 2011).
2. Michael Walzer, *Spheres of Justice: A Defense of Pluralism and Equality* (New York: Basic, 1983).
3. Jennifer Clapp, *Food*, 2nd ed. (Cambridge: Polity Press, 2016), p. 20.
4. Sue Donaldson and Will Kymlicka, *Zoopolis: A Political Theory of Animal Rights* (Oxford: Oxford University Press, 2011).
5. Walzer, *Spheres of Justice*, p. xiv.
6. "Different political arrangements enforce, and different ideologies justify, different distributions of membership, power, honor, ritual eminence, divine grace, kinship and love, knowledge, wealth, physical security, work and leisure, rewards and punishments, and a host of goods more narrowly and materially conceived—food, shelter, clothing, transportation, medical care, commodities of every sort, and all the odd things (paintings, rare books, postage stamps) that human beings collect. And this multiplicity of goods is matched by a multiplicity of distributive procedures, agents, and criteria." Walzer, p. 3.

7. Walzer, p. 8.
8. "Distributive criteria and arrangements are intrinsic not to the good-in-itself but to the social good. If we understand what it is, what it means to those for whom it is a good, we understand how, by whom, and for what reasons it ought to be distributed. All distributions are just or unjust relative to the social meanings of the goods at stake." Walzer, pp. 8–9.
9. "I call a good dominant if the individuals who have it, because they have it, can command a wide range of other goods." Walzer, p. 10.
10. Walzer, p. 19.
11. Michael Walzer, "Involuntary Association," in *Politics and Passion: Toward a More Egalitarian Liberalism* (New Haven, CT: Yale University Press, 2004), p. 19.
12. Walzer, "Involuntary Association," p. 18.
13. Michael Walzer, "Politics and Passion," in *Politics and Passion*, p. 126.
14. Richard Bulliet et al., *The Earth and Its Peoples: A Global History, Volume I* (Boston: Houghton Mifflin, 2008).
15. W. K. Kellogg Foundation, "Perceptions of the U.S. Food System: What and How Americans Think about Their Food," 2012, accessed January 2017, http://www.topospartnership.com/wp-content/uploads/2012/05/Food-Systems.pdf; European Commission, "Europeans, Agriculture, and the Common Agricultural Policy," *Eurobarometer* 80.2, March 2014, http://ec.europa.eu/commfrontoffice/publicopinion/archives/ebs/ebs_410_en.pdf; European Commission Directorate-General for Agriculture and Rural Development, *Report on the Results of the Public Consultation on the Review of the EU Policy on Organic Agriculture,* September 19, 2013, https://ec.europa.eu/agriculture/sites/agriculture/files/consultations/organic/final-report-full-text_en.pdf.
16. U.S. Department of Agriculture, National Agricultural Statistics Service, modified May 3, 2019, https://www.nass.usda.gov/AgCensus.
17. Food Chain Workers Alliance, *The Hands that Feed Us: Challenges and Opportunities for Workers Along the Food Chain*, June 6, 2012,http://foodchainworkers.org/wp-content/uploads/2012/06/Hands-That-Feed-Us-Report.pdf.
18. "International Markets and U.S. Trade," U.S. Department of Agriculture, Economic Research Service, 2015, https://www.ers.usda.gov/topics/international-markets-us-trade.
19. Clapp, *Food*, p. 20.
20. For an optimistic account of how new food technologies can improve the lives of animals, see Wayne Pacelle, *The Humane Economy: How Innovators and Enlightened Consumers Are Transforming the Lives of Animals* (New York: HarperCollins, 2016).
21. Forward contracts were known to exist in ancient Rome, Greece, Mesopotamia, and probably elsewhere. Aristotle mentions them in *Politics* $1259^{a}1$–$1259^{a}35$. Kim Oosterlinck, "History of Forward Contracts," in *The New Palgrave Dictionary of Economics*, online edition, ed. Steven N. Durlauf and Lawrence E. Blume (New York: Springer, 2009).
22. David M. Newberry, "Futures Markets, Hedging and Speculation," in *The New Palgrave Dictionary of Economics*, ed. Steven N. Durlauf and Lawrence E. Blume (New York: Springer, 2008), pp. 521–526.
23. Clapp, *Food*, p. 120.
24. Clapp, *Food*, p. 121.

25. Jennifer Clapp and Sarah J. Martin, "Agriculture and Finance," in *Encyclopedia of Food and Agricultural Ethics*, ed. Paul B. Thompson and David M. Kaplan (New York: Springer, 2014), pp. 86–94.
26. Matias E. Margulis, "Land Acquisitions for Food and Fuel," in *Encyclopedia of Food and Agricultural Ethics*, pp. 1325–1332.
27. Sean Field, "The Financialization of Food and the 2008–2011 Food Price Spikes," *Environment and Planning* 48, no. 11 (2016): 2272–2290.
28. Sasha Breger Bush, *Derivatives and Development: A Political Economy of Global Finance, Farming, and Poverty* (New York: Palgrave MacMillan, 2012).
29. Philip McMichael, "The Land Grab and Corporate Food Regime Restructuring," *Journal of Peasant Studies* 39, no. 3–4 (2012): 681–701.
30. Food and Agriculture Organization of the United Nations, *The State of Agricultural Commodity Markets: Trade and Food Security*, (Rome: FAO, 2015), http://www.fao.org/3/a-i5090e.pdf.
31. Olivier De Schutter, "How Not to Think of Land-Grabbing: Three Critiques of Large-Scale Investment in Farmland," *Journal of Peasant Studies* 38, no. 2 (2011): 249–279.
32. Jennifer Clapp and Peter Dauvergne, *Paths to a Green World: The Political Economy of the Global Environment,* 2nd ed. (Cambridge, MA: MIT Press, 2011).
33. For counter-arguments concerning the dire consequences of commodity speculation on food prices, food security, and land grabbing, see Robert Paarlberg, *Food Politics: What Everyone Needs to Know*, 2nd ed. (New York: Oxford University Press, 2013). Paarlberg has a more optimistic view of modernization than Clapp and I do. Science and technology can, of course, solve some social and environmental problems but not injustices and inequalities caused by poverty and financialization.
34. Karl Marx, "Letter from Marx to Arnold Ruge, 1843," in *The Marx-Engels Reader*, ed. Robert C. Tucker, 2nd ed. (New York: W. W. Norton & Company, 1978), pp. 135.
35. Sasha Breger Bush, *Derivatives and Development*.
36. Warren Belasco, *Appetite for Change: How Counterculture Took on the Food Industry* (Ithaca, NY: Cornell University Press, 1987).
37. See www.slowfood.com.
38. Declaration of Nyéléni, February 27, 2007, http://www.nyeleni.org/spip.php?article290.
39. See La Via Campesina, https://viacampesina.org/en.
40. Food and Agricultural Organization of the United Nations, *Report on the World Food Summit, 13–17 November, 1996* (Rome: FAO, 1996), http://www.fao.org/docrep/003/x0736m/x0736m00.htm.
41. For an overview of the different versions and inconsistencies in recent iterations of the concept of food sovereignty, see Raj Patel, "What does food sovereignty look like?" *Journal of Peasant Studies* 36, no. 3 (2009): 663–706.
42. "Doha Declarations," The World Trade Organization, November 14, 2001, https://www.wto.org/english/thewto_e/minist_e/min01_e/mindecl_e.htm.
43. Clapp, *Food*, pp. 137–143.
44. Clapp, pp. 137–143.

45. Jennifer Clapp, *Food Security and International Trade: Unpacking Disputed Narratives*, Food and Agricultural Organization of the United Nations, (Rome: FAO, 2015), http://www.fao.org/3/a-i5160e.pdf.
46. Clapp, *Food Security*, pp. 12–17.
47. Clapp, pp. 19–28.
48. Tony Weis, *The Ecological Hoofprint: The Global Burden of Industrial Livestock* (New York: Zed, 2013), p. 1.
49. Food and Agricultural Organization of the United Nations, *Livestock's Long Shadow: Environmental Issues and Options*, (Rome: FAO, 2006), http://www.fao.org/3/a-a0701e.pdf.
50. Weis, *The Ecological Hoofprint*, pp. 2–9.
51. Weis, p. 2.
52. For a classic statement of modernization theory, see Seymour Martin Lipset, *Political Man* (New York: Anchor, 1960).
53. Weis, *Ecological Hoofprint*, p. 71.
54. Lizzie Collingham, *The Taste of Empire: How Britain's Quest for Food Shaped the Modern World* (New York: Basic, 2017).
55. Marion Nestle, *Food Politics* (Berkeley, CA: University of California Press, 2003), pp. 29–51.
56. Maxine Chen, "The Meat Hook: Satiating Asia's Demand for Meat," Mongabay, April 27, 2017, https://news.mongabay.com/2017/04/the-meat-hook-satiating-asias-demand-for-beef.
57. Chen, "The Meat Hook."
58. Weis, *Ecological Hoofprint*, pp. 26–52.
59. Weis, pp. 26–52.
60. "Animal Production," FAO Animal Production and Health Division, accessed June 2016, http://www.fao.org/agriculture/animal-production-and-health/en/.
61. Bill and Melinda Gates Foundation, *Agricultural Development: Strategy Overview*, August 2011, https://docs.gatesfoundation.org/documents/agricultural-development-strategy-overview.pdf.
62. Bill and Melinda Gates Foundation, *Agricultural Development*.
63. World Bank, *World Development Indicators 2017* (Washington, DC: 2017), https://openknowledge.worldbank.org/handle/10986/26447?show=full.
64. For arguments that animals deserve rights on the basis of sentience and selfhood (not because they meet a threshold of complex mental abilities), see Paola Cavalieri, *The Animal Question: Why Nonhuman Animals Deserve Human Rights* (Oxford: Oxford University Press, 2001); Gary L. Francione, *Animals as Persons: Essays on the Abolition of Animal Exploitation* (New York: Columbia University Press, 2008); and Gary Steiner, *Animals and the Moral Community: Mental Life, Moral Status, and Kinship* (New York: Columbia University Press, 2008).
65. Michael Walzer, "Cultural Rights," in *Politics and Passion*, pp. 44–65.
66. Sue Donaldson and Will Kymlicka, *Zoopolis: A Political Theory of Animal Rights* (Oxford: Oxford University Press, 2011).
67. Donaldson and Kylmlicka, pp. 50–69.
68. Donaldson and Kylmlicka, pp. 50–69.
69. Donaldson and Kylmlicka, p. 107.

70. Food and Agriculture Organization of the United Nations, *The State of World Fisheries and Aquaculture 2018* (Rome: FAO, 2018), http://www.fao.org/3/i9540en/I9540EN.pdf.
71. Eliot Michaelson and Andrew Reisner, "Ethics for Fish," in *The Oxford Handbook of Food Ethics*, ed. Anne Barnhill, Mark Budolfson, and Tyler Doggett (New York: Oxford University Press, 2017).
72. Eliza Barclay, "Why There's Less Meat on Many American Plates," NPR, June 27, 2012, https://www.npr.org/sections/thesalt/2012/06/27/155837575/why-theres-less-red-meat-served-on-many-american-plates.
73. European Union Agriculture and Rural Development, *EU Agricultural Outlook: Prospect for the EU Agricultural Markets and Income 2016–2026*, December 2016, https://ec.europa.eu/agriculture/sites/agriculture/files/markets-and-prices/medium-term-outlook/2016/2016-fullrep_en.pdf.
74. Oliver Milman and Stuart Leavenworth, "China's Plan to Cut Meat Consumption by 50% Cheered by Climate Campaigners," *Guardian*, June 20, 2016, https://www.theguardian.com/world/2016/jun/20/chinas-meat-consumption-climate-change.
75. Anna Edney, "Lab-Grown Meat Startups Backed by Bill Gates, Tyson Foods Face FDA Oversight," *Bloomberg News*, June 15, 2018, https://www.bloomberg.com/news/articles/2018-06-15/lab-grown-meat-backed-by-gates-tyson-foods-faces-u-s-oversight.
76. "Mad Sausage," mercyforanimals, March 11, 2013, https://www.youtube.com/watch?v=PNFfJJBwBjY.
77. Alex Horton, "Tucker Carlson Suggested Immigrants Make the U.S. 'Dirtier'—And It Cost Fox News an Advertiser," *Washington Post*, December 15, 2018, https://www.washingtonpost.com/business/2018/12/15/tucker-carlson-suggested-immigrants-make-us-dirtier-it-cost-fox-news-an-advertiser/?utm_term=.4d5ab9cc38c4.
78. George Lakoff, *Moral Politics: How Liberals and Conservatives Think*, 2nd ed. (Chicago: University of Chicago Press, 2000), pp. 65–107.
79. Lakoff, *Moral Politics*, pp. 65–107.
80. Klaus Morales, "Brazil Adopts Stronger Pictures on Cigarette Packages in Anti-Smoking Campaign," *British Medical Journal*, 336 (2008): 1333.
81. Gonzalo Palomo-Vélez, Joshua M. Tybur, and Mar van Vugt, "Unsustainable, Unhealthy or Disgusting? Comparing Different Persuasive Messages Against Meat Consumption," *Journal of Environmental Psychology* 58, (August 2018): 63–71.
82. Fred Amofa Yamoah and David Eshun Yawson, "Assessing Supermarket Food Shopper Reaction to Horsemeat Scandal in the UK," *International Review of Management and Marketing* 4, no. 2 (2014): 98–107.
83. J. Chung et al., "Media Framing and Perception of Risk for Food Technologies: The Case of 'Pink Slime,'" in *Food Futures: Ethics, Science and Culture*, ed. I. Anna S. Olsson, Sofia M. Araújo, and M. Fátima Vieira (Wageningen, Netherlands: Wageningen Academic, 2016), pp. 315–320.
84. Ying Kei Tse et al., "Insight from the Horsemeat Scandal: Exploring the Consumers' Opinion of Tweets Toward Tesco," *Industrial Management and Data Systems* 116, no. 6 (2017): 1178–1200.
85. Emily Laber-Warren, "Unconscious Reactions Separate Liberals and Conservatives," *Scientific American*, September 1, 2012, https://www.scientificamerican.com/article/calling-truce-political-wars.

86. John Rawls, *Political Liberalism* (New York: Columbia University Press, 1993), pp. 144–150.

6. FOOD EXISTENTIALISM

1. I take Kierkegaard, Nietzsche, Sartre, and Heidegger to be representative of existentialism, even though the first two preceded the use of the term and Heidegger explicitly said he was not an existentialist.
2. Leon Kass, *The Hungry Soul: Eating and the Perfecting of Our Nature* (Chicago: University of Chicago Press, 1994), pp. 19–27.
3. Maurice Merleau-Ponty, *Phenomenology of Perception*, trans. Colin Smith (New York: Routledge Classics University Press, 2002), p. 137.
4. Merleau-Ponty, p. 138.
5. Merleau-Ponty, p. 475.
6. Merleau-Ponty, p. 102.
7. Merleau-Ponty, p. 102.
8. Jean-Paul Sartre, *Being and Nothingness*, trans. Hazel E. Barnes (New York: Philosophical Library, 1962), p. 329.
9. Sartre, p. 327.
10. Sartre, p. 354.
11. Paul Ricoeur, *Freedom and Nature: The Voluntary and Involuntary*, trans. Erazim V. Kohák (Evanston, IL: Northwestern University Press, 1966), pp. 4–19.
12. Ricoeur, p. 85.
13. Ellyn Satter, "Hierarchy of Food Needs," *Journal of Nutrition Education and Behavior* 39, no. 5 (2018): 187–188.
14. Gudrun Sproesser et al., "The Eating Motivation Survey: Results from the USA, India, and Germany," *Public Health Nutrition* 21, no. 3 (2018): 515–525.
15. Herbert Marcuse, *One-Dimensional Man: Studies in the Ideology in Advanced Industrial Society* (London: Routledge & Kegan Paul, 1964).
16. Hubert Dreyfus is the leading proponent of a reading of Heidegger as a philosopher of social practices and skillful coping as an alternative to the cognitive and perceptual focus of Modern epistemic and phenomenological traditions. Hubert Dreyfus, *Being-in-the-World: A Commentary on Heidegger's Being in Time, Division I* (Cambridge, MA: MIT Press, 1990).
17. Lisa Feldman Barrett, *How Emotions Are Made: The Secret Life of the Brain* (Boston: Houghton Mifflin Harcourt, 2017).
18. Daniel Kelly and Nicolae Morar, "Against the Yuck Factor: On the Ideal Role for Disgust in Society," *Utilitas* 26, no. 2 (2014): 153–177.
19. Douglas Rushkoff, *Coercion: Why We Listen to What "They" Say* (New York: Riverhead, 1999).
20. Gabriel Marcel, *The Mystery of Being Vol. 1: Reflection and Mystery*, trans. G. S. Fraser (New York: Gateway, 1960), p. 149.
21. Brian Treanor, "Gabriel Marcel," *Stanford Encyclopedia of Philosophy*, March 2016, https://plato.stanford.edu/entries/marcel.
22. Jane Bennett, *Vibrant Matter: A Political Ecology of Things* (Durham: Duke University Press, 2010), p. 51.

23. Suzana Herculano-Houzel, *The Human Advantage: How Our Brains Became Remarkable* (Cambridge, MA: MIT Press, 2016).
24. Richard Wrangham, *Catching Fire: How Cooking Made Us Human* (New York: Basic, 2009).
25. Kim Sterelny, *The Evolved Apprentice: How Evolution Made Humans Unique* (Cambridge, MA: MIT Press, 2012).
26. Marvin Harris, *The Sacred Cow and the Abominable Pig: Riddles of Food and Culture* (New York: Simon & Schuster, 1987).
27. For analyses of how national cuisines came about, see Arjun Appadurai, "How to Make a National Cuisine: Cookbooks in Contemporary India," *Comparative Studies in Society and History* 30, no. 1 (January 1988): 3–24 and Katarzyna J. Cwiertka, *Modern Japanese Cuisine: Food, Power, and National Identity* (New York: Reaktion, 2006). For an argument that a national cuisine is an artifice and that cuisines are genuinely regional and only ideologically national, see Sydney Mintz, *Tasting Food, Tasting Freedom: Excursions into Eating, Culture, and the Past* (Boston: Beacon Press, 1997).
28. For arguments about the lack of uniformity in culinary globalization, see James L. Watson, ed., *Golden Arches East: McDonald's in East Asia* (Palo Alto, CA: Stanford University Press, 2006); for how local cuisines interact with colonialism and globalism without necessarily being assimilated, see Richard Wilk, *Home Cooking in the Global Village: Caribbean Food from Buccaneers to Ecotourists* (New York: Berg, 2006); for a defense of the virtues of *terroir* in the face of industrialization, see Amy B. Trubek, *The Taste of Place: A Cultural Journey into Terroir* (Berkeley, CA: University of California Press, 2009).
29. B. W. Higman, *How Food Made History* (Hoboken, NJ: Wiley-Blackwell, 2011).
30. Isabelle de Solier, *Food and the Self: Consumption, Production, and Material Culture* (London: Bloomsbury, 2013).
31. Pierre Emmanuel, "Is France Being Americanized?" *Atlantic*, June 1958, https://www.theatlantic.com/magazine/archive/1958/06/is-france-being-americanized/376248.
32. Danny Lewis, "Italian City Bans New 'Ethnic' Restaurants," *Smithsonian Magazine*, March 4, 2016, https://www.smithsonianmag.com/smart-news/italian-city-bans-new-ethnic-restaurants-180958283.
33. Benedetta Grasso, "Polenta vs. Cous Cous: Legally Banning Ethnic Food from Northern Italy," *iItaly*, April 9, 2010, http://www.iitaly.org/magazine/dining-in-out/articles-reviews/article/polenta-vs-cous-cous-legally-banning-ethnic-food.
34. Nina Siegal, "New Slaughtering Rules Pit Dutch Religious Freedoms Against Animal Rights," *New York Times*, December 31, 2017, https://www.nytimes.com/2017/12/31/world/europe/netherlands-kosher-halal-animal-rights.html.
35. It might seem that they could form a political alliance in an overlapping consensus, except Rawls maintains that political justice applies only to "reasonable comprehensive doctrines," which would rule out the racist nationalists. John Rawls, *Political Liberalism* (New York: Columbia University Press, 1993), pp. 144–150.
36. Michael Twitty, "Culinary Justice: Defining a Theory of Gastronomic Sovereignty," University of Michigan, March 28, 2017, https://www.youtube.com/watch?v=7DL7yY3r-ig.
37. Twitty, "Culinary Justice."

38. Lisa Heldke, *Exotic Appetites: Ruminations of a Food Adventurer* (New York: Routledge, 2003).
39. Martin Heidegger, *Being and Time*, trans. John Macquarrie and Edward Robinson (New York: Harper & Row, 1962), pp. 78–91.
40. Heidegger, pp. 91–102.
41. Ron Mallon, *The Construction of Human Kinds* (Oxford: Oxford University Press, 2016).
42. Hilde Nelson, *Holding On and Letting Go: The Social Practice of Personal Identities* (New York: Oxford University Press, 2014), p. 87.
43. Nick Fiddes, *Meat: A Natural Symbol* (London: Routledge, 1991).
44. Marta Zaraska, *Meathooked: The History and Science of Our 2.5-Million-Year Obsession with Meat* (New York: Basic, 2016), p. 103–118.
45. Carol Nemeroff and Paul Rozin, "'You Are What You Eat': Applying the Demand-Free 'Impressions' Technology to an Unacknowledged Belief," *Ethos* 17, no. 1 (1989): 50–69.
46. Paul Rozin et al., "Is Meat Male? A Quantitative Multimethod Framework to Establish Metaphoric Relationships," *Journal of Consumer Research* 39, no. 3 (October 1, 2012): 629–643.
47. Daniel Kelly and Nicolae Morar, "I Eat, Therefore I Am: Disgust at the Intersection of Food and Identity," in *The Oxford Handbook of Food Ethics*, ed. Anne Barnhill, Mark Budolfson, and Tyler Doggett (New York: Oxford University Press, 2017), pp. 637–657.
48. Stephen R. L. Clark, "Vegetarianism and the Ethics of Virtue," in *Food for Thought: The Debate over Eating Meat*, ed. Steve F. Sapontzis (New York: Prometheus, 2004), pp. 138–151.
49. Quoted in Marta Zaraska, *Meathooked*, p. 158.
50. Rebecca Kukla, "Shame, Seduction, and Character in Food Messaging," in *The Oxford Handbook of Food Ethics*, pp. 593–613.
51. Kelly and Morar, "I Eat, Therefore I Am," p. 650.
52. Rebecca M. Puhl and Chelsea A. Heuer, "Obesity Stigma: Important Considerations for Public Health," *American Journal of Public Health* 100, no. 6 (June 2010): 1019–1028.
53. Carole M. Counihan and Steven L. Kaplan, eds., *Food and Gender: Identity and Power* (New York: Routledge, 1998), pp. 1–12.
54. Emily J. H. Contois, "Gender and Dieting," in *Encyclopedia of Food and Agricultural Ethics*, ed. Paul B. Thompson and David M. Kaplan (New York: Springer, 2014), pp. 1081–1087.
55. Leah Selim, "Gender Inequality and Food Insecurity," in *Encyclopedia of Food and Agricultural Ethics*, pp. 1087–1093.
56. Alison N. C. Reiheld, "Gender Norms and Food Behavior," in *Encyclopedia of Food and Agricultural Ethics*, pp. 1094–1100.
57. Ron Mallon and Daniel Kelly, "Making Race out of Nothing: Psychologically Constrained Social Roles," in *The Oxford Handbook of Philosophy of Social Science*, ed. Harold Kincaid (New York: Oxford University Press, 2012), pp. 507–532.
58. Iris Marion Young, *Justice and the Politics of Difference* (Princeton, NJ: Princeton University Press, 1991).

59. Virgil Hawkins, "'Shithole' Countries? The Media's Portrayal of Africa Reconsidered," *Fair Observer*, January 16, 2018, https://www.fairobserver.com/region/africa/donald-trump-shithole-countries-media-africa-coverage-news-headlines-87600.
60. Teju Cole, "The White-Savior Industrial Complex," *Atlantic*, March 21, 2012, https://www.theatlantic.com/international/archive/2012/03/the-white-savior-industrial-complex/254843.
61. Andy Baker, "Media Portrayals of Africa Promote Paternalism," *Washington Post*, March 5, 2015, https://www.washingtonpost.com/news/monkey-cage/wp/2015/03/05/media-portrayals-of-africa-promote-paternalism.
62. "Voices: Have You Ever Had a Lunchbox Moment?" *NBC News Asian America*, May 3, 2016, https://www.nbcnews.com/news/asian-america/voices-have-you-ever-had-lunch-box-moment-n566411.
63. "Have You Ever Had a Lunchbox Moment?"
64. Hannah Kim, "My Lunchbox Moment: A Day in the Life of an Asian American," *Odyssey*, May 9, 2016, https://www.theodysseyonline.com/lunch-box-moment.
65. Maniaxzero, "Have you ever had a 'lunchbox moment'? I know I have," Reddit, May 5, 2016, https://www.reddit.com/r/asianamerican/comments/4ioqnj/have_you_ever_had_a_lunchbox_mo.
66. Animals can take some stances on their lives, albeit not as many as we can. Mammals are generally aware of their own bodies and their own agency, but it is hard to tell if they are aware of their personality traits, attitudes, and opinions, and how much they compare themselves to others. Alain Morain, "What Are Animals Conscious Of?" in *Experiencing Animal Minds*, ed. Julie Smith and Robert Mitchell (New York: Columbia University Press, 2012), pp. 246–260.
67. Heidegger, *Being and Time*, p. 223.
68. Michel Foucault, *Discipline and Punish: The Birth of the Prison*, trans. Allan Sheridan (New York: Vintage Press, 1975).
69. Drew DeSilver, "What's on Your Table? How America's Diet Has Changed over the Decades," Pew Research Center, December 13, 2016, http://www.pewresearch.org/fact-tank/2016/12/13/whats-on-your-table-how-americas-diet-has-changed-over-the-decades.
70. DeSilver, "What's on Your Table?".
71. U.S. Department of Health and Human Services and U.S. Department of Agriculture, *2015–2020 Dietary Guidelines for Americans*, 8th ed., December 2015, https://health.gov/dietaryguidelines/2015/guidelines.
72. Brock Bastian et al., "Don't Mind Meat? The Denial of Mind to Animals Used for Human Consumption," *Personality and Social Psychology Bulletin* 38, no. 2 (2012): 247–256.
73. Charles Stahler, "How Many People Are Vegan?" The Vegetarian Resource Group, accessed May 2019, https://www.vrg.org/nutshell/Polls/2019_adults_veg.htm. Accessed May 2019.
74. Martha C. White, "We Now Spend More at Restaurants Than at Grocery Stores," *Money*, June 15, 2016, http://money.com/money/4370620/food-spending-restaurants-versus-groceries.
75. Karen Hamrick, "Americans Spend an Average of 37 Minutes a Day Preparing and Serving Food and Cleaning Up," United States Department of Agriculture Economic Research Service, November 7, 2016, https://www.ers.usda.gov/amber-waves/2016

/november/americans-spend-an-average-of-37-minutes-a-day-preparing-and-serving-food-and-cleaning-up.

76. Eddie Yoon, "The Grocery Industry Confronts a New Problem: Only 10% of Americans Love Cooking," *Harvard Business Review*, September 22, 2017, https://hbr.org/2017/09/the-grocery-industry-confronts-a-new-problem-only-10-of-americans-love-cooking.
77. Annemarie Kuhns and Michelle Saksena, "Food Purchase Decisions of Millennial Households Compared to Other Generations," United States Department of Agriculture Economic Research Service, EIB-168, December 2017, https://www.ers.usda.gov/webdocs/publications/86401/eib-186.pdf.
78. Eric Robinson et al., "Eating Attentively: A Systematic Review and Meta-Analysis of the Effects of Food Intake Memory and Awareness on Eating," *American Journal of Clinical Nutrition* 97, no. 4 (April 2013): 728–742.
79. Sapna Maheshwari, "When Is a Burrito More Than a Burrito? When It Is a Lifestyle," *New York Times*, July 29, 2018, https://www.nytimes.com/2018/07/29/business/media/lifestyle-brands-marketing.html.
80. Maheshwari, "When Is a Burrito More Than a Burrito?"
81. Heidegger, *Being and Time*, p. 230.
82. Heidegger, p. 420.
83. Heidegger, p. 220.
84. Dreyfus, *Being-in-the-World*, 242.
85. Heidegger, *Being and Time*, p. 223.
86. Heidegger, p. 437.
87. Dreyfus, *Being-in-the-World*, p. 315.
88. Marcuse, *One-Dimensional Man*, pp. 56–83.
89. For example, Jean-Paul Sartre, *Search for a Method*, trans. Hazel E. Barnes (New York: Vintage, 1965).
90. For example, Karl Jaspers, *The Origin and Goal of History*, trans. Michael Bullock (London: Routledge & Kegan Paul, 1953).
91. For the relationship between alienation and reification, see Georg Lukács, *History and Class Consciousness: Studies in Marxist Dialectics*.
92. Paul Ricoeur, *History and Truth*, trans. Charles Kelbley (Evanston, IL: Northwestern University Press, 1965), p. 13.

BIBLIOGRAPHY

Abdul-Matin, Ibrahim. *Green Deen: What Islam Teaches about Protecting the Planet*. San Francisco: Berrett-Koehler, 2010.

Achaya, K. T. *Indian Food: A Historical Companion*. Delhi: Oxford University Press, 1998.

Alexander, Kevin. "Why 'Authentic' Food is Bullshit." *Thrillist*, July 15, 2017. https://www.thrillist.com/eat/nation/why-authentic-food-is-bullshit.

Alkon, Alison Hope, and Julian Agyeman, eds. *Cultivating Food Justice: Race, Class, and Sustainability*. Cambridge, MA: MIT Press, 2011.

Amer, Muhammad, Tugrul U. Daim, and Antonie Jetter. "A Review of Scenario Planning." *Futures* 46 (2013): 23–40.

American Association for the Advancement of Science. "Statement by the AAAS Board of Directors on Labeling of Genetically Modified Foods, American Associate for the Advancement of Science." October 20, 2012. https://www.aaas.org/sites/default/files/AAAS_GM_statement.pdf.

American Heart Association. "Food as Fuel Before, During and After Workouts." Updated January 2015. https://www.heart.org/en/healthy-living/healthy-eating/eat-smart/nutrition-basics/food-as-fuel-before-during-and-after-workouts..

American Psychiatric Association. *Diagnostic and Statistical Manual of Mental Disorders*. 5th ed. New York: American Psychiatric Publishing, 2013.

Appadurai, Arjun. "How to Make a National Cuisine: Cookbooks in Contemporary India." *Comparative Studies in Society and History* 30, no. 1 (1988): 3–24.

Aussie Farms Repository. "Age of Animals Slaughtered." Accessed September 2018. http://www.aussieabattoirs.com/facts/age-slaughtered.

Bakalar, Nicholas. "Red Meat Increases the Risk of Dying from 8 Diseases." *New York Times*, May 15, 2017. https://www.nytimes.com/2017/05/15/well/eat/red-meat-increases-risk-of-dying-from-8-diseases.html.

Baker, Andy. "Media Portrayals of Africa Promote Paternalism." *Washington Post*, March 5, 2015. https://www.washingtonpost.com/news/monkey-cage/wp/2015/03/05/media-portrayals-of-africa-promote-paternalism.

Barclay, Eliza. "Why There's Less Meat on Many American Plates." *National Public Radio*, June 27, 2012. https://www.npr.org/sections/thesalt/2012/06/27/155837575/why-theres-less-red-meat-served-on-many-american-plates.

Barrett, Lisa Feldman. *How Emotions Are Made: The Secret Life of the Brain*. Boston: Houghton Mifflin Harcourt, 2017.

Bastian, Brock, Steve Loughnan, Nick Haslam, and Helena R. M. Radke. "Don't Mind Meat? The Denial of Mind to Animals Used for Human Consumption." *Personality and Social Psychology Bulletin* 38, no. 2 (2012): 247–256.

Belasco, Warren. *Appetite for Change: How Counterculture Took on the Food Industry*. Ithaca: Cornell University Press, 1987.

Belasco, Warren. *Meals to Come: A History of the Future of Food*. Berkeley, CA: University of California Press, 2006.

Bennett, Jane. *Vibrant Matter: A Political Ecology of Things*. Durham: Duke University Press, 2010.

Berndsen, Mariëtte, and Joop van der Pligt. "Ambivalence Towards Meat." *Appetite* 42, no. 1 (February 2004): 71–78.

Berry, Wendell. *Bringing It to the Table: On Farming and Food*. Berkeley, CA: Counterpoint, 2009.

Bill and Melinda Gates Foundation. *Agricultural Development: Strategy Overview*. August, 2011. https://docs.gatesfoundation.org/documents/agricultural-development-strategy-overview.pdf.

Billinghurst, Thomas. "Is 'Shmeat' the Answer? In Vitro Meat Could be the Future of Food." *Gulf News*. May 2, 2013. https://gulfnews.com/going-out/restaurants/is-shmeat-the-answer-in-vitro-meat-could-be-the-future-of-food-1.1176127.

Blum, Lawrence A. *Friendship, Altruism and Morality*. London: Routledge and Kegan Paul, 1980.

Boisvert, Raymond D. "Convivialism: A Philosophical Manifesto." *Pluralist* 5, no. 2 (2010): 57–68.

Boisvert, Raymond D., and Lisa Heldke. *Philosophers at Table: On Food and Being Human*. London: Reaktion, 2016.

Bollier, David, and Silke Helfrich, eds. *The Wealth of the Commons: A World Beyond Market and State*. Amherst: Levellers Press, 2013.

Borghini, Andrea. "What Is a Recipe?" *Journal of Agricultural and Environmental Ethics* 28, no. 4 (2015): 719–38.

Bourdieu, Pierre. *Distinction: A Social Critique of the Judgment of Taste*. Translated by Richard Nice. Cambridge, MA: Harvard University Press, 1984.

Bratanova, Boyka, Christin-Melanie Vauclair, Nicolas Kervyn, Sandy Schuman, Robert Wood, and Olivier Klein. "Savouring Morality. Moral Satisfaction Renders Food of Ethical Origin Subjectively Tastier." *Appetite* 91 (August 2015): 137–49.

Bratskeir, Kate. "11 Food Companies Removing Artificial Colors and Flavors by 2018." *Huffington Post*, July 28, 2015. https://www.huffingtonpost.com/entry/11-companies-that-plan-to-remove-artificial-flavors-before-2019_us_55b6a777e4b0074ba5a5d327.

Bulliet, Richard, Pamela Crossley, Daniel Headrick, Stephen Hirsch, and Lyman Johnson. *The Earth and Its Peoples: A Global History, Volume I*. Boston: Houghton Mifflin, 2008.

Burke, Edmund. *A Philosophical Enquiry into the Origin of Our Ideas of the Sublime and Beautiful*. Edited by James T. Boulton. South Bend, IN: University of Notre Dame Press, 1968.

Bush, Sasha Breger. *Derivatives and Development: A Political Economy of Global Finance, Farming, and Poverty*. New York: Palgrave MacMillan, 2012.

Carroll, Noël. "Hume's Standard of Taste." *Journal of Aesthetics and Art Criticism* 43, no. 2 (Winter 1984): 181–194.

Carruthers, Peter. *The Animals Issue: Moral Theory in Practice*. New York: Cambridge University Press, 2002.

Castle, Stephen, and Doreen Carvajal. "Counterfeit Food More Widespread than Suspected." *New York Times*, June 26, 2013. http://www.nytimes.com/2013/06/27/business/food-fraud-more-widespread-than-suspected.html.

Cavalieri, Paola. *The Animal Question: Why Nonhuman Animals Deserve Human Rights*. Oxford: Oxford University Press, 2001.

Center for Science in the Public Interest. "Chemical Cuisine." Accessed September 2018. http://www.cspinet.org/reports/chemcuisine.html.

Charon, Rita, and Martha Montello. *Stories Matter: The Role of Narratives in Medical Ethics*. New York: Routledge, 2002.

Chen, Maxine. "The Meat Hook: Satiating Asia's Demand for Meat." Mongabay, April 27, 2017. https://news.mongabay.com/2017/04/the-meat-hook-satiating-asias-demand-for-beef.

Chignell, Andrew. "Can We Really Vote with Our Forks?: Opportunism and the Threshold Chicken." In *Philosophy Comes to Dinner: Arguments about the Ethics of Eating*, edited by Andrew Chignell, Terence Cuneo, and Matthew C. Halteman, 182–202. New York: Routledge, 2015.

Chiles, James R. *Inviting Disaster: Lessons from the Edge of Technology*. New York: Harper Business, 2002.

Chung, J., K. Runge, L.Y.F. Su, D. Brossard, and D. Scheufele. "Media Framing and Perception of Risk for Food Technologies: The Case of 'Pink Slime.'" In *Food Futures: Ethics, Science and Culture*, edited by I. Anna S. Olsson, Sofia M. Araújo, and M. Fátima Vieira, 315–320. Wageningen, Netherlands: Wageningen Academic, 2016.

Clapp, Jennifer. *Food*. 2nd ed. Cambridge: Polity Press, 2016.

Clapp, Jennifer. *Food Security and International Trade: Unpacking Disputed Narratives*. Food and Agricultural Organization of the United Nations. Rome: FAO, 2015. http://www.fao.org/3/a-i5160e.pdf.

Clapp, Jennifer, and Peter Dauvergne. *Paths to a Green World: The Political Economy of the Global Environment*. 2nd ed. Cambridge, MA: MIT Press, 2011.

Clapp, Jennifer, and Sarah J. Martin. "Agriculture and Finance." In *Encyclopedia of Food and Agricultural Ethics*, edited by Paul B. Thompson and David M. Kaplan, 86–94. New York: Springer, 2014.

Clark, Stephen R. L. "Vegetarianism and the Ethics of Virtue." In *Food for Thought: The Debate over Eating Meat*, edited by Steve F. Sapontzis, 138–151. New York: Prometheus, 2004.

Cole, Teju. "The White-Savior Industrial Complex." *Atlantic*, March 21, 2012. https://www.theatlantic.com/international/archive/2012/03/the-white-savior-industrial-complex/254843.

Collingham, Lizzie. *The Taste of Empire: How Britain's Quest for Food Shaped the Modern World*. New York: Basic, 2017.

Contois, Emily J. H. "Gender and Dieting." In *Encyclopedia of Food and Agricultural Ethics*, edited by Paul B. Thompson and David M. Kaplan, 1081–1087. New York: Springer, 2014.

Counihan, Carole M., and Stephen L. Kaplan, eds. *Food and Gender: Identity and Power*. New York: Routledge, 1998.

Craig, W. J., and A. R. Magels, "Position of the American Dietetic Association: Vegetarian Diets." *Journal of the American Dietetic Association* 109, no. 7 (2009): 1266–1282.

Cwiertka, Katarzyna J. *Modern Japanese Cuisine: Food, Power, and National Identity*. New York: Reaktion, 2006.

Danto, Arthur. *Narration and Knowledge*. New York: Columbia University Press, 1985.

Davidson, Donald. "On the Very Idea of a Conceptual Scheme." In *Inquiries into Truth and Interpretation*. 2nd ed. Oxford: Clarendon Press, 2001.

Davis, Ellen F. *Scripture, Culture, and Agriculture: An Agrarian Reading of the Bible*. Albany, NY: SUNY Press, 2004.

De Schutter, Olivier. "How Not to Think of Land-Grabbing: Three Critiques of Large-Scale Investment in Farmland." *Journal of Peasant Studies* 38, no. 2 (2011): 249–279.

DeSilver, Drew. "What's on Your Table? How America's Diet Has Changed over the Decades." Pew Research Center, December 13, 2016. http://www.pewresearch.org/fact-tank/2016/12/13/whats-on-your-table-how-americas-diet-has-changed-over-the-decades.

de Solier, Isabelle. *Food and the Self: Consumption, Production, and Material Culture*. London: Bloomsbury, 2013.

DeVore, John. "Life in Chains: Finding Home at Taco Bell." *Eater*, November 5, 2014. https://www.eater.com/2014/11/5/7155501/life-in-chains-kfc-taco-bell.

Dickie, George. *The Century of Taste: The Philosophical Odyssey of Taste in the Eighteenth Century*. New York: Oxford University Press, 1996.

Dinnerstein, Leonard. *Antisemitism in America*. New York: Oxford University Press, 1995.

Donaldson, Sue, and Will Kymlicka. *Zoopolis: A Political Theory of Animal Rights*. Oxford: Oxford University Press, 2011.

Dreyfus, Hubert. *Being-in-the-World: A Commentary on Heidegger's Being in Time, Division I*. Cambridge, MA: MIT Press, 1990.

Drucker, Steven. *Altered Genes, Twisted Truth: How the Venture to Genetically Engineer Our Food Has Subverted Science, Corrupted Government, and Systematically Deceived the Public*. White River Junction, VT: Clear River Press, 2015.

Edney, Anna. "Lab-Grown Meat Startups Backed by Bill Gates, Tyson Foods Facing FDA Oversight." *Bloomberg News*, June 15, 2018. https://www.bloomberg.com/news/articles/2018-06-15/lab-grown-meat-backed-by-gates-tyson-foods-faces-u-s-oversight.

Ehrlich, Paul. *The Population Bomb*. New York: Ballantine, 1971.

Emmanuel, Pierre. "Is France Being Americanized?" *Atlantic*, June 1958. https://www.theatlantic.com/magazine/archive/1958/06/is-france-being-americanized/376248.

Engel, Mylan. "Do Animals Have Rights and Does it Matter if They Don't?" In *The Moral Rights of Animals*, edited by Mylan Engel and Gary Lynn Comstock, 39–64. Lanham, MD: Lexington, 2016.

Ergil, Marnae, and Kevin Ergil. *Pocket Atlas of Chinese Medicine*. Valencia, CA: TPS, 2009.

Estes, J. Worth. "Food as Medicine." In *Cambridge World History of Food*, edited by Kenneth Kiple and Kriemhild Coneè Ornelas, 1534–1553. Cambridge: Cambridge University Press, 2000.

European Commission. *A Decade of EU-funded GMO Research (2001–2010)*. https://ec.europa.eu/research/biosociety/pdf/a_decade_of_eu-funded_gmo_research.pdf.

European Commission. "EU Agricultural Outlook: Prospect for the EU agricultural market and income 2016–2026." *European Union Agriculture and Rural Development*, December 2016. https://ec.europa.eu/agriculture/markets-and-prices/medium-term-outlook_en

European Commission. "Europeans, Agriculture, and the Common Agricultural Policy." *Eurobarometer* 80.2, March 2014. http://ec.europa.eu/commfrontoffice/publicopinion/archives/ebs/ebs_410_en.pdf.

European Commission Directorate-General for Agriculture and Rural Development, 2013. *Report on the Results of the Public Consultation on the Review of the EU Policy on Organic Agriculture*. September 19, 2013. https://ec.europa.eu/agriculture/sites/agriculture/files/consultations/organic/final-report-full-text_en.pdf.

Fairlie, Simon. *Meat: A Benign Extravagance*. White River Junction, VT: Chelsea Green, 2010.

Feagin, Susan L. "Mill and Edwards on the Higher Pleasures," *Philosophy* 58, no. 224 (1983): 244–252.

Feyeraband, Paul. *Against Method: Outline of an Anarchist Theory of Knowledge*. New York: Verso Press, 1975.

Fick, Gary W. *Food, Farming, and* Faith. Albany, NY: SUNY Press, 2008.

Fiddes, Nick. *Meat: A Natural Symbol*. London: Routledge, 1991.

Field, Sean. "The Financialization of Food and the 2008–2011 Food Price Spikes." *Environment and Planning* 48, no. 11 (2016): 2272–2290.

Fireman, Gary D, Ted E. McVay, and Owen J. Flanagan, eds. *Narrative and Consciousness: Literature, Psychology, and the Brain*. New York: Oxford University Press, 2003.

Fisher, Jennifer Orlet, Diane C. Mitchell, Helen Smiciklas-Wright, Leann Lipps Birch. "Parental Influences on Young Girls' Fruit and Vegetable, Micronutrient, and Fat Intakes." *Journal of the American Dietetics Association* 102, no. 1 (2002): 58–64.

Fisher, Robert William. "Disgust as Heuristic." *Ethical Theory and Moral Practice* 19, no. 3 (2016): 679–693.

Fleming, Amy. "Restaurant Menu Psychology: Tricks to Make Us Order More." *Guardian*, May 8, 2013. https://www.theguardian.com/lifeandstyle/wordofmouth/2013/may/08/restaurant-menu-psychology-tricks-order-more.

Fona International. "Flavor Descriptors." Accessed February 2017. https://www.fona.com/discover-fona/FlavorDescriptors_Discover.

Food and Agricultural Organization of the United Nations. "Animal Production and Health." FAO Agriculture and Consumer Protection Department. Accessed June 2016. http://www.fao.org/ag/againfo/home.htm.

Food and Agricultural Organization of the United Nations. *Livestock's Long Shadow: Environmental Issues and Options*. Rome: FAO, 2006. http://www.fao.org/3/a-a0701e.pdf.

Food and Agricultural Organization of the United Nations. "Major Cuts in Greenhouse Gas Emissions from Livestock within Reach." September 26, 2013. http://www.fao.org/news/story/en/item/197608/icode.

Food and Agricultural Organization of the United Nations. *Report on the World Food Summit, 13–17 November, 1996*. Rome: FAO, 1996. http://www.fao.org/docrep/003/x0736m/x0736m00.htm.

Food and Agriculture Organization of the United Nations. *The State of Agricultural Commodity Markets: Trade and Food Security*. Rome: FAO, 2015. http://www.fao.org/3/a-i5090e.pdf.

Food and Agricultural Organization of the United Nations. *The State of Food Insecurity in the World 2015*. Rome: FAO, 2015. http://www.fao.org/3/a-i4646e.pdf.

Food and Agricultural Organization of the United Nations. *The State of World Fisheries and Aquaculture*. Rome: FAO, 2018. http://www.fao.org/3/i9540en/I9540EN.pdf.

Food and Agricultural Organization of the United Nations. *World Livestock 2011: Livestock in Food Security*. Rome: FAO, 2011. http://www.fao.org/3/i2373e/i2373e.pdf.

Food Chain Workers Alliance. *The Hands that Feed Us: Challenges and Opportunities for Workers Along the Food Chain*. June 6, 2012. http://foodchainworkers.org/wp-content/uploads/2012/06/Hands-That-Feed-Us-Report.pdf.

Foster, John Bellamy. *Marx's Ecology: Materialism and Nature*. New York: Monthly Review Press, 2000.

Foucault, Michel. *Discipline and Punish: The Birth of the Prison*. Translated by Allan Sheridan. New York: Vintage Press, 1975.

Fox, Eve. "The Case for Eating Older Animals." *Modern Farmer*, January 2015. https://modernfarmer.com/2015/01/case-eating-older-animals.

Francione, Gary L. *Animals as Persons: Essays on the Abolition of Animal Exploitation*. New York: Columbia University Press, 2008.

Francione, Gary L. "The Problem of Happy Meat and the Importance of Vegan Education." In *The Philosophy of Food*, edited by David M. Kaplan, 169–189. Berkeley, CA: University of California Press, 2012.

Francione, Gary L., and Anna Charlton. *Eat Like You Care: An Examination of the Morality of Eating Animals*. New York: Exampla Press, 2013.

Frank, Arthur. *The Wounded Storyteller: Body, Illness, and* Ethics. Chicago: University of Chicago Press, 1995.

Fraser, David. "Animal Ethics and Food Production in the Twenty-First Century." In *The Philosophy of Food*, edited by David M. Kaplan, 190–213. Berkeley, CA: University of California Press, 2012.

Freyfogle, Eric T., ed. *The New Agrarianism: Land, Culture, and the Community of Life*. Washington, DC: Island Press, 2001.

Funk, Cary, and Brian Kennedy. "Public Opinion About Genetically Modified Foods and Trust in Scientists Connected with These Foods." Pew Research Center,

December 1, 2016. http://www.pewinternet.org/2016/12/01/public-opinion-about-genetically-modified-foods-and-trust-in-scientists-connected-with-these-foods.

Gadamer, Hans-Georg. *Truth and Method*. Translated by Joel Weinsheimer. 2nd ed. New York: Continuum, 1989.

Gold, Jonathan. "Crullers That Bloom in Spring." *LA Weekly*, March 21, 2007. https://www.laweekly.com/restaurants/crullers-that-bloom-in-spring-2147969.

Gold, Jonathan. "Pie's the Limit." *Los Angeles Times*, October 7, 1993. http://articles.latimes.com/1993-10-07/food/fo-42909_1_pie-n-burger-burger.

Goode, Jamie. "Wine and the Brain." In *Questions of Taste: The Philosophy of Wine*, edited by Barry Smith, 79–98. New York: Oxford University Press, 2007.

Gottlieb, Roger, and Anupama Joshi. *Food Justice*. Cambridge, MA: MIT Press, 2013.

Grandin, Temple. *Human Livestock Handling: Understanding Livestock Behavior and Building Facilities for Healthier Animals*. North Adams, MA: Storey, 2008.

Grasso, Benedetta. "Polenta vs. Cous Cous: Legally Banning Ethnic Food from Northern Italy." *iItaly*, April 9, 2010. http://www.iitaly.org/magazine/dining-in-out/articles-reviews/article/polenta-vs-cous-cous-legally-banning-ethnic-food.

Griffin, Lisa Kern. "Narrative, Truth, and Trial." *Georgetown Law Journal* 101 (2013): 281–335.

Grimm, Gebra Cuyun, Lisa Harnack, and Mary Story. "Factors Associated with Soft Drink Consumption in School-Aged Children." *Journal of the American Dietetics Association* 104, no. 8 (2004): 1244–1249.

Haidt, Jonathan, Clark McCauley, and Paul Rozin. "Individual Differences in Sensitivity to Disgust: A Scale Sampling Seven Domains of Disgust Elicitor." *Personality and Individual Differences* 16, no. 5 (1994): 701–713.

Hamrick, Karen. "Americans Spend an Average of 37 Minutes per Day Preparing and Serving Food and Cleaning Up." United States Department of Agriculture Economic Research Service, November 7, 2016. https://www.ers.usda.gov/amber-waves/2016/november/americans-spend-an-average-of-37-minutes-a-day-preparing-and-serving-food-and-cleaning-up.

Harding, Luke. "Victim of cannibalism agreed to be eaten." *Guardian*, December 4, 2003. https://www.theguardian.com/world/2003/dec/04/germany.lukeharding.

Harman, Elizabeth. "Eating Meat as a Morally Permissible Moral Mistake." In *Philosophy Comes to Dinner: Arguments about the Ethics of Eating*, edited by Andrew Chignell, Terence Cuneo, and Matthew C. Halteman, 215–231. New York: Routledge, 2015.

Harris, Marvin. *The Sacred Cow and the Abominable Pig: Riddles of Food and Culture*. New York: Simon & Schuster, 1987.

Hauter, Wenonah. *Foodopoly: The Battle over the Future of Food and Farming in America*. New York: New Press, 2012.

Havermans, Remco C., Tim Janssen, Janneke C. A. H. Giesen, Anne Roefs, and Anita Jansen. "Food Liking, Food Wanting and Sensory-Specific Satiety." *Appetite* 52, no. 1 (2009): 222–225.

Hawkins, Virgil. "'Shithole' Countries? The Media's Portrayal of Africa Reconsidered." *Fair Observer*, January 28, 2018. https://www.fairobserver.com/region/africa/donald-trump-shithole-countries-media-africa-coverage-news-headlines-87600.

Heidegger, Martin. *Being and Time*. Translated John Macquarrie and Edward Robinson. New York: Harper & Row, 1962.

Heldke, Lisa. "An Alternative Ontology of Food: Beyond Metaphysics." *Radical Philosophy Review* 15, no. 1 (2012): 67–88.

Heldke, Lisa. *Exotic Appetites: Ruminations of a Food Adventurer*. New York: Routledge, 2003.

Hellwig, Monika K. "Eucharist." In *Encyclopedia of Religion*, edited by Lindsay Jones. 2nd ed. New York: Macmillan Reference, 2004.

Herculano-Houzel, Suzana. *The Human Advantage: How Our Brains Became Remarkable*. Cambridge, MA: MIT Press, 2016.

Hess, Charlotte, and Elinor Ostrum, eds. *Understanding Knowledge as a Commons: From Theory to Practice*. Cambridge, MA: MIT Press, 2007.

Higman, B. W. *How Food Made History*. Hoboken, NJ: Wiley-Blackwell, 2011.

Hogan, C. Michael, "Archaea." In *The Encyclopedia of Earth*. www.eoearth.org.

Horton, Alex. "Tucker Carlson Suggested Immigrants Make the U.S. Dirtier—And It Cost Fox News an Advertiser." *Washington Post*, December 15, 2018. https://www.washingtonpost.com/business/2018/12/15/tucker-carlson-suggested-immigrants-make-us-dirtier-it-cost-fox-news-an-advertiser/?utm_term=.4d5ab9cc38c4.

Hume, David. "Of the Standard of Taste." In *Essays: Moral, Political, and Literary*. Boston: Little, Brown, & Company, 1987.

Hutto, Daniel B. *Folk Psychological Narratives: The Sociocultural Basis for Understanding Reasons*. Cambridge, MA: MIT Press, 2008.

Inbar, Yoel, David A. Pizarro, and Paul Bloom. "Conservatives are More Easily Disgusted than Liberals." *Cognition and Emotion* 23, no. 4 (2009): 714–725.

Jaspers, Karl. *The Origin and Goal of History*. Translated by Michael Bullock. London: Routledge & Kegan Paul, 1953.

Kant, Immanuel. *Critique of Judgment*. Translated by Werner Pluhar. Indianapolis, IN: Hackett, 1987.

Kant, Immanuel. *The Groundwork for the Metaphysics of Moral*. Translated by James W. Ellington. 3rd ed. Indianapolis, IN: Hackett, 1993.

Kant, Immanuel. *The Metaphysics of Morals*. Translated by Mary Gregor. New York: Cambridge University Press, 1991.

Kant, Immanuel. "To Perpetual Peace: A Philosophical Sketch." In *Perpetual Peace and Other Essays*. Translated by Ted Humphrey. Indianapolis, IN: Hackett, 1983: 107–143.

Kass, Leon. *The Hungry Soul: Eating and the Perfecting of Our Nature*. Chicago: University of Chicago Press, 1994.

Kass, Leon. "The Wisdom of Repugnance." *New Republic* 216, no. 22 (1997): 17–26.

Kazez, Jean. *Animal Kind: What We Owe to Animals*. New York: Wiley-Blackwell, 2010.

Keith, Lierre, *The Vegetarian Myth: Food, Justice, and Sustainability*. Oakland, CA: PM Press, 2009.

Kelly, Daniel. *Yuck!: The Nature and Moral Significance of Disgust*. Cambridge, MA: MIT Press, 2011.

Kelly, Daniel, and Nicolae Morar. "Against the Yuck Factor: On the Ideal Role for Disgust in Society." *Utilitas* 26, no. 2 (2014): 153–177.

Kelly, Daniel, and Nicolae Morar, "I Eat, Therefore I Am: Disgust at the Intersection of Food and Identity." In *The Oxford Handbook of Food Ethics,* edited by Anne Barnhill, Mark Budolfson, and Tyler Doggett, 637–657. New York: Oxford University Press, 2017.

Kershaw, Sarah. "Using Menu Psychology to Entice Diners." *New York Times*, December 22, 2009. https://www.nytimes.com/2009/12/23/dining/23menus.html.

Kim, Hannah. "My Lunchbox Moment: A Day in the Life of an Asian American." *Odyssey*, May 9, 2016. https://www.theodysseyonline.com/lunch-box-moment.

Kirby, David. *Animal Factory: The Looming Threat of Industrial Pig, Dairy, and Poultry Farms to Humans and the Environment*. New York: St. Martin's Press, 2010.

Kliman, Todd. "Debunking the Myth of Authenticity." *Lucky Peach,* no. 1 (July 2011): 82–92.

Koeppel, Dan. *Banana: The Fate of Fruit that Changed the World*. New York: Plume, 2008.

Kolnai, Aurel. *On Disgust*. Edited by Barry Smith and Carolyn Korsmeyer. Chicago: Open Court, 2004.

Konnikova, Maria. "What We Really Taste When We Drink Wine." *New Yorker*, July 11, 2014. https://www.newyorker.com/science/maria-konnikova/what-we-really-taste-when-we-drink-wine.

Korsgaard, Christine M. "Interacting with Animals: A Kantian Account." In *The Oxford Handbook of Animal Ethics*, edited by Tom L. Beauchamp and R. G. Frey, 91–118. New York: Oxford University Press, 2011.

Korsmeyer, Carolyn. "Ethical Gourmandism." In *The Philosophy of Food*, edited by David M. Kaplan, 87–102. Berkeley, CA: University of California Press, 2012.

Korsmeyer, Carolyn. *Making Sense of Taste: Food and Philosophy*. Ithaca, NY: Cornell University Press, 1999.

Korsmeyer, Carolyn. *Savoring Disgust: The Foul and the Fair in Aesthetics*. New York: Oxford University Press, 2011.

Kuhn, Thomas. *The Essential Tension*. Chicago: University of Chicago Press, 1977.

Kuhns, Annemarie, and Michelle Saksena. "Food Purchase Decisions of Millennial Households Compared to Other Generations." United States Department of Agriculture Economic Research Service, EIB-168, December 2017. https://www.ers.usda.gov/webdocs/publications/86401/eib-186.pdf.

Kukla, Rebecca. "Shame, Seduction, and Character in Food Messaging." In *The Oxford Handbook of Food Ethics*, edited by Anne Barnhill, Mark Budolfson, and Tyler Doggett, 593–613. New York: Oxford University Press, 2017.

Laber-Warren, Emily. "Unconscious Reactions Separate Liberals and Conservatives." *Scientific American*, September 1, 2012. https://www.scientificamerican.com/article/calling-truce-political-wars.

Lakoff, George. *Moral Politics: How Liberals and Conservatives Think*. 2nd ed. Chicago: University of Chicago Press, 2000.

Landy, Justin F., and Geoffrey P. Goodwin. "Does Incidental Disgust Amplify Moral Judgment? A Meta-Analytic View of Experimental Evidence." *Perspectives on Psychological Science* 10, no. 4 (2015): 1018–1036.

Larson, Nicole, and Mary Story. "A Review of Environmental Influences on Food Choices." *Annals of Behavioral Medicine* 38, no. 1 (2009): 56–73.

Levinson, Jerrold. "Hume's Standard of Taste: The Real Problem." *Journal of Aesthetics and Art Criticism* 60, no. 3 (Summer 2002): 227–238.

Lewis, Danny. "Italian City Bans New 'Ethnic' Restaurants." *Smithsonian Magazine*, March 4, 2016. https://www.smithsonianmag.com/smart-news/italian-city-bans-new-ethnic-restaurants-180958283.

Lipset, Seymour Martin. *Political Man*. New York: Anchor, 1960.

Logue, Alexandra W. *The Psychology of Eating and Drinking*. 4th ed. New York: Routledge, 2014.

Lowe, Peggy. "Working 'The Chain,' Slaughterhouse Workers Face Lifelong Injuries." *National Public Radio*, August 11, 2016. https://www.npr.org/sections/thesalt/2016/08/11/489468205/working-the-chain-slaughterhouse-workers-face-lifelong-injuries.

Lukács, Georg. *History and Class Consciousness: Studies in Marxist Dialectics*. Translated by Rodney Livingston. Cambridge, MA: MIT Press, 1972.

MacIntyre, Alasdair. *After Virtue: A Study in Moral Theory*. Notre Dame, IN: University of Notre Dame Press, 1981.

Magdoff, Fred, John Foster, and Frederick H. Buttel, eds. *Hungry for Profit: The Agribusiness Threat to Farmers, Food, and the Environment*. New York: Monthly Review Press, 2000.

Maheshwari, Sapna. "When is a Burrito More Than a Burrito? When It Is a Lifestyle." *New York Times*, July 29, 2018. https://www.nytimes.com/2018/07/29/business/media/lifestyle-brands-marketing.html.

Mallon, Ron. *The Construction of Human Kinds*. Oxford: Oxford University Press, 2016.

Mallon, Ron, and Daniel Kelly. "Making Race out of Nothing: Psychologically Constrained Social Roles." In *The Oxford Handbook of Philosophy of Social Science*, edited by Harold Kincaid, 507–532. New York: Oxford University Press, 2012.

Marcel, Gabriel. *The Mystery of Being Vol. 1: Reflection and Mystery*. Translated by G. S. Fraser. New York: Gateway, 1960.

Marcuse, Herbert. *One-Dimensional Man: Studies in the Ideology in Advanced Industrial Society*. London: Routledge & Kegan Paul, 1964.

Margulis, Matias E. "Land Acquisitions for Food and Fuel." In *Encyclopedia of Food and Agricultural Ethics*, edited by Paul B. Thompson and David M. Kaplan, 1325–1332. New York: Springer, 2014.

Martin, Adrienne M. "Factory Farming and Consumer Complicity." In *Philosophy Comes to Dinner: Arguments about the Ethics of Eating*, edited by Andrew Chignell, Terence Cuneo, and Matthew C. Halteman, 203–214. New York: Routledge, 2015.

Marx, Karl. "Letter from Marx to Arnold Ruge, 1843." In *The Marx-Engels Reader*, edited by Robert C. Tucker. New York: W. W. Norton & Company, 1978.

Masson, Jeffrey Moussaieff. *The Pig Who Sang to the Moon: The Emotional World of Farm Animals*. New York: Ballantine, 2003.

May, Joshua. "Does Disgust Influence Moral Judgment?" *Australasian Journal of Philosophy* 92, no. 1 (2014): 125–141.

May, Joshua. "Why Do Politicians Appeal to Our Disgust?" *Birmingham News*, May 5, 2016. https://www.al.com/opinion/index.ssf/2016/05/why_do_politicians_appeal_to_o.html.

McArdle, Megan. "'Authentic' Food Is Not What You Think It Is." *Bloomberg*, February 24, 2017. https://www.bloomberg.com/view/articles/2017-02-24/-authentic-food-is-not-what-you-think-it-is.

McCarthy, Cormac. *The Road*. New York: Vintage, 2006.

McMichael, Philip. "The Land Grab and Corporate Food Regime Restructuring." *Journal of Peasant Studies* 39, no. 3–4. (2012): 681–701.

McPherson, Tristram. "Why I Am a Vegan." In *Philosophy Comes to Dinner: Arguments about the Ethics of Eating*, edited by Andrew Chignell, Terence Cuneo, and Matthew C. Halteman, 73–91. New York: Routledge, 2015.

Mellon, Margaret. "Biotechnology—A Failed Promise." Union of Concerned Scientists, August 25, 2011. https://blog.ucsusa.org/margaret-mellon/biotechnology-a-failed-promise.

Mercy for Animals. "Mad Sausage." March 11, 2013. https://www.youtube.com/watch?v=PNFfJJBwBjY.

Merleau-Ponty, Maurice. *Phenomenology of Perception*. Translated by Colin Smith. New York: Routledge Classics University Press, 2002.

Michaelson, Eliot, and Andrew Reisner. "Ethics for Fish." In *The Oxford Handbook of Food Ethics*, edited by Anne Barnhill, Mark Budolfson, and Tyler Doggett, 189–208. New York: Oxford University Press, 2017.

Michelfelder, Diane P. "Technological Ethics in a Different Voice." In *Technology and the Good Life?*, edited by Eric Higgs, Andrew Light, and David Strong, 219–233. Chicago: University of Chicago Press, 2000.

Mill, John Stuart. *Utilitarianism*. 2nd ed. Indianapolis, IN: Hackett, 2002.

Miller, William Ian. *The Anatomy of Disgust*. Cambridge, MA: Harvard University Press, 1997.

Milman, Oliver, and Stuart Leavenworth. "China's Plan to Cut Meat Consumption by 50% Cheered by Climate Campaigners." *Guardian*, June 20, 2016. https://www.theguardian.com/world/2016/jun/20/chinas-meat-consumption-climate-change.

Mintz, Sidney. *Sweetness and Power: The Place of Sugar in Modern History*. New York: Penguin, 1986.

Mintz, Sidney. *Tasting Food, Tasting Freedom: Excursions into Eating, Culture, and the Past*. Boston: Beacon Press, 1997.

Monroe, Dave. "Can Food Be Art? The Problem of Consumption." In *Food and Philosophy: Eat, Think, and Be Merry*, edited by Fritz Allhoff and Dave Monroe, 133–144. New York: Blackwell, 2007.

Morain, Alain. "What Are Animals Conscious Of?" In *Experiencing Animal Minds*, edited by Julie Smith and Robert Mitchell, 246–260. New York: Columbia University Press, 2012.

Morales, Klaus. "Brazil Adopts Stronger Pictures on Cigarette Packages in Anti-Smoking Campaign." *British Medical Journal*, 336 (2008): 1333.

Morgan, Carissa J., Candace C. Croney, and Nicole J. Olynk Widmar, "Exploring Relationships Between Ethical Consumption, Lifestyle Choices, and Social Responsibility." *Advances in Applied Sociology* 6, no. 5 (May 2016): 199–216.

Mufson, Beckett, "This Guy Served His Friends Tacos Made from His Amputated Leg." Vice.com, June 12, 2018. https://www.vice.com/en_us/article/gykmn7/legal-ethical-cannibalism-human-meat-tacos-reddit-wtf.

National Academies of Sciences, Engineering, and Medicine. *Genetically Engineered Crops: Experiences and Prospects*. Washington, DC: National Academies Press, 2016. https://doi.org/10.17226/23395.

NBC News Asian America, "Voices: Have You Ever Had a Lunchbox Moment?" May 3, 2016. https://www.nbcnews.com/news/asian-america/voices-have-you-ever-had-lunch-box-moment-n566411.

Nelson, Hilde. *Holding On and Letting Go: The Social Practice of Personal Identities*. New York: Oxford University Press, 2014.

Nelson, Hilde, ed. *Stories and Their Limits: Narrative Approaches to Bioethics*. New York: Routledge, 1997.

Nemeroff, Carol, and Paul Rozin. "'You Are What You Eat': Applying the Demand-Free 'Impressions' Technology to an Unacknowledged Belief." *Ethos* 17, no. 1 (1989): 50–69.

Nestle, Marion. *Food Politics*. Berkeley, CA: University of California Press, 2003.

New York Times Magazine. "Put Your Ethics Where Your Mouth Is," April 20, 2012. Accessed June 2014. www.nytimes.com/interactive/2012/04/20/magazine/ethics-eating-meat.html.

Newberry, David M. "Futures Markets, Hedging and Speculation." In *The New Palgrave Dictionary of Economics*, edited by Steven N. Durlauf and Lawrence E. Blume, 521–526. New York: Springer, 2008.

Nielsen Company. "We Are What We Eat: Healthy Eating Trends from Around the World." January 2015. https://www.nielsen.com/content/dam/nielsenglobal/eu/nielseninsights/pdfs/Nielsen%20Global%20Health%20and%20Wellness%20Report%20-%20January%202015.pdf.

Niman, Nicolette Hahn. *Defending Beef: The Case for Sustainable Meat Production*. White River Junction, VT: Chelsea Green, 2014.

Novotaste. "Flavour descriptors," August 30, 2017. http://www.novotaste.com/content/flavour-descriptors.

Nussbaum, Martha C. *Cultivating Humanity: A Classical Defense of Reform of Liberal Education*. Cambridge, MA: Harvard University Press, 1998.

Nussbaum, Martha C. *Hiding from Humanity: Disgust, Shame, and the Law*. Princeton, NJ: Princeton University Press, 2004.

Nussbaum, Martha C. *Loves Knowledge: Essays on Philosophy and Literature*. New York: Oxford, 1992.

Nyéléni. "Declaration of Nyéléni," February 27, 2007. http://www.nyeleni.org/spip.php?article290.

O'Connor, Cailin, and James Owen Weatherall. *The Misinformation Age: How False Beliefs Spread*. New Haven, CT: Yale University Press, 2018.

Ogden, Jane, Nicola Coop, Charlotte Cousins, Rebecca Crump, Laura Field, Sarah Hughes, and Nigel Woodger. "Distraction, the Desire to Eat and Food Intake. Toward an Expanded Model of Mindless Eating." *Appetite* 62, no. 1 (2013): 119–126.

Ohlson, Kristin. *The Soil Will Save Us: How Scientists, Farmers, and Foodies Are Healing the Soil to Save the Planet*. Emmaus, PA: Rodale, 2014.

Oosterlinck, Kim. "History of Forward Contracts." In *The New Palgrave Dictionary of Economics*, edited by Steven N. Durlauf and Lawrence E. Blume, online edition. New York: Springer, 2009.

Paarlberg, Robert. *Food Politics: What Everyone Needs to Know.* 2nd ed. New York: Oxford University Press, 2013.

Pacelle, Wayne. *The Humane Economy: How Innovators and Enlightened Consumers are Transforming the Lives of Animals.* New York: HarperCollins, 2016.

Palomo-Vélez, Gonzalo, Joshua M. Tybur, and Mar van Vugt. "Unsustainable, Unhealthy or Disgusting? Comparing Different Persuasive Messages Against Meat Consumption." *Journal of Environmental Psychology* 58, (August 2018): 63–71.

Patel, Raj. "What Does Food Sovereignty Look Like?" *Journal of Peasant Studies* 36, no. 3 (2009): 663–706.

Perullo, Nicola. *Taste as Experience: The Philosophy and Aesthetics of Food.* New York: Columbia University Press, 2016.

Piqueras-Fiszman, Betina, Agnes Giboreau, and Charles Spence. "Assessing the Influence of the Color of the Plate on the Perception of a Complex Food in a Restaurant Setting." *Flavour* 2, no. 24 (2013).

Plato. *Republic.* Translated by G. M. A. Grube. Indianapolis, IN: Hackett, 1992.

Pollan, Michael. *In Defense of Food: An Eater's Manifesto.* New York: Penguin, 2009.

Pollan, Michael. *Omnivore's Dilemma: A Natural History of Four Meals.* New York: Penguin Press, 2006.

Puhl, Rebecca M., and Chelsea A. Heuer. "Obesity Stigma: Important Considerations for Public Health." *American Journal of Public Health* 100, no. 6 (June 2010): 1019–1028.

Quine, W. V. O. "Ontological Relativity." In *Ontological Relativity and Other Essays.* New York: Columbia University Press, 1969.

Rachels, James. "The Basic Argument for Vegetarianism." In *Food for Thought: The Debate over Eating Meat*, edited by Steve Sapontzis, 70–80. New York: Prometheus, 2004.

Rachels, James. "Vegetarianism." In *The Oxford Handbook of Animal Ethics*, edited by Tom L. Beauchamp and R. G. Frey, 877–905. New York: Oxford University Press, 2011.

Rawls, John. *Political Liberalism.* New York: Columbia University Press, 1993.

Ray, Krishnendu. *The Ethnic Restauranteur.* New York: Bloomsbury Academic, 2016.

Reiheld, Alison N. C. "Gender Norms and Food Behavior." In *The Encyclopedia of Food and Agricultural Ethics*, edited by Paul B. Thompson and David M. Kaplan, 1094–1100. New York: Springer, 2014.

Ricoeur, Paul. *Freedom and Nature: The Voluntary and Involuntary.* Translated by Erazim V. Kohák. Evanston, IL: Northwestern University Press, 1966.

Ricoeur, Paul. *History and Truth.* Translated by Charles Kelbley. Evanston, IL: Northwestern University Press, 1965.

Ricoeur, Paul. *Oneself as Another.* Translated by David Pellauer. Chicago: University of Chicago Press, 1992.

Ricoeur, Paul. *Time and Narrative 1.* Translated by Kathleen Blamey and David Pellauer. Chicago: University of Chicago Press, 1984.

Robin, Maria-Monique. *The World According to Monsanto.* New York: New Press, 2012.

Robinson, Eric, Paul Aveyard, Amanda Daley, Kate Jolly, Amanda Lewis, Deborah Lycett, and Suzanne Higgs. "Eating Attentively: A Systematic Review and Meta-Analysis of the Effects of Food Intake Memory and Awareness on Eating." *The American Journal of Clinical Nutrition* 97, no. 4 (April 2013): 728–742.

Rosner, Helen. "That Guy Who Won That Thing: What Jonathan Gold Meant for Food Writing." *New Yorker*, July 24, 2018. https://www.newyorker.com/culture/annals-of-gastronomy/that-guy-who-won-that-thing-what-jonathan-gold-meant-for-food-writing.

Rozin, Paul. "Disgust." In *Handbook of Emotions*, edited by Michael Lewis and Jeannette M. Haviland, 757–776. New York: Guilford, 1993.

Rozin, Paul, and April E. Fallon. "A Perspective on Disgust." *Psychological Review* 94, no. 1 (1987): 23.

Rozin, Paul, Julia M. Hormes, Myles S. Faith, and Brian Wansink. "Is Meat Male? A Quantitative Multimethod Framework to Establish Metaphoric Relationships." *Journal of Consumer Research* 39, no. 3 (October 2012): 629–643.

Rushkoff, Douglas. *Coercion: Why We Listen to What "They" Say.* New York: Riverhead, 1999.

Sandler, Ronald L. *Food Ethics: The Basics.* New York: Routledge, 2014.

Sanford, Whitney. *Growing Stories from India: Religion and the Fate of Agriculture.* Lexington, KY: University of Kentucky Press, 2011.

Santo, Alysia, and Lisa Iaboni. "What's in a Prison Meal?" *Marshall Project*, July 7, 2015. https://www.themarshallproject.org/2015/07/07/what-s-in-a-prison-meal.

Sartre, Jean-Paul. *Being and Nothingness.* Translated by Hazel E. Barnes. New York: Philosophical Library, 1962.

Sartre, Jean-Paul. *Search for a Method.* Translated by Hazel E. Barnes. New York: Vintage, 1965.

Satter, Ellyn. "Hierarchy of Food Needs." *Journal of Nutrition Education and Behavior* 39, no. 5 (2018): 187–188.

Schlosser, Eric. *Fast Food Nation: The Dark Side of the All-American Meal.* New York: Houghton Mifflin, 2001.

Schmidt, Samantha. "Anorexic Woman Weighing 69 Pounds Has the Right to Starve, Court Rules." *Washington Post*, November 22, 2016. https://www.washingtonpost.com/news/morning-mix/wp/2016/11/22/anorexic-woman-weighing-69-pounds-has-a-right-to-starve-court-rules.

Schnall, Simone, Jennifer Benton, and Sophie Harvey. "With a Clean Conscience." *Psychological Science* 19, no. 12, (2008): 1219–1222.

Schnall, Simone, Jonathan Haidt, Gerald L. Clore, and Alexander H. Jordan. "Disgust as Embodied Moral Judgment." *Personality and Social Psychology Bulletin* 34, no. 8 (2008): 1096–1109.

Schwartz, Judith D. *Cows Save the Planet and Other Improbable Ways of Restoring Soil to Heal the Earth.* White River Junction, VT: Chelsea Green, 2013.

Scruton, Roger. "The Conscientious Carnivore." In *Food for Thought: The Debate over Eating Meat*, edited by Steve Sapontzis, 81–91. New York: Prometheus, 2004.

Searle, John. *The Construction of Social Reality.* New York: Free Press, 1995.

Selim, Leah. "Gender Inequality and Food Insecurity." In *Encyclopedia of Food and Agricultural Ethics*, edited by Paul B. Thompson and David M. Kaplan, 1087–1093. New York: Springer, 2014.

Shaffer, Michael. "Taste, Gastronomic Expertise, and Objectivity." In *Food and Philosophy: Eat, Think, and Be Merry*, edited by Fritz Allhoff and David Monroe, 73–87. New York: Blackwell, 2007.

Shah, Anup. "Poverty Facts and Statistics." *Global Issues*, January 7, 2013. http://www.globalissues.org/article/26/poverty-facts-and-stats.

Sheikh, Knvul. "How Gut Bacteria Tell Their Hosts What to Eat." *Scientific American*, April 25, 2017. https://www.scientificamerican.com/article/how-gut-bacteria-tell-their-hosts-what-to-eat.

Shepherd, Gordon M. *Neurogastronony: How the Brain Creates Flavor and Why It Matters*. New York: Columbia University Press, 2010.

Shields, Meg. "The Future of Food: Five Ominous Trends in Science Fiction Cuisine." *Film School Rejects*, March 14, 2017. https://filmschoolrejects.com/science-fiction-food-trends-6ecccad9b291.

Shurpin, Yehuda. "Is the Lab-Created Burger Kosher?: The Halachic Standing of Lab-Created Meat." Chabad.org. www.chabad.org/library/article_cdo/aid/2293219/jewish/Is-the-Lab-Created-Burger-Kosher.

Sibley, Frank. "Aesthetic Concepts." In *Approach to Aesthetics: Collected Papers on Philosophical Aesthetics*, edited by John Benson, Betty Redfern, Jeremy Roxbee Cox, 1–23. Oxford: Oxford University Press.

Sibley, Frank. "Tastes, Smells, and Aesthetics." In *Approach to Aesthetics: Collected Papers on Philosophical Aesthetics*, edited by John Benson, Betty Redfern, and Jeremy Roxbee Cox, 207–255. Oxford: Clarendon Press, 2001.

Siegal, Nina. "New Slaughter Rules Pit Dutch Religious Freedoms Against Animal Rights." *New York Times*, December 31, 2017. https://www.nytimes.com/2017/12/31/world/europe/netherlands-kosher-halal-animal-rights.html.

Sinclair, Upton. *The Jungle*. New York: Doubleday, 1906.

Singer, Peter. *Animal Liberation*. New York: Random House, 1990.

Singer, Peter, and Jim Mason. *The Ethics of What We Eat*. Emmaus, PA: Rodale, 2007.

Smith, Barry. "The Objectivity of Tastes and Tastings." In *Questions of Taste: The Philosophy of Wine*, edited by Barry Smith, 41–78. New York: Oxford University Press, 2007.

Sorensen, Glorian, Anne M. Stoddard, Tamara Dubowitz, Elizabeth M. Barbeau, Judy Ann Bigby, Karen M. Emmons, Lisa F. Berkman, and Karen E. Peterson. "The Influence of Social Context on Changes in Fruit and Vegetable Consumption: Results of the Healthy Directions Studies." *American Journal of Public Health* 97, no. 7 (2007): 1216–1227.

Sproesser, Gudrun, Matthew B. Ruby, Naomi Arbit, Paul Rozin, Harald T. Schupp, and Britta Renner. "The Eating Motivation Survey: Results from the USA, India, and Germany." *Public Health Nutrition* 21, no. 3 (2018): 515–525.

Stahler, Charles. "How Many People Are Vegan?" The Vegetarian Resource Group. https://www.vrg.org/nutshell/Polls/2019_adults_veg.htm.

Steiner, Gary. *Animals and the Moral Community: Mental Life, Moral Status, and Kinship*. New York: Columbia University Press, 2008.

Sterelny, Kim. *The Evolved Apprentice: How Evolution Made Humans Unique*. Cambridge, MA: MIT Press, 2012.

Sugden, Joanna, and Aditi Malhotra. "In India, Lab-Grown Meat Still Taboo," *Wall Street Journal*, August 6, 2013. https://blogs.wsj.com/indiarealtime/2013/08/06/lab-grown-beef-still-taboo.

Sweeney, Kevin W. "Hunger is the Best Sauce: The Aesthetics of Food." In *The Philosophy of Food*, edited by David M. Kaplan, 52–68. Berkeley, CA: University of California Press, 2012.

Swirski, Peter. *Of Literature and Knowledge*. New York: Routledge, 2007.

Telfer, Elizabeth. *Food for Thought: Philosophers and Food*. New York: Routledge, 1996.

Thompson, Paul B. "Shall We Dine? Confronting the Strange and Horrifying Story of GMOs in Our Food." In *Food and Philosophy: Eat, Think, and Be Merry*, edited by Fritz Allhoff and Dave Monroe, 208–220. New York: Blackwell, 2007.

Todd, Cain. *The Philosophy of Wine: A Case of Truth, Beauty, and Intoxication*. Montreal: McGill-Queen's University Press, 2011.

Torgan, Carol. "Vegetarian Diets Linked to Lower Mortality." National Institutes of Health, June 10, 2013. https://www.nih.gov/news-events/nih-research-matters/vegetarian-diets-linked-lower-mortality.

Treanor, Brian. "Gabriel Marcel." *Stanford Encyclopedia of Philosophy*, March, 2016. https://plato.stanford.edu/entries/marcel.

Trubek, Amy B. *The Taste of Place: A Cultural Journey into Terroir*. Berkeley: University of California Press, 2009.

Tse, Ying Kei, Minhao Zang, Bob Doherty, Paul Chappell, and Philip Garnett. "Insight from the Horsemeat Scandal: Exploring the Consumers' Opinion of Tweets Toward Tesco," *Industrial Management and Data Systems* 116, no. 6 (2017): 1178–1200.

Tucker, Mary Evelyn, and Duncan Ryuken Williams. *Buddhism and Ecology: The Interconnection of Dharma and* Deeds. Cambridge, MA: Harvard University Press, 1998.

Twitty, Michael. "Culinary Justice: Defining a Theory of Gastronomic Sovereignty." University of Michigan, March 28, 2017. https://www.youtube.com/watch?v=7DL7yY3r-ig.

Union of Concerned Scientists. "CAFOs Uncovered: The Untold Costs of Confined Animal Feeding Operations," April 2008. https://www.ucsusa.org/food_and_agriculture/our-failing-food-system/industrial-agriculture/cafos-uncovered.html.

Union of Concerned Scientists. "Monsanto's Claims for Their Genetically Engineered Crops Seem Too Good to be True—But What Are the Alternatives?" February 2012, https://www.ucsusa.org/publications/ask/2012/modern-farming.html

U.S. Department of Agriculture, Economic Research Service. "International Markets and U.S. Trade." https://www.ers.usda.gov/topics/international-markets-us-trade.

U.S. Department of Health and Human Services and U.S. Department of Agriculture. *2015–2020 Dietary Guidelines for Americans*. 8th ed. https://health.gov/dietaryguidelines/2015/guidelines.

U.S. Food and Drug Administration. "Adverse Event Reports Allegedly Related to 5-Hour Energy, Monster and Rockstar." November 2012. http://www.fda.gov

/OfficeofFoods/CFSAN/CFSANFOIAElectronicReadingRoom/UCM328270.pdf.

U.S. Food and Drug Administration. "Consumer Info About Food from Genetically Engineered Plants." https://www.fda.gov/food/food-new-plant-varieties/consumer-info-about-food-genetically-engineered-plants.

U.S. Food and Drug Administration. "Dietary Supplements." https://www.fda.gov/ForConsumers/ConsumerUpdates/ucm153239.htm.

U.S. Food and Drug Administration. "Food Dressings and Flavorings," Code of Federal Regulations, 21 CFR 169.

U.S. Food and Drug Administration. "Frequently Asked Questions about Medical Foods, Second Edition." https://www.fda.gov/downloads/Food/GuidanceRegulation/GuidanceDocumentsRegulatoryInformation/UCM500094.pdf.

U.S. Food and Drug Administration. "Guidance for Industry: Distinguishing Liquid Dietary Supplements from Beverages." https://www.fda.gov/downloads/Food/GuidanceRegulation/GuidanceDocumentsRegulatoryInformation/DietarySupplements/UCM381220.pdf.

U.S. Food and Drug Administration. "Medicines in Our Home: Caffeine and Your Body." http://www.fda.gov/downloads/Drugs/ResourcesForYou/Consumers/BuyingUsingMedicineSafely/UnderstandingOver-the-CounterMedicines/UCM205286.pdf.

U.S. Food and Drug Administration. "Substances Added to Food (formerly EAFUS)." https://www.fda.gov/food/food-additives-petitions/substances-added-food-formerly-eafus.

U.S. Food and Drug Administration. "Warning Letter: Hampton Creek Foods," August 12, 2015. www.fda.gov/ICECI/EnforcementActions/WarningLetters/2015/ucm458824.htm.

Vegetarian Research Group. "How Many Adults in the U.S. are Vegetarian and Vegan?" https://www.vrg.org/nutshell/faq.htm#poll

Vivero-Pol, Jose Luis, Tomaso Ferando, Olivier de Schutter, and Ugo Mattei, eds. *Routledge Handbook of Food as a Commons*. New York: Routledge, 2018.

Wadhera, Devina, and Elizabeth D. Capaldi-Phillips. "A Review of Visual Cues Associated with Food Acceptance and Consumption." *Eating Behaviors* 15, no. 1 (January 2014): 132–143.

Walker, Margaret Urban. *Moral Understandings: A Feminist Study in Ethics*. 2nd ed. New York: Routledge, 2007.

Walton, Kendall. "Categories of Art." *Philosophical Review* 73, no. 3 (July 1970): 334–367.

Walzer, Michael. "Involuntary Association." In *Politics and Passion: Toward a More Egalitarian Liberalism*. New Haven, CT: Yale University Press, 2004.

Walzer, Michael. "Politics and Passion." In *Politics and Passion: Toward a More Egalitarian Liberalism*. New Haven, CT: Yale University Press, 2004.

Walzer, Michael. *Spheres of Justice: A Defense of Pluralism and Equality*. New York: Basic, 1983.

Watson, James L. ed. *Golden Arches East: McDonald's in East Asia*. Palo Alto, CA: Stanford University Press, 2006.

Wein, Harrison. "Risk in Red Meats?" National Institutes of Health, March 26, 2012. www.nih.gov/news-events/nih-research-matters/risk-red-meat.

Weis, Tony. *The Ecological Hoofprint: The Global Burden of Industrial Livestock*. New York: Zed, 2013.

White, Martha C. "We Now Spend More at Restaurants Than at Grocery Stores." *Money*, June 15, 2016. http://money.com/money/4370620/food-spending-restaurants-versus-groceries.

Widdicombe, Lizzie. "The End of Food: Has a Tech Entrepreneur Come Up with a Product to Replace Our Meals?" *New Yorker*, May 5, 2014. https://www.newyorker.com/magazine/2014/05/12/the-end-of-food

Wilk, Richard. *Home Cooking in the Global Village: Caribbean Food from Buccaneers to Ecotourists*. New York: Berg, 2006.

Williams, Bernard. "A Critique of Utilitarianism." In *Utilitarianism: For and Against*, edited by Bernard Williams and J. J. C. Smart, 108–118. New York: Cambridge University Press, 1973.

Winerip, Michael. "You Call That a Tomato?" *New York Times*, June 24, 2013. https://www.nytimes.com/2013/06/24/booming/you-call-that-a-tomato.html.

Wirzba, Norman, ed. *The Essential Agrarian Reader: The Future of Culture, Community, and the Land*. New York: Counterpoint, 2004.

Wisnewski, J. Jeremy. "Cannibalism." In *Encyclopedia of Food and Agricultural Ethics*, edited by Paul B. Thompson and David M. Kaplan, 279–286. New York: Springer, 2014.

W. K. Kellogg Foundation. "Perceptions of the U.S. Food System: What and How Americans Think about Their Food." Accessed January 2016. http://www.topospartnership.com/wp-content/uploads/2012/05/Food-Systems.pdf.

Wood, Gordon S. *The Radicalism of the American Revolution*. New York: Vintage, 1991.

World Bank. *World Development Indicators 2017*. Washington, DC: 2017. https://openknowledge.worldbank.org/handle/10986/26447?show=full.

World Health Organization. "Food Safety: Frequently Asked Questions on Genetically Modified Food," May 2014. http://www.who.int/foodsafety/areas_work/food-technology/faq-genetically-modified-food/en.

The World Trade Organization. "Doha Declarations," November 14, 2001. https://www.wto.org/english/thewto_e/minist_e/min01_e/mindecl_e.htm.

Wrangham, Richard. *Catching Fire: How Cooking Made Us Human*. New York: Basic, 2009.

Yamoah, Fred Amofa, and David Eshun Yawson. "Assessing Supermarket Food Shopper Reaction to the Horsemeat Scandal in the UK." *International Review of Management and Marketing* 4, no. 2 (2014): 98–107.

Yoon, Eddie. "The Grocery Industry Confronts a New Problem: Only 10% of Americans Love Cooking." *Harvard Business Review*, September 22, 2017. https://hbr.org/2017/09/the-grocery-industry-confronts-a-new-problem-only-10-of-americans-love-cooking.

Young, Iris Marion. *Justice and the Politics of Difference*. Princeton, NJ: Princeton University Press, 1991.

Young, Sera. *Craving Earth: Understanding Pica—The Urge to Eat Clay, Starch, Ice, and Chalk*. New York: Columbia University Press, 2011.

Zamore, Mary L., ed. *The Sacred Table: Creating a Jewish Food Ethic*. New York: CCAR Press, 2011.

Zampini, Massimiliano, Daniel Sanabria, Nicola Phillips, and Charles Spence. "The Multisensory Perception of Flavor: Assessing the Influence of Color Cues on Flavor Discrimination Responses." *Food Quality and Perception* 18, no. 7 (2007): 975–984.

Zaraska, Marta. *Meathooked: The History and Science of Our 2.5-Million-Year Obsession with Meat*. New York: Basic, 2016.

INDEX

CPSIA information can be obtained
at www.ICGtesting.com
Printed in the USA
JSHW081509060723
44314JS00001B/161

9 780231 167918